Performance Studies

✧ ✧

The Interpretation of Aesthetic Texts

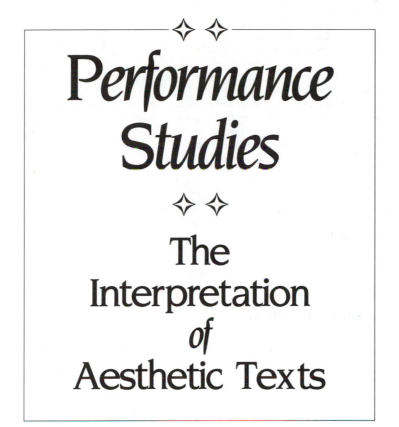

Performance Studies

The Interpretation of Aesthetic Texts

Ronald J. Pelias

Southern Illinois University, Carbondale

ST. MARTIN'S PRESS   NEW YORK

Editor: Cathy Pusateri
Managing editor: Patricia Mansfield
Project editor: Suzanne Holt
Production supervisor: Alan Fischer
Text design: Leon Bolognese & Associates, Inc.
Graphics: G&H Soho, Ltd.
Cover design and art: Butler Udell

Library of Congress Catalog Card Number: 90-71638
Copyright © 1992 by St. Martin's Press, Inc.

Manufactured in the United States of America.
65432
fedcba

For information, write:
St. Martin's Press, Inc.
175 Fifth Avenue
New York, NY 10010

ISBN: 0-312-04732-0

ACKNOWLEDGMENTS

From *Preface to a Twenty Volume Suicide Note,* copyright © 1961 by Amiri Baraka. Reprinted by permission of Sterling Lord Literistic, Inc.

"Poem," copyright © 1964 by Frank O'Hara. Reprinted by permission of City Lights Books.

"The Second Coming" reprinted with permission of Macmillan Publishing Company from *The Poems of W. B. Yeats: A New Edition,* edited by Richard J. Finneran. Copyright © 1924 by Macmillan Publishing Company, renewed 1952 by Bertha Georgie Yeats.

From Lattimore, trans., *The Iliad of Homer, Book 18,* lines 461–616, pp. 387–91. Reprinted by permission of The University of Chicago Press.

"Borges and I" from *In a Personal Anthology,* by Jorge Luis Borges. Copyright © 1967, 1978 by Grove Press. Reprinted by permission.

From *Sandino's Daughters* by Margaret Randall. Copyright 1981 by Margaret Randall. Reprinted by permission of New Star Books, Ltd., Publishers.

From *Dream Children* by Gail Godwin. Copyright © 1976 by Gail Godwin. Reprinted by permission of Alfred A. Knopf, Inc.

In Westminster Abbey by John Betjeman. Copyright © 1959 by John Betjeman and John Murray (Publishers) Ltd. Reprinted by permission.

From *Hard Times: An Oral History of the Great Depression* by Studs Terkel. Copyright © 1970 by Studs Terkel. Reprinted by permission of Pantheon Books, a division of Random House, Inc.

"The Hospital Window" and "A Blessing" reprinted from *Poems 1957–1967* copyright © 1967 by James Dickey. Wesleyan University Press by permission of the University Press of New England.

"Big Boy" by Theresa M. Carilli. Permission granted by Theresa M. Carilli.

From Valerius Babrius (trans. Hull), *Aesop's Fables, Nos. 50 and 108.* Copyright © 1960 by The University of Chicago Press. All rights reserved. Reprinted by permission.

Acknowledgments and copyrights are continued at the back of the book on page 245, which constitutes an extension of the copyright page.

Preface: To the Instructor

P erformance Studies: The Interpretation of Aesthetic Texts is an undergraduate textbook that asks students to use performance as a means of understanding the artistic utterances of others. To suggest that performance is a way of learning reminds us of a long tradition in the discipline of oral interpretation. Characteristic of this tradition is a careful and detailed focus on literary texts. Such a focus encourages students to translate their literary insights from the page to the stage and, in so doing, to increase their knowledge of literature. We have described this translation process as a communicative, artistic, therapeutic, and critical act. It is communicative in that literature in performance is a transaction between speakers and listeners. It is artistic in that literature in performance is a theatrical event. It is therapeutic in that literature in performance is a means of self-discovery. It is critical in that literature in performance is an explication of a literary work. This tradition is the foundation for the present textbook.

The oral interpretation tradition, however, is not static. We have continued to build upon its theoretical perspectives. In recent years, we have given increasing attention to the concept of human communication as a performance act. Explaining communication in theatrical terms allows us to see all communication acts as spoken by actors who have specific motives and exist in particular scenes. We have come to realize that our specialized training in performance places us in a particularly strong position to view communication in these terms. Not only have we called upon performance terminology to explore communication, we have become even more convinced that the act of doing performance, of giving voice and body to others, is a powerful way of knowing. In short, we believe in the value of performance as a mode of inquiry. It is for this reason that the present textbook uses the label *performance studies* as the best description of current interests. Even so, this book is perhaps best read and understood as a continuation of the long and rich traditions of oral interpretation. The book keeps the word *interpretation* in its title not only to honor our history, but also to identify an informing perspective.

No undergraduate textbook in performance studies could adequately address all the subjects that are presently commanding attention from scholars in our field. This book restricts itself to four central thrusts. First, it encourages students to examine various types of aesthetic texts. It asks students not only to look at traditional literary forms, but also to embrace any communicative act that possesses aesthetic qualities. It invites students to consider all utterances, written and oral, that speakers structure in a unified and expressive manner as appropriate material for performance. Second, the book challenges students to create aesthetic performances. It calls upon students to become performing artists, engaged in aesthetic transactions. Third, the book presents students with an extended discussion of performance as a methodology. It shows students how to use their voice and body as well as empathic skills as tools for examining the aesthetic texts of others. Fourth, the book offers students a detailed description of the participatory and evaluative role of the audience in aesthetic events. It urges students as audience members to take an active part in the aesthetic exchange. In general, then, the book invites each student to assume the tasks of textual critic, artistic performer, and performance critic. By the end of the book, students should be able to:

1. understand aesthetic communication as performative, dramatistic acts, as carefully constructed utterances that present the most engaging thoughts of humankind,
2. possess greater sensitivity to aesthetic texts, recognizing their distinct forms and characteristics,
3. use performance as a method for examining human communication, and
4. have increased their critical abilities to give informed and precise evaluations of artistic performances.

In keeping with these interests, the textbook is divided into four parts. Part I, "Performance Studies in Perspective," offers students an overview and working definition of performance studies as well as a brief history of the field. Part II provides students with several procedures for exploring the aesthetic texts of others. Chapter 4 presents the dramatistic method. Chapter 5 develops the idea that the performer's voice and body are analytic tools for examining aesthetic texts. Chapter 6 focuses upon the performer's empathic skills for understanding others. Part III, "The Nature of Aesthetic Texts in Aesthetic Transactions," describes the typical qualities of aesthetic utterances and discusses the dynamics of aesthetic transactions. Part IV turns to the performative and evaluative roles of the audience.

Throughout the textbook, students will find probes to help in their learning. The probes function in a number of ways, including serving as study questions, exercises, topics for in-class discussion, and potential assignments. Some of the probes students can work with on their own; others would benefit from the instructor's guidance. In addition to the probes, the book includes two appendixes, a bibliography of aesthetic texts, and a glossary to aid instruction. Appendix A offers several aesthetic texts for classroom discussion. It is not intended, however, as an anthology for the course. The Bibliography of Aesthetic Texts points students to a number of sources for their performance material. Appendix B presents a sample dramatistic analysis written by an undergraduate student.

Considerable thanks are in order to a number of people for their insights and support during the preparation of this book. I am particularly grateful to Linda Park-Fuller, Bruce Henderson, Beverly Whitaker Long, Robert Overstreet, and Carol Simpson Stern. Their careful reading of earlier drafts of the book helped shape the final product. I am also very grateful to Sharon Bebout, Amy Burt, Darrin Hicks, Kevin Kelch, and Tami Spry who worked on the Bibliography of Aesthetic Texts and the Glossary. To Jill Taft-Kaufman, Mary H. Pelias, Cathy Pusateri, and James VanOosting, I give my special thanks.

Ronald J. Pelias

Preface: To the Student

This is a book about performing. It asks you to do what all performers do—to take on another's voice and body, to become another person. It invites you to put on stage the words of other people. Not just any words, but words that have artistic value. Throughout this book, we will refer to such language as aesthetic communication. Doing performance and working with aesthetic communication are common activities. Such practices are familiar daily experiences. Let us pause for a moment to consider some of our everyday actions in these terms.

We are constantly engaged in acts of performance. Not only do we watch them regularly on television and films, but we produce them for others in our everyday encounters. We tell stories for the enjoyment of our friends. We share the latest joke we have heard. We participate in ceremonies that mark important occasions in our lives. We quote what others say in order to mock them or to ponder their thoughts. We give speeches in our classes and for various organizations. We tease and mimic our acquaintances. We often create such utterances more for their expressive than for their practical value. We enjoy playing with language, using it to entertain ourselves and others. We recognize that some performance acts are more pleasing than others. Some engage us more fully; some demand greater attention. In short, we create and evaluate many performances as we go about our daily lives. In doing so, we are often producing aesthetic communication acts.

As the above paragraph implies, this book looks at two primary types of aesthetic communication. First, it considers performance itself as an aesthetic act. In other words, performance is an art form that demands of its practitioners what all the arts demand: a willingness of the artists to give of themselves, learn their crafts, and take risks. Second, it assumes that the language or texts that performers present are aesthetic. We often find compelling texts for performance when we read traditional literature. Performers have a long history of taking poems, short stories, novels, and plays to the stage. Performing such literary works requires no defense; people have enjoyed the performance of literature for many centuries. But performers are surely not restricted to just these kinds of texts. Aesthetic utterances occur not only in written form, but also in everyday talk. Aesthetic acts are very much a part of our speech environment. As we shall see, performers may look beyond traditional literary works in their efforts to find aesthetic texts for presentation.

Performance is also central to this book — as the basis for studying aesthetic texts. This book assumes that performance is a powerful method for exploring other people. It allows the performer to live in another's sensibility, to take on another's voice and body, to think in keeping with another's mind. Such a process permits a profound encounter with others. Performance offers experiences for our lives. Doing performance is a way of producing understanding. It is a means for coming to know others.

This is also a book about listening to performances. By listening to what performers present, we can also learn. Performers stage performances not only for their own benefit, but also for ours. By attending to what they offer, we share in their discoveries and benefit from their efforts. In doing so, we take on an obligation to give to performers. At a minimum, we must give our focused attention, but we should be willing to share our critical responses as well. Performers want and deserve feedback. Our responsibility to performers is to offer responses that are not just mere flattery but are carefully constructed insights into their work.

This book, then, has four central goals. First, it challenges you to create aesthetic performances. It summons you to become a performing artist. To help you achieve this end, the book provides specific suggestions about performance work, offering techniques for presenting your own and others' aesthetic communication. Second, the book encourages you to examine various types of aesthetic texts. It gives a detailed account of the common qualities of aesthetic acts and makes a case for seeing a wide array of communicative acts as aesthetic. Third, the book urges you to use performance as a method of inquiry. It shows how doing performance work generates insights and identifies specific procedures that performers can follow to make their encounters with aesthetic texts productive. Fourth, the book asks you to become an informed critic of artistic performances. It establishes a vocabulary and several models for making sense of performance events and develops an argument for what constitutes valid evaluations.

The book also relies upon probes to aid your learning. These probes are used to elaborate upon points, to put into practice particular concepts, to demonstrate the complexity of some issues, to develop specific performance skills, and so on. Some probes you may find difficult; others, fairly easy. In either case, you will benefit from trying to work through the probes.

By the end of the semester, you will probably surprise yourself with the quality of your performance work. You will see what it means to be a performing artist. You will understand why people have found performance wonderfully engaging. You will know the joys of an aesthetic encounter. You will learn from others' aesthetic acts. You will discover what makes for rich discussions of artistic performances. In short, you will experience communication at its most profound and most seductive.

Contents

Preface: To the Instructor   v
Preface: To the Student   viii

PART I
Performance Studies in Perspective   1

Chapter 1   Understanding Performance   3

Human Communication as Performance   3
The Drama and the Dramatistic in Performance   7
Artistic Performances   8
Approach of the Textbook   12
Notes   13
Suggested Readings   13

Chapter 2   A Definition of Performance Studies   15

Performance Studies Defined   15
The Performing Audience   22
The Challenge of Performance   23
Notes   24
Suggested Readings   24

Chapter 3   A Historical Account of Performance Studies   26

Literacy and the Nature of Consciousness   26
Performance and Literary Periods of Western Culture   31
   Greek and Roman Antiquity   31
   Medieval Age   32
   Renaissance   34
   Neo-Classical Period   35
   Romantic Era   36
   Twentieth Century   38

New Conceptions of Performance Practice   40
Notes   41
Suggested Readings   42

PART II
Exploring the Aesthetic Communication of Others 45

Chapter 4 **The Dramatistic Approach 47**

Fundamental Assumptions of Dramatism 47
The Pentad 48
The Speakers of Aesthetic Communication 51
The Aesthetic Communication of Speakers 56
Some Final Notes for the Performer 60
Notes 62
Suggested Readings 62

Chapter 5 **The Voice and Body as Analytic Tools 64**

Exploring Others through Voice and Body 64
Dimensions of the Voice 68
Dimensions of the Body 73
Working with the Voice and Body 78
Notes 85
Suggested Readings 85

Chapter 6 **Empathy: The Understanding and Sharing of Feelings 87**

Empathy Defined 87
The Empathic Process 90
  Recognition 90
  Convergence 93
  Adoption 94

Empathy and Performance 95
Notes 98
Suggested Readings 99

PART III
The Nature of Aesthetic Texts in
Aesthetic Transactions 101

Chapter 7 **The Language of Aesthetic Texts in Aesthetic Transactions 103**

The Classification of Aesthetic Texts 103
The Participants and Language in Aesthetic Transactions 107
  Participants 107
  Language 109

Notes 116
Suggested Readings 117

Chapter 8 The Structures of Aesthetic Texts in Aesthetic Transactions   119

Structuring the Whole   119
  Point of View   120
  Forces in Conflict   121
  Sequence   124

Structuring the Parts   129
  Audience   129
  Character   130
  Character Speech   131
  Sound and Rhythm   132

Notes   137
Suggested Readings   138

**PART IV
The Performative and Evaluative Roles
of the Audience   139**

Chapter 9 The Performative Role of the Audience   141

The Performer as Audience   141
The Audience as Performer   144
Participation and Competence within Aesthetic Transactions   147
Notes   150
Suggested Readings   151

Chapter 10 The Evaluative Role of the Audience   152

The Evaluative Act   152
Evaluative Models   156
Issues in Evaluation   159
  Text-centered Issues   159
  Performer-centered Issues   162
  Performance-centered Issues   163

Evaluation and Ethics   165
Notes   167
Suggested Readings   167

Appendix A   Aesthetic Texts for Discussion   169
  The Shield of Achilleus, *Homer*   171
  Borges and I, *Jorge Luis Borges*   175
  It Is a Beauteous Evening, *William Wordsworth*   175
  From Sandino's Daughters: Testimonies of Nicaraguan Women in
    Struggle, *Margaret Randall*   176

A Sorrowful Woman, *Gail Godwin*   178
In Westminster Abbey, *John Betjeman*   183
From Hard Times, *Studs Terkel*   184
The Hospital Window, *James Dickey*   186
Big Boy, *Theresa M. Carilli*   187
The Fox and the Woodcutter, *from Aesop's Fables*   190
The Gasoline Wars, *Jean Thompson*   191
The Merry Chase, *Gordon Lish*   200
My Breath, *Orpingalik*   204
From Battered Women, Shattered Lives, *Kathleen H. Hofeller*   206
The Do-All Ax, *Harold Courlander*   212
Excerpt from a Conversational Improvisation Rehearsal, *Bryan K. Crow*   214
Twirler, *Jane Martin*   220
Women's Laughter, *Marge Piercy*   222
Address to the National Institute of Arts and Letters, 1971, *Kurt Vonnegut, Jr.*   223

Appendix B   Sample Dramatistic Analysis   229
The Focus of Attention in Edmund Spencer's "One Day I Wrote Her Name," *Joey Barton*   229

Bibliography of Aesthetic Texts   233

Glossary   238

Index   247

Performance Studies

✧ ✧

The Interpretation of Aesthetic Texts

PART I
✦ ✦

Performance Studies in Perspective

CHAPTER 1

Understanding Performance

P art I provides an orientation to the field of performance studies. Chapter 1 argues that we can view all human communication as an act of performance. We shall see how we could define performance quite broadly before focusing our interests on artistic performances. Chapter 1, then, specifies the scope of this textbook. Chapter 2 offers a definition of performance studies, and Chapter 3 presents a history of performance studies.

Human Communication as Performance

All human communication is an act of performance. In its most general sense, performance is the executing of an action. Performance also provides some language or vocabulary that helps explain how people communicate. To illustrate this viewpoint, we might follow a hypothetical student, Eric, through a typical day to see if we can understand his behavior in performance terms.

Eric begins the morning by getting ready for school. He does his daily exercise routine, combs his hair, and dresses. With each of these activities we could view him as preparing for the performances that he will engage in during the day. He assesses how his body performs and then judges whether his clothing is a suitable costume for the roles he will have to play that day. Eric's actions so far are private or backstage, "warm-ups" for the day's activities.

After leaving the house, Eric makes his way to school. In doing so, he follows the rules of the road, playing the role, perhaps unconsciously, of the private citizen who obeys the law. Once at school, Eric plays the familiar role of student in a series of classes. He recognizes that his instructors have expectations about the language students should use in the classroom. In his second class, Eric wants to make a point and rehearses in his own mind what he plans to say. When the instructor calls on him, however, the rehearsal fails to pay off. Eric blows his lines by saying something he did not intend.

Throughout the day, Eric encounters various friends. Playing the role of friend, Eric's language is usually more casual, less carefully planned than in the classroom. Eric recognizes that his friends view him in a variety of ways —as witty, attentive, distant, supportive, and so on. His perception of their views feeds into how Eric sees himself. By talking with his friends, he comes to realize that they look at him in certain ways and expect certain behaviors from him. They anticipate that Eric will engage in certain scripts, and Eric is more likely than not to fulfill their expectancies.

Eric also realizes that his talk is, in part, determined by how he perceives each of his friends. With some friends, he typically enjoys intense discussions about political issues; with others, he often reflects upon past high-school days. Eric and his friends, then, take on the role of friend or audience for each other, selecting language that is appropriate to the role. They decide on scripts to present in each other's presence and they understand to some extent why they present them in certain contexts.

After school, Eric goes to his part-time job at McDonald's. He is quite aware that much of his behavior at work has been carefully scripted and that the restaurant has been thoughtfully designed for maximum efficiency and economy. The manager insists that Eric greet customers with the standard line "May I help you?", that Eric always respond to a request for "a small order of fries" with the gentle corrective "Regular?", that Eric present himself as friendly and polite, and so on. The boldly printed menu above the cashiers, the drive-up window, the napkin dispensers, the food trays, and the trash receptacles are all designed to move customers through their meals with speed. Even the tile flooring, the plastic chairs, and the brightly painted walls encourage customers to eat quickly and leave.

Eric starts home after his shift at work. On the way, he stops at the grocery store to buy a few things. Here he plays the role of customer, exchanging a few socially scripted words with the cashier:

Eric: Hi, how are you?
Cashier: Fine, thanks. [Rings up groceries.] That will be $5.87. Thanks for shopping at ———. [Returns change.]
Eric: Thank you. Have a nice night.
Cashier: You too.

Both Eric and the cashier know that the most efficient way to complete the transaction is to stick to their predictable, socially set lines.

Once home, Eric greets his roommate. They share stories of interest from the day's events. They both play the role of storyteller and, in so doing, decide what is worth telling and how they might best tell it. In the telling, they make sense of their world, not only for each other, but also for themselves. Soon, Eric begins to unwind from his performances of the day. He takes off his shoes, pulls his shirt from his pants, and collapses into his favorite chair. Eric's performances are once again private, done for himself and judged by himself.

Try to explain your own day in performance terms. Describe moments when you felt as if you were on stage. Think of times when you felt a need to adjust your clothing in order to be appropriately costumed. Specify any predictable scripts you performed. Identify particular scenes (e.g., restaurants, business offices, friend's home) that appeared staged. What distinct roles did you play?

To what extent does thinking of yourself as an actor engaged in an ongoing theatrical performance help you describe your day? To what extent does general performance terminology (e.g., costume, backstage, warm-ups, role, language, rehearsal, script, audience, staged, lines, storyteller) allow you to understand your own and others' behavior?

This brief sketch of Eric's day suggests that there is considerable power in conceiving of human communication as performance. Performance, as a model for explaining human action, specifies how people communicate with themselves and one another.[1] The example of Eric's day helps clarify this line of thinking in several ways.

First, all communicative acts are performances, done on various private or public stages. When people speak, they do so within a particular situation. Eric's speech is influenced by the contexts in which he finds himself. Eric speaks differently, for instance, in class and at work. Eric, then, performs upon various stages — theatrical settings that influence his talk.

Second, all communication is motivated by particular desires. Human actions carry specific intentions, are driven by conscious and unconscious thoughts and feelings. When Eric speaks to his roommate, he has particular goals or aims. Maybe he wants his roommate to do more of the chores around the apartment, or maybe he wishes that his roommate would stop studying and join him at a party next door. More generally, he may hope that his actions appear warm and considerate, that his stories seem witty and entertaining, that his talk sounds intelligent, and so on. Eric's communication, then, is not random; it is motivated, propelled by his desires and intentions.

Third, all communication is scripted by (1) cultural and linguistic expectations and (2) the unique characteristics of each individual speaker. People are both products and makers of their culture. They follow established principles or conventions for using language and participating in their culture and, at the same time, generate their own talk, placing their individual stamp on what they say. Eric's speech reflects his membership in a particular community, a social group that has contributed significantly to who Eric is. Eric knows what is expected of him if he wishes to follow the "rules" of his culture. Eric is also a unique individual, capable of creating his own talk, his own original scripts. His contributions in part define his culture. As a participating cultural member, Eric communicates with others and, in so doing, helps determine how his culture might be understood.

Fourth, all communication is a process in which people create meaning. In trying to communicate their thoughts and feelings through language, people most often feel they can use language effectively enough to make others understand them. When Eric speaks to his instructor, his friends, and others, he trusts that he can translate his thoughts and feelings into articulated speech, a process of putting his meaning into spoken language. What Eric decides to say is also an indication, implicitly or explicitly, of what he thinks is worth saying. In this sense, all of Eric's statements are statements of value. As Eric considers his feelings and observations, he selects what he believes merits speech.

Finally, all communication is open to interpretation. Eric's talk is interpreted by others to express certain meanings and values. Perhaps Eric and those with whom he communicates share a similar sense of what Eric says. Or perhaps a considerable discrepancy exists between what Eric believes he said and what others think Eric means. In short, sometimes others see Eric as a successful communicator, and sometimes they do not. All communication, then, is an interpretive process in which people attribute meaning and value to speech.

It should be clear that to think of human communication as performance is to reject the stereotypic, negative connotations sometimes associated with performance. To perform in the presence of others is not a means of hiding one's "real self." It is not a question of concealing who one really is behind a number of public roles. The root of performance is to make, to do, not to fake. Performance is a process in which individuals display and create themselves through the roles they elect to portray. One's "real self" is a composite of all these roles. People are what they do. They define themselves by their actions, by their talk. Thus, we might best classify humankind not as *homo sapiens*, the intelligent species, but as *homo histrio*, the performing species.[2] This label suggests that people fundamentally are performing creatures (*histrio*) who engage in an ongoing process of giving speech to their thoughts and feelings. Through the act of performing, people make their lives meaningful and define themselves.

The Drama and the Dramatistic in Performance

It is a short step from viewing all communication as performance to understanding that all performances are dramatic. Through the concept of drama, we might define performance in greater detail. Drama, particularly within the Western tradition, is typically associated with conflict — forces pulling in opposite directions. Having to separate from a close friend when leaving for college, for example, places in conflict the desire to attend college and the wish to stay with the friend. Even the simple greeting "Hi, how are you?" is in conflict with other ways of greeting people. As these commonplace examples show, all human speech stands in contrast to other potential ways of speaking. Conflict is inherent in choice: to make one statement is to deny others. In this sense, everyday existence is dramatic, a source of tension or conflict. Human action is a conscious or unconscious decision to select one option from among a world of possibilities.

It might seem strange to argue that ordinary, everyday lives are dramatic. To think of life, communication, or performances as dramatic, however, is simply to recognize the complexity of the human condition. Whether alone or speaking with others, individuals cannot escape the ongoing dramas of their daily lives. While personal dramas are more intense, profound, and involving at some times than at others, people are always dramatic beings in a dramatic world. The dramas in which people participate clearly are not restricted to literary plays. Rather, drama is a way of being in the world. To take an action is to set in motion a drama of one's own making.

As suggested, each human communication is an action performed upon a social stage, a drama engaged in by motivated individuals in specific contexts. Embedded in this claim is the idea that all human communication possesses what are called dramatistic features: a speaker or speakers saying particular things in a particular manner for a particular reason in a particular time and place to a particular audience. We can summarize these dramatistic qualities in seven basic questions that we can ask of all communication:

Who?	speaker(s)
What?	saying particular things
How?	in a particular manner
Why?	for a particular reason
When?	in a particular time
Where?	in a particular place
To whom?	to a particular audience

Throughout this book, these questions will gain importance. For now, it is important to recognize the dramatistic nature of human speech, to understand that all communication is a performance act requiring a speaker in a specific context.

PROBE 2   Isolate two incidents from your day—one in which you were deeply involved and one in which you were only involved to a limited degree. How might these events be seen as dramatic? How would you describe these events in keeping with the seven dramatistic questions? In what ways is thinking about an incident in these terms instructive?

Artistic Performances

By now it should be clear that we can define all human communication as performance, dramatic in nature and possessing dramatistic features. This broad view allows for rich and compelling explanations of all human action, and it helps us understand the nature of performance itself. In contrast to this expansive view is a more specific definition of performance, one that links performance with the artistic. Such a connection is more in keeping with the typical connotations of performance. Even so, artistic performances encompass a considerable variety of communicative acts. To help establish the range and nature of the artistic performance events that this textbook examines, several examples should prove instructive.

Richard Lewis, in *I Breathe a New Song: Poems of the Eskimo*, describes a typical song duel between two Eskimos:

> In East Greenland, Eskimos control feuds and resolve disputes by song duels. Two men—sometimes two women—having become enemies, give vent to their anger once a year. With one drum between them they enter a small circle that has been scratched in the tundra, and take turns drumming and singing. Surrounded by an audience whose verdict is laughter, each seeks to direct this laughter toward his opponent.
>
> Opening songs are often composed long in advance, even rehearsed in private. The introduction may be borrowed from some old, well-known song. The melodies and refrains may be inherited—property left by a father to his son, for example. But the burden is original, full of personal accusations, sneering references, word tricks and subtle allusions.
>
> The duelist begins with a great show of modesty, then gradually unmasks his fire. He says one thing, outwardly innocent, but means something quite different. The audience understands and, unless the victim

parries each thrust, matching point for point, he is soon laughed from the circle. The highest form of dueling consists in bringing your opponent to a full stop.[3]

Richard Schechner, writing of the Tiwi society of north Australia, offers another example:

A Tiwi elder accuses a young man of adultery by coming to the center of the village, preferably on a feast day so he can be sure of a large crowd, and calling the offender out. The old man is painted from head to toe in white. In one hand he carries some ceremonial spears and in the other hunting spears. A crowd arranges itself in an ellipse with the old man at one elongated end and the young man at the other. Everyone in the village, and often outsiders too, are present — men, women, children, dogs. They sit, stand, move about, according to their excitement. The young man is naked, except for a few strokes of white coloring applied to his flanks. The more white he wears the more defiant he declares himself to be. Perhaps he carries a spear or two or only a throwing stick. The old man begins a harangue of about 20 minutes duration. He details the young man's worthlessness and ingratitude — talking not only of the offence at hand but the whole life of the young man. The old man stamps his feet and chews his beard: he puts on a good show. The young man shows his good form by taking in this verbal assault in silence. When the harangue is over the old man throws a hunting spear at the young man. The young man dodges — which is not hard to do because the old man is old and he is throwing from 40 to 50 feet away. But if the young man moves too far away at his end of the ellipse, the crowd jeers at him. If the old man is wild in his throws, he is jeered. The trial/duel continues until the young man has dodged enough spears to prove his prowess, but not too many to appear insolent. Allowing himself to be hit takes greatest skill and the crowd enjoys a young man who takes a spear in the fleshy part of the thigh or the upper arm. There is much blood and no permanent harm. The young man's bravery and humility have been demonstrated while the old man's authority and dignity have been repaired. The crowd, entertained, happily applauds both parties to the dispute.[4]

Schechner goes on to explain that the question of guilt is not the issue. Whether or not the young man yields to the authority of the elderly man is the fundamental concern. If he fails to do so, he is driven from the community or killed.

Another example comes from Richard Bauman's description of comedian Dick Gregory's childhood experiences. After quoting from Gregory's autobiographical account of how he used humor as a young kid to become an accepted member of his community, Bauman notes:

Through performance, Gregory is able to take control of the situation, creating a social structure with himself at the center. His first performances are ones in which he takes control by the artful use of deprecatory humor that the other boys had formally directed at him. The joking is still at his own expense, but he has transformed the situation, through performance, into one in which he gains admiration for his performance skills. Then, building on the control he gains through performance, he is able, by strategic use of his performance skills, to transform the situation still further, turning the humor aggressively against those who had earlier victimized him in a manner related to and reminiscent of verbal dueling. In a very real sense, Gregory emerges from the performance encounters in a different social position vis-à-vis the other boys from the one he occupied before he began to perform, and the change is a consequence of his performance in those encounters.[5]

What do these three examples suggest about the range and nature of the performance events that this book explores? First, most members of the Eskimo, Tiwi, and Black communities would view the described events of their respective cultures as performances. Members of each culture could also isolate communication events that they would label not as performance, but simply as a part of common, everyday talk. This suggests that performance is culturally defined, viewed as a special form of communication. People recognize certain events as performance and distinguish them from ordinary communication practice. Oscar G. Brockett starts his *History of the Theatre* by drawing upon this distinction:

> Theatrical and dramatic elements are present in every society, no matter how complex or unsophisticated it is. These elements are as evident in our own political campaigns, parades, sports events, religious services, and children's make-believe as they are in the dances and ceremonies of primitive peoples. Nevertheless, most participants do not consider such activities to be primarily theatrical, even when they make use of spectacle, dialogue, and conflict. Consequently, it is usual to acknowledge a distinction between the theatre as a form of art and the incidental use of theatrical elements in other activities. This distinction is especially important here, for it would be impossible to construct a coherent history of all the theatrical devices found in humanity's diverse undertakings through the ages. Therefore, this book is primarily about the theatre as an institution — its origin and subsequent development.[6]

Following Brockett's lead, we need to distinguish between artistic performances and the performance aspects of all communication events. Although looking beyond artistic performance events to the "theatrical and dramatic elements present in every society" is likely to enrich the understanding of performance as an art form, this book, like Brockett's text, is primarily interested in artistic performances.

Second, all three examples suggest that artistic performance occurs in a variety of settings and calls for various theatrical trappings. Performance recognizes no territorial bounds; it emerges on the tundra, in the village, in the inner city. The participants employ whatever elements cultural and theatrical conventions dictate to create their performances, be they drums, spears, or street clothes. To find artistic performance events, we can look beyond the proscenium arch and lit stage.

Third, all three examples demonstrate the social and cultural power of artistic performance. Performance skills may determine individual worth. A community may welcome or reject people as a result of their performance behavior. People make judgments as to the appropriateness, intelligence, and technical proficiency, to name just a few critical criteria, of an individual's performance — judgments likely to have social consequences for the individual. Embedded in every culture is an implicit set of performance norms — rules or guidelines for performance behavior. To break from these expectations is to break from the culture. Performance is a communicative act embodying cultural norms and values. In this way, performance has the power to maintain cultural traditions and beliefs. Yet performance also has the power to transform culture. By stretching the limits of cultural expectations, by providing alternative visions, performance can bring about change.

Try to envision a time when your own performance behavior either enhanced or lessened your membership in a given group (i.e., Girl Scouts, fraternity, athletic team, drama club). Describe your performance behavior in detail, and explain why it did or did not prove effective.

PROBE 3

Finally, all three examples involve one type of artistic performance behavior — verbal dueling. Many other forms of verbal art exist: for example, offering cultural myths and rituals; presenting jokes, puns, parables, stories, and personal narratives; delivering speeches, sermons, and lectures; and staging literature (poetry, prose, and drama). Perhaps most striking is the fact that quite disparate cultures display many of the same types of verbal art. As the examples above show, we find verbal dueling in Eskimo, Tiwi, and American Black communities. Playing with language is a universal human trait, a performance act reaching toward and, at times, achieving art.

So far, we have argued that all human communication possesses a performative and dramatic nature; that we typically view performance as a communicative event distinct from ordinary talk, an artistic act that exists in a variety of forms and settings; and that performance is a social and cultural event that has the power to solidify and modify cultural values. Given these claims, how shall we approach performance in this book?

Approach of the Textbook

First, the concern of this book is with artistic communication events. While all communication is performative, not all communication is artistic. Following Oscar G. Brockett's distinction between artistic and everyday communication events, this book focuses only upon artistic performance acts. Throughout this book, such performance events are called aesthetic. Aesthetics is the study of the arts, based on analysis of the qualities or dimensions of art works and of how people respond to the arts. Part III explores in detail the qualities of aesthetic communication and describes the factors influencing responses to such communication acts.

Further, the book does not embrace all performance events that we might label aesthetic. It restricts itself to the live performance of verbal art, aesthetic speech. The book excludes such performance events as dance, music, and mime. Likewise, the book does not address film and television performances. Students interested in such performance events can usually find other courses at their respective schools that speak to the performative and aesthetic nature of these art forms. For the same reason, the theatrical presentation of plays receives only minimal attention. This book, then, confines itself to the performance of certain types of aesthetic communication. These types of communication, however, represent quite a large field, including literary, conversational and ceremonial forms.

In particular, this book uses the term *aesthetic communication* to refer to (1) the written or oral text selected by the performer to be presented on stage and (2) the actual presentation given by the performer. Both are aesthetic communication acts. Creating an aesthetic text, however, is a quite different task from performing that text. Performers typically stage the texts that others have created. As they place others' aesthetic texts within a theatrical framework, they are communicating what others have previously said. The performers' creativity revolves around working with others' aesthetic texts. Thus, the performers' task is to translate aesthetic texts found in a number of contexts to the stage, to place others' aesthetic communication within a theatrical setting. In doing so, performers frame or hold up others' aesthetic texts for consideration. The primary interest of this book, then, is to develop the performer's ability to present the aesthetic texts of others on stage.

Finally, the book focuses upon the presentation of aesthetic texts by the solo performer. While many aesthetic performance events involve more than one performer, this book assumes that all presentations for this course will be made by the individual performer, a single person working alone on stage. Even in cases when an aesthetic text that a performer has chosen to do has more than one speaker or character, the performer works alone. This book does not address group performance.

The book, then, recognizes the performative nature of all communicative acts and the variety of aesthetic communication events. It limits itself, however, to the individual performer's artistic presentation on stage of another's aesthetic speech. The rest of this book is an attempt to increase students' sensitivity to the verbal art of others and to develop students' performance skills so that they may evoke such communication on stage.

Notes

1. A number of writers have pursued the connections between performance and communication. For example, see Kenneth Burke, *A Grammar of Motives* (New York: Prentice-Hall, 1945); Erving Goffman, *The Presentation of Self in Everyday Life* (Garden City, NY: Doubleday Anchor Books, 1959); A. Paul Hare, *Social Interaction as Drama: Applications from Conflict Resolution* (Beverly Hills, CA: Sage, 1985); Richard Schechner and Mady Schuman, eds., *Ritual, Play, and Performance: Readings in the Social Sciences/Theatre* (New York: Seabury Press, 1976); James E. Combs and Michael W. Mansfield, eds., *Drama in Life: The Uses of Communication in Society* (New York: Hastings House, 1976); and Victor Turner, *From Ritual to Theatre: The Human Seriousness of Play* (New York: Performing Arts Journal Publication, 1982).
2. For a detailed discussion of these concepts, see Dwight Conquergood, "Communication and Performance: Dramaturgical Dimensions of Everyday Life," in *The Jensen Lectures: Contemporary Communication Studies*, ed. John Sisco (Tampa: University of South Florida, 1983), 24–43.
3. Richard Lewis, *I Breathe a New Song: Poems of the Eskimo* (New York: Simon & Schuster, 1971), 22–23.
4. Richard Schechner, *Performance Theory*, rev. ed. (New York: Routledge, 1988), 35–36.
5. Richard Bauman, *Verbal Art as Performance*, 2nd ed. (Prospect Heights, IL: Waveland Press, 1984), 44–45.
6. Oscar G. Brockett, *History of the Theatre*, 5th ed. (Boston: Allyn & Bacon, 1987), 1.

Suggested Readings

Bauman, Richard. *Verbal Art as Performance*. Rowley, MA: Newbury House, 1977.
Bauman, Richard. *Story, Performance, Event: Contextual Studies in Oral Narrative*. Cambridge: Cambridge University Press, 1986.
Burke, Kenneth. *A Grammar of Motives*. New York: Prentice-Hall, 1945.
Burns, Elizabeth. *Theatricality: A Study of Convention in the Theatre and in Social Life*. London: Longman, 1972.

Combs, James E., and Michael W. Mansfield, eds. *Drama in Life: The Uses of Communication in Society*. New York: Hastings House, 1976.

Conquergood, Dwight. "Communication and Performance: Dramaturgical Dimensions of Everyday Life." In *The Jensen Lectures: Contemporary Communication Studies*, edited by John Sisco, 24–43. Tampa: University of South Florida, 1983.

Farb, Peter. *Word Play: What Happens When People Talk*. New York: Bantam, 1976.

Fine, Elizabeth C., and Jean Haskell Speer. "A New Look at Performance." *Communication Monographs* 44(1977): 374–89.

Fisher, Walter R. *Human Communication as Narration: Toward a Philosophy of Reason, Value, and Action*. Columbia: University of South Carolina Press, 1987.

Goffman, Erving. *The Presentation of Self in Everyday Life*. Garden City, NY: Doubleday Anchor Books, 1959.

Hornby, Richard. *Drama, Metadrama, and Perception*. Lewisburg, PA: Bucknell University Press, 1986.

Issacharoff, Michael, and Robin F. Jones, eds. *Performing Texts*. Philadelphia: University of Pennsylvania Press, 1988.

Lyman, Stanford M., and Marvin B. Scott. *The Drama of Social Reality*. New York: Oxford University Press, 1975.

Poirier, Richard. *The Performing Self*. New York: Oxford University Press, 1971.

Sayre, Henry M. *The Object of Performance: The American Avant-Garde Since 1970*. Chicago: University of Chicago Press, 1989.

Schechner, Richard. *Between Theatre & Anthropology*. Philadelphia: University of Pennsylvania Press, 1985.

Schechner, Richard. *Performance Theory*, rev. ed. New York: Routledge, 1988.

Schechner, Richard, and Mady Schuman, eds. *Ritual, Play, and Performance: Readings in the Social Sciences/Theatre*. New York: Seabury Press, 1976.

Schechner, Richard, and Willa Appel, eds. *By Means of Performance: Intercultural Studies of Theatre and Ritual*. Cambridge: Cambridge University Press, 1990.

Turner, Victor. *Dramas, Fields, and Metaphors: Symbolic Action in Human Society*. Ithaca, NY: Cornell University Press, 1974.

Turner, Victor. *From Ritual to Theatre: The Human Seriousness of Play*. New York: Performing Arts Journal Publications, 1982.

Turner, Victor. *The Anthropology of Performance*. New York: Performing Arts Journal Publications, 1986.

Turner, Victor, and Edward M. Bruner, eds. *Anthropology as Experience*. Urbana: University of Illinois Press, 1986.

Wilshire, Bruce. *Role Playing and Identity: The Limits of Theatre as Metaphor*. Bloomington: Indiana University Press, 1982.

CHAPTER 2

A Definition of Performance Studies

$\boxed{A}$s suggested in Chapter 1, we could define performance studies to encompass a broad range of subjects, including all of the performing arts or, even more generally, all of human communication. As noted, this textbook foregoes such a large scope in favor of identifying the field of performance studies with the presentation of the aesthetic texts of others within a theatrical framework. This chapter clarifies that focus by offering the specific perspective on performance studies that informs this book.

Performance Studies Defined

Performance studies is not a new field. For most of this century, it was carried out as an academic discipline under the label oral interpretation. In keeping with the traditions of oral interpretation, its primary subjects are performance and aesthetic texts. Performance also is its method for understanding aesthetic acts, its tool for analyzing aesthetic communication. Thus, the central interest of performance studies is *the process of dialogic engagement with one's own and others' aesthetic communication through the means of performance*. This claim requires some explanation.

Performance is a communicative process. All performances are transactional communication events between speakers and listeners. The participants share in an ongoing, dynamic interrelationship, a communicative process that triggers their sensitivity, not only to what is being said verbally, but to their nonverbal behavior as well. The communicative process of speakers and listeners is also influenced by the context in which they speak, the style or manner of their speech, their understanding of one another as individuals and as members of a particular social and cultural group, their general attitudes as well as their specific attitudes toward one another, and so on. In short, performance, like all communication events, is a complex process calling upon the participants' interpretive and behavioral skills.

At times, participants may feel that their communicative skills are sufficient—that they have understood one another. At other times, they may decide that their skills are inadequate—that they have not understood one another. Given the complexity of the communicative process, it is not surprising that communication breaks down, that there are times when people face the frustration of not understanding or of not being understood. All people experience their own inadequacy to communicate and feel the urge to cry out, like T. S. Eliot's Sweeney, "But I've gotta use words when I talk to you."[1] Meaning, then, emerges in the act of communication, in the transactional process of the participants. It is not something one person gives another. Instead, people create meaning through dialogue, through talk. People construct meaning in the process of communication.

PROBE 1   Call to mind a time when you felt that the person with whom you were speaking did not understand what you were trying to say. Answer the following questions about this communication breakdown.

1. How would you explain the communication failure? In what distinct ways did you and your listener understand what you were trying to say? Who was responsible for the breakdown? Explain. How could you alter this exchange in order to increase communication effectiveness?
2. Based upon your analysis of this situation, how might you argue that communication is a dynamic, ongoing process in which the participants create meaning?

Thinking of performance as a transactional communication process leads to the second part of the initial claim. Performance calls for a *dialogic engagement*. Dialogue refers most commonly to conversation between two people. Someone might describe two people who are talking with one another as being "in dialogue." In the same sense, what characters in a play say to one another is their dialogue. At the most basic level, then, dialogue implies an exchange, a communicative transaction. At least two voices come into play.

The voices of primary concern to performers are their own, those within aesthetic texts, and those of audience members. Performers' fundamental interest, then, is the dialogue that takes place between themselves and aesthetic texts and between themselves and audience members. Ideally, all participants enter dialogue in an earnest attempt to understand one another. True dialogue calls upon the participants to pursue their communicative task in sympathy, in a sincere desire to comprehend. Such a pursuit does not demand that the participants agree with each other, only that the participants seek understanding. When performers engage in a dialogue with aesthetic texts, their first task is to make sense of what is being said. Likewise, when performers open up a dialogue between themselves and audience members, they strive to make their presentations meaningful. The exchange is a struggle for genuine communication, a transaction that no single voice monopolizes. The ideal dialogue denies isolation. In short, performers hear, in the most profound sense, another voice. To hear in a profound way suggests an engaged self—a self taking on another, making an imaginative leap into another world.

When genuine dialogic engagement occurs between a performer and an aesthetic text, the performer encounters another voice. The aesthetic text enters the performer until its words can be spoken as if they were the performer's own. To allow another voice to speak in one's presence, to have a genuine conversation with another, to enjoy an intimate merger of self and other—that is the performer's ultimate goal. When performers neglect this goal, they deny their human potential and silence those who seek to be heard.

When staging others, however, performers do not abandon themselves. It is a process of letting the other live within the performer so that for a time the performer comes to know the other in an intimate way. Performers maintain a sense of self-identity in order to question points of difference, to understand new ways of seeing the world, and to feel what perhaps cannot be articulated. In a dialogic engagement, performers never confuse themselves with others—they remain open, sensitive, alive to others while keeping themselves in check as points of reference. An audience member attending a theatrical event, no matter how deeply involved with the production, would not run on stage to stop a murder or to expose the villain. The self asserts itself, reminding the audience member of the role the member is to play in the event. In a similar manner, no matter how fully engaged performers become in the world of the other, a part of themselves remains secure in their own world. Ironically, it is their ability to keep a claim on themselves that allows them to know others. They recognize their similarities and differences; they note points of comparison and contrast.

A dialogic engagement can also occur when performers encounter their own aesthetic texts. As an example, assume that someone, Jessica, wrote a poem for an English class expressing her affection for someone with whom she is no longer involved. Assume further that a few years after she wrote this piece, she discovers it in her desk. As she begins to read it, she must reconstruct her previous self, taking into account the attitudes and feelings she once held. Her feelings and attitudes may not have changed, or they may have changed to a significant degree. In either case, her challenge is to engage in genuine dialogue with herself in order to determine how the "self" of her poem compares with her present self. Given this example, it should be clear that a performer may present *one's own or others'* aesthetic texts.

PROBE 2   Think of some situation in which you were in dialogue with yourself. Did you genuinely listen to both aspects of yourself? Did you experience a dialogic engagement with yourself? If so, describe the experience.

Much of what we have said thus far could apply to all ideal communication events. Communication is a transactional process that functions best when the participants seek a dialogic engagement with one another. The next aspect of the chapter-opening claim, however, specifies a particular type of communication: *aesthetic*.

Throughout the centuries, artists and scholars have struggled to define the term *aesthetic*. In its most general sense, the aesthetic refers to artistic beauty. It is not surprising, then, that people commonly associate craft and creativity with definitions of the aesthetic. Craft, when connected to the aesthetic, is the skillful use of artistic material. It implies technical knowledge, proficiency, and expertness with an artistic medium; in short, it is artistic know-how. Thus, artists, using their skills, mold into artistic form what they wish to express. In doing so, they may be creative. Creativity implies the presentation of a new or fresh insight, an original invention, an independent perception from the imagination. We could argue, then, that the aesthetic occurs when an artist combines technique with creativity. For our present purposes, however, we need a more fully developed definition. Based upon the theatrical and literary tradition, how else might we understand the aesthetic?

We can begin with the point, made in Chapter 1, that aesthetic communication is culturally defined. Members of a given culture are likely to deem certain communicative acts as aesthetic. They recognize aesthetic speech as a particular kind of communication, distinct from other ways of communicating. In this sense, aesthetic communication is a separate category, or class, of communication events. To separate various communication acts is to acknowledge that people try to make speech function in particular ways. In essence, some communicative acts are used for aesthetic ends, some are not. Presentations of a poem, speech, story, joke, or essay are some familiar examples of speech used for aesthetic purposes. This is not to say that such communicative acts cannot have multiple functions. Dr. Martin Luther King's famous "I Have a Dream" speech, for instance, not only is an aesthetic act, it also is a call for social change, a historical marker of the civil rights movement, and so on. Nevertheless, people typically understand when communicative acts are aesthetic. Such an awareness emerges in part because speakers shape their aesthetic communication in particular ways, usually generating certain kinds of reactions from listeners.

The second point to recognize about aesthetic communication, then, is that speakers are likely to create aesthetic acts such that they possess certain unique qualities, qualities typically not found in everyday talk. Just what these qualities might be has been the subject of much argument. The contention of this book, as developed in Chapters 7 and 8, is that aesthetic communication is a creative act in which a speaker structures language in a unified and expressive manner. Aesthetic speakers shape or mold their talk into appealing patterns. They unify their utterances so that all parts of their speech contribute to what they want to say. They express themselves in language that is sensuous, figurative, rhythmic, and reflexive. In doing so, they are likely to create audience reaction.

In aesthetic communication, then, aesthetic speakers elicit certain kinds of responses from their listeners. An aesthetic reaction to a communicative act suggests that it has demanded audience involvement. Audience members become engaged in the communication event. Aesthetic acts heighten their senses, stir their emotions, question their knowledge. To be in the presence of the aesthetic is to be transported — carried into another world. One's sense of self is paradoxically both suspended and enlivened. One surrenders oneself in order to be captivated. In this act of magical transformation, individuals become more than they were. To make such claims is simply to identify the compelling power of art. Art, an enticing public offering, requests full mental and physical participation. It is a seductive invitation asking only that individuals bring themselves. Such participation, however, is only possible when audience members recognize what role they are to play in the aesthetic exchange and possess the competencies to do so.

Given the above discussion, we may define aesthetic communication as a culturally specified act in which a speaker structures language in a unified and expressive manner, triggering audience response. Aesthetic communication calls upon speakers and listeners to become engaged in the power of art, to accept their respective roles, and to possess the necessary competencies for the exchange to take place. When the participants meet these conditions, an aesthetic transaction occurs.

PROBE 3   The following exercises and questions are designed to help you reflect about the nature of aesthetic communication.

1. It was noted that aesthetic communication is culturally defined. Identify which of the following carry artistic status
   within our culture:

Television news	Rock concert
Ceramics	Weaving
Juggling	Photography
Cooking	Paint by numbers
Radio drama	Film

   Have our perceptions of any of the above changed over time?
   In other words, would we consider to be art certain things that
   we would not have viewed as such at another point in time?
       Do we designate particular people within our culture to
   decide what communicative acts are artistic? If so, whom do
   we authorize to determine which communicative acts merit
   artistic status? How is this accomplished within our culture?
   Are the authorities always granted final judgment?

2. Examine the list of communicative acts identified below:

Poetry reading	Biography
Sermon	Friend's joke
Newspaper editorial	Football cheer
Jump-rope rhyme	Novel
Love letter	Political speech

   Recalling your own experience with each of these communicative acts, answer the following: Which communicative acts
   were aesthetic? What criteria are you using to make your assessment? How would you argue for the criteria you are
   using? How do your criteria compare to the criteria outlined
   in the discussion of aesthetic communication?

Through the means of performance is the final aspect of our initial claim.
Performance offers an experience, an encounter with another sensibility. Experience allows for learning, for new knowledge. Accordingly, performance

The Performance Process

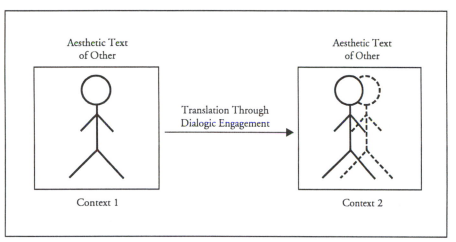

FIGURE 2.1

can function as a mode of inquiry, a method for understanding the aesthetic communication of others. Thus, performance becomes an experiential, investigative tool facilitating comprehension. The performer's primary concern lies with using performance as a way of knowing rather than as an artifact or product. The performer pursues performance work in order to make experience intelligible.

To make experience intelligible through the means of performance is a process of enactment in which performers willingly let others speak through them. Enactment requires that they take on another, vocally and bodily. In so doing, they empower others through their presence. They offer a public space in which the other can be heard. Their obligation is to do the other justice by placing the other rather than themselves in the foreground.

To make experience intelligible through the means of performance is also an act of translation. It is the process of translating aesthetic texts from one communicative context to another. Performers take aesthetic texts — whether found on the page, in private discussions, in rituals, in personal narratives, or wherever — and place them within a theatrical context, or frame. In doing so, performers create an equivalent aesthetic act — something that is and is not their own. Thus, performers take aesthetic texts from a variety of communicative contexts to the theatrical stage and offer them for consideration. When aesthetic texts are translated to the stage, they are held up, framed for scrutiny and examination.[2] Figure 2.1 graphically demonstrates the dynamics of the performer's translation process.

Translation is a tricky and delicate process. Poet Miller Williams, discussing the translation of poems from one language to another, offers a description of what is involved:

When I am translating I want the poet to be able to speak through me. I want to know his work well enough so that I move from metaphor to metaphor at his pace, to vibrate as it were with him so that I can look at something and respond to it as he would. I want to create the poem that he would have created had English been his language. When we talk about the translator's humility, we're not talking about piousness, or even a humble deference, but the kind of humility that causes one actor to be quiet backstage when another one is working. Part of the humility is the awareness of the inability to say all we want to say, to say enough of what the original poet said. There's an essential futility, the futility of an act we can't help trying to perform. It's part of the terror of any writing, but also its motive.[3]

Williams' description applies not only to poets working between languages, but also to performers. The performer's task is to engage in genuine dialogue and to present others by translating the other's vibrant presence to the stage. Williams' comments also remind us that performers must approach those they stage with respect. Performance, publicly offered, is the evidence of understanding. Respect for others is the performer's ultimate critical standard. Performing, the challenging and inviting process of standing in for another, is the concern of this book. Knowing the complexity and richness of aesthetic communication, performers may wonder if they are up to the task. They stand humble but are motivated to present others so that they may learn.

The Performing Audience

Thus far, we have given little attention to the audience in our discussion. For the most part, we have focused on the individual performer's dialogic relationship to the aesthetic communication of others. Yet, performance suggests the presence of an audience, an audience distinct from the performer. When people think of theatrical events, they typically assume that there will be an audience for the performance. Audience members usually are people who have gathered to focus upon some event. They typically function both as a group and as individuals.

As a group, audience members recognize theatrical conventions for proper audience behavior. Knowing when it is permissible to laugh, to talk, to enter and exit, and to go onto the stage are some familiar conventions. Performers might invite the audience to break such theatrical conventions; but unless performers extend such an invitation, the spectator who fails to follow the "rules" for theatrical behavior will be viewed as highly inappropriate. As a group, audience members also feed upon each others' reactions to the theatrical event. Laughing, for example, often is contagious. That is why a comic film usually seems funnier at the movie theatre than in one's home. Obeying theatrical conventions and sharing responses to a theatrical event indicate that the audience is actively participating in the theatrical process. The audience, in short, is performing a public role, set by tradition and dependent upon the unfolding theatrical event.

Describe an incident from your own experience in which (1) an audience member failed to follow an expected theatrical convention and (2) the audience response seemed to be intensified because of the presence of other spectators.

PROBE 4

As individuals, each audience member also performs a private role. Each spectator strives to make sense of the theatrical presentation. Although the audience members are likely to construe the event in some shared ways, each individual constructs a private vision, based upon personal schemes for making sense of the world. The theatrical event is likely to strike each individual somewhat differently. One person, for example, might find the performance very moving, another only moderately so, and another not at all. This "sense maker" role points to the transactional nature of communication. Each person plays a role in the communicative process. Like the performer who strives for a dialogic engagement with the aesthetic texts of others, the ideal audience member remains open, ready to enter the communicative exchange, receptive to the aesthetic communication the performer offers. Acting within the boundaries of theatrical conventions and sharing responses with other spectators aids audience members in their sense-making task, but a dialogic engagement is ultimately a private decision. This book invites the reader to play the roles of performer and audience member, and to decide in favor of dialogic engagement.

The Challenge of Performance

Playing the roles of performer and audience member is perhaps more familiar than one would at first expect. As suggested in Chapter 1, we can consider all communication a performance act. Even more to the point, many everyday communication events are aesthetic. In daily conversation, people often tell stories or jokes. They participate in social rituals, such as initiations into clubs or religious groups. They give speeches and toasts. They use language in playful ways, mimicking others, faking arguments, telling obvious lies, and so on. These types of aesthetic communication are very much a part of everyone's speech environment. People frequently take on the role of performer or audience member in such communication events.

To play the roles of performer and audience member in the spirit of this book, however, requires somewhat more than people typically give in their everyday communication. For performers, the task involves studying the aesthetic texts of others and presenting those texts on stage. In working with others' aesthetic texts, performers explore those texts in detail. They rely upon their analytic and empathic abilities, as well as their vocal and bodily behaviors, to understand others' aesthetic texts. In staging aesthetic texts, performers strive for artistic expression, an aesthetic encounter between themselves and the audience members. To do so, they learn the techniques of their art.

Playing the role of audience member requires an attentive and reflective stance. Good listeners are not passive; they are actively engaged in the ongoing transaction. They are sensitive to the given performance, always striving for understanding. They watch the performance carefully, noting the choices the performer has made. They think about what the performer presents in order to learn and to determine how they might help the performer. In short, they are accountable to themselves and to the performer.

Notes

1. T. S. Eliot, "Sweeney Agonistes," in *Collected Poems 1909–1962* (New York: Harcourt, Brace & World, 1970), 123.
2. The translation process can also center upon the movement from the theatrical or social stage to another medium. A considerable amount of work, for example, has been devoted to devising schemes for recording performance in print. See Elizabeth C. Fine, *The Folklore Text: From Performance to Print* (Bloomington: Indiana University Press, 1984) for an extended discussion of this issue.
3. Miller Williams, "The Sanctioned Babel," in *Acts of Mind: Conversations with Contemporary Poets*, ed. Richard Jackson (University, AL: University of Alabama Press, 1983), 11–12.

Suggested Readings

Bacon, Wallace A. "An Aesthetics of Performance." *Literature in Performance* 1 (November 1980): 1–9.

Bacon, Wallace A. *The Art of Interpretation*, 3rd ed. New York: Holt, Rinehart & Winston, 1979.

Berleant, Arnold. *The Aesthetic Field: A Phenomenology of Aesthetic Experience*. Springfield, IL: Charles C. Thomas, 1970.

Conquergood, Dwight. "Between Experience and Meaning: Performance as a Paradigm for Meaningful Action." In *Renewal and Revision: The Future of Interpretation*, edited by Ted Colson, 26–59. Denton, TX: NB Omega, 1986.

Fine, Elizabeth C. *The Folklore Text: From Performance to Print.* Bloomington: Indiana University Press, 1984.

Lee, Charlotte I., and Timothy Gura. *Oral Interpretation*, 7th ed. Boston: Houghton Mifflin, 1987.

Long, Beverly Whitaker, and Mary Frances HopKins. *Performing Literature: An Introduction to Oral Interpretation.* Englewood Cliffs, NJ: Prentice-Hall, 1982.

Pelias, Ronald J., and James VanOosting. "A Paradigm for Performance Studies." *Quarterly Journal of Speech* 73(1987): 219–31.

Roloff, Leland H. "Performer, Performing, Performance: Toward a Psychologicalization of Theory." *Literature in Performance* 3 (April 1983): 13–24.

Roloff, Leland H. *The Perception and Evocation of Literature.* Glenview, IL: Scott, Foresman, 1973.

Strine, Mary. "Between Meaning and Representation: Dialogic Aspects of Interpretation Scholarship." In *Renewal and Revision: The Future of Interpretation*, edited by Ted Colson, 69–91. Denton, TX: NB Omega, 1986.

Strine, Mary S., Beverly Whitaker Long, and Mary Frances HopKins. "Research in Interpretation and Performance Studies: Trends, Issues, Priorities." In *Speech Communication: Essays to Commemorate the 75th Anniversary of the Speech Communication Association*, edited by Gerald M. Phillips and Julia T. Wood, 181–204. Carbondale: Southern Illinois University Press, 1990.

CHAPTER 3

A Historical Account of Performance Studies

H istory offers perspective, a way of situating oneself in time. To understand the present often requires a grasp of the past. Ideas, concepts, and
theories do not emerge in a vacuum; they evolve over time through dialogue
and debate, through changes in cultural values and attitudes, and through a
belief in the future. To outline a history of performance studies, then, is to
provide a framework for understanding current practices. The task of this
chapter is to sketch briefly the long and complex history of performance
studies.

Performance studies derives part of its richness from the variety of van-
tage points historians bring to the field. Most typically, performance-studies
historians trace the past in terms of two overlapping frameworks: (1) literacy
and the nature of consciousness, and (2) performance and literary periods of
Western culture. In recent years, historians have also looked at performance
practices across cultures and beyond formal, theatrical settings. Each of these
schemes offers historical insights into performance studies.

Literacy and the Nature of Consciousness

Modern *Homo sapiens* have been on earth for approximately 30,000–50,000
years. Writing, however, is a relatively recent phenomenon, dating back only
to about 6,000 years ago. Initially, writing was limited by the available mate-
rials. Wet clay, dried animal skins (parchment, vellum), and strips of tree
bark (papyrus) served as paper. Styluses, goose quills, and brushes func-
tioned as pens. Not until the twelfth century was paper manufactured in Europe.[1] Print was not available to the European public until the mid-fifteenth
century, when Johannes Gutenberg invented the movable-type press. Walter
Ong, in his fascinating *Orality and Literacy*, claims: "Indeed, language is so

overwhelmingly oral that of all the many thousands of languages — possibly tens of thousands — spoken in the course of human history only around 106 have ever been committed to writing to a degree sufficient to have produced literature, and most have never been written at all. Of the some 3,000 languages spoken that exist today only some 78 have a literature."[2] For the most part, then, the use of human language has an oral rather than written history. Despite its limited history, once the written word becomes a cultural fact, profound changes in human consciousness occur. Significant differences in perceiving and apprehending the world exist between cultures with more or less exposure to writing.

In oral cultures, language moves in the world of sound. Words have no visual presence. Sound penetrates, approaches from all directions; the ear has no particular point of view. Sound enters the listener, making language an event, a simultaneous happening with the environment. The world is processed with an auditory bias. Hearing is privileged: there is no such thing as "looking something up" in a book. In contrast, cultures that possess the technology of writing are accustomed to relying upon the written word. Written language stores what is valued within a culture. Whatever is worth knowing is recorded. The written word is the trusted word. To increase the reliability of the written word, grammatical and stylistic rules are established. Seeing, not hearing, is believing. It is common in literate cultures to prove a point by reference to a book. Such a procedure is literally unthinkable in nonliterate cultures. Literate cultures depend upon written, not oral, record keeping.

Script cultures have the ability to write but not the capacity to produce writing in print form. In general, script cultures emerge prior to print cultures, often carrying many of the biases of their oral past as they reach into their print future. Initially, people tend to give the scribes' written word little regard. Most often, they view it as a poor substitute for what oral practices could accomplish or as a dangerous, magical power best left in the hands of a few privileged members of society. Over time, however, the technology of writing proves too alluring to resist. Scribes gain some value in the eyes of their community, which begins to see them as craftspersons, offering a service to those who wish to have something written. Most members of the culture feel little, if any, obligation to learn how to write. In this sense, scribes are not authors, but recorders of others' oral thoughts. To copy is not a question of plagiarism but a paid-for service, as one might today get from a brick mason or an electrician. Once a culture integrates the technology of writing into its daily life, writing gains momentum. More and more people come to value and to depend upon writing. In doing so, they exchange their auditory bias for a visual one. Writing becomes a private matter, and a sense of authorship emerges. As writing penetrates a culture, the way people think changes.

PROBE 1

It is most difficult, if not impossible, for members of a print culture to think about certain words without forming a mental image of the words themselves. After reading the following words, try to think of them without reference to their written form:

Flower	Philosophy
Whisper	But
Smart	Speech
The	Insight
Believe	Therefore

Which of these words are the most difficult to consider without thinking of the word itself? Which words made you reflect upon how language functions? In what ways could a member of an oral culture make similar reflections? Explain.

Writing and, to a much greater extent, print alter the social structure of previously oral cultures. The economic, sociological, and political systems, as well as the historical beliefs, personal psychologies, and communication patterns of members of the community, change. In *The Gutenberg Galaxy*, Marshall McLuhan suggests that the shift from an oral to a print culture encourages changes such as, to name just a few, the rise of nationalism in government, assembly-line manufacturing, the separation of art and science in learning, and the development of perspective in painting.[3] Such changes result from adopting a new sensory relationship to language, from exchanging an ear for an eye.

Writing turns language into a thing or object. It unfolds one word at a time, in a sequential, linear order. It demands analytic thought, a personal, private act. Writing names, labels, and classifies; it unifies and orders thought. Literacy instills the visual bias of logic and rationality and offers a heightened sense of order and control over the environment. In oral cultures, people learn by apprenticeship, by listening and doing. In print cultures, people learn by reading, by studying and reflecting. Language is interiorized, divorced from sound. Memorization, a highly developed and essential ability in oral cultures, becomes a neglected skill of limited use. Thus, humans are a product of their own inventions. Print, an extension of the eye, develops new sensibilities, new ways of perceiving. A description of the performance practices in an oral and print culture may make these ideas more concrete.

One of the best pictures of performance practice from an oral culture comes from ancient Greece, where, prior to the introduction of writing, performers were known as singers. The most famous, of course, is Homer, whose epic poems, the *Iliad* and the *Odyssey*, contain many telling descriptions of the singer. The *Odyssey*, in particular, gives considerable time to two singers, Demodokos and Phemius. Homer portrays both of these singers as divinely inspired by the gods, privileged and prized members of a noble court, and capable of delighting and enchanting an audience. Odysseus, the central character in the *Odyssey*, claims: "For with all peoples upon the earth singers are entitled/to be cherished and to their share of respect, since the Muse has taught them/her own way, and since she loves all the company of singers."[4] Odysseus is brought to tears listening to Demodokos' song: "So the famous singer sang his tale, but Odysseus/melted, and from under his eyes the tears ran down, drenching/his cheeks."[5]

The singers not only enchanted and entertained audiences, but, more importantly, were cultural historians. Since the early Greeks did not have writing, they needed some method to transmit their cultural heritage from generation to generation. Through the singers' verse, the Greeks learned and maintained their culture. The singers' songs were a record, an oral history that perpetuated traditions and fostered a sense of continuity.

The Greek singers could call upon a number of techniques to help with the performance task of carrying on Greek traditions and values. Based upon their study of modern Yugoslav singers, Milman Parry and his student, Albert B. Lord, deduced the Greek singers' methods. Lord notes that singers, using the lyre as musical accompaniment, created what they wanted to say at the same time as they were performing.[6] Since composition and performance occurred simultaneously, singers needed strategies to help with their presentations. One scheme that the singers employed was to go into performance with a body of set formulas and themes. Lord defines a formula as "a group of words which is regularly employed under the same metrical conditions to express a given essential idea."[7] Singers, working with a set metrical pattern (dactylic hexameter, a pattern of one stressed syllable followed by two unstressed syllables, repeated six times), relied upon formulas to complete a poetic line. Such formulaic metrical phrases as "rosy-fingered dawn," "roan-red steed," "Zeus the cloud-gatherer" and "tall Hektor of the shining helm" could be used to satisfy the verse structure and to convey a given thought. Singers knew thousands of often-repeated formulas that they could call upon whenever needed. Singers also structured their tales around certain themes—the arming of the hero, the battle between heroes, the long journey, and so on. Such themes were woven together to create the tale. In general, then, formulas allowed singers to work within certain metrical demands, and themes provided them with organizational patterns for constructing their tales.

Equally significant, formulas and themes helped with memorization. On hearing a new tale, singers did not memorize the story word for word. Instead, by remembering the tale in terms of themes, they could retell it by structuring the themes in their own pattern and by calling upon their vast number of available formulas. Relying upon a stockpile of formulas and themes, singers could compose and elaborate their songs for an extended period of time. Under the demands of oral composition, singers had to depend on these devices. Singing repeated formulas and themes in a particular meter not only allowed singers to remember their songs, but also helped the audience to retain the tales. Remembering what was sung was indeed important, since performance was a means of publication, a public act of repeating cultural knowledge.

Print cultures encourage a quite different set of performance practices. First, a clear separation emerges between the creative acts of writing and performing. While writers at times may perform their own work, people generally see writing and performing as distinct skills and judge them by different standards. The playwright and the actor, for example, are unique members of the theatrical community. Each fulfills a given function: one writes plays, the other performs them. Usually, the actor's first job is to memorize, word for word, what the playwright has written. In most cases, composition during performance occurs only if the actor has failed to remember the lines. The actor typically feels an obligation to the written word.

Second, in a print culture performance, as a distinct art from writing, is no longer the primary means of publication. Writers publish books; their art survives without oral performance. Performers, on the other hand, rely to a large extent on the printed word. The written word is often the basis of their work. Performers depend upon writers much more than writers depend upon performers.

Finally, performers in print cultures do not carry the same responsibility to maintain cultural continuity as do the performers in oral cultures. Print cultures have a tendency to lock performance into its entertainment function. While performance in print cultures may, for example, deal with historical or religious subjects, seldom do people look to performers as the authorities on historical and religious matters. As print becomes firmly established within a culture, formal performance events evolve into products to sell. Performance is no longer an integral part of everyday life; it is a commodity. In this sense, performance simply becomes one of many available forms of entertainment. Throughout this book, we shall challenge the notion of performance as mere entertainment. For now, however, looking at the history of performance studies in terms of Western chronology should help us trace the roots of the field.

Performance and Literary Periods of Western Culture

Performance studies historians commonly identify Greek and Roman antiquity, the medieval age, the Renaissance, the neo-classical period, the romantic era, and the twentieth century as the primary performance and literary periods of Western culture. Based upon this chronology, we shall explore the performance practices and the central literary forms and figures associated with each period. The close link between performance practice and literature suggests that performers are performers of something—and that "something" is, in the broadest sense of the term, literature. The Latin root of *literature* points to the written word. To conceive of literature as only a written form, however, can be misleading. Few people, for example, would question whether Homer's epics are literature, even though they existed for many centuries before being put in writing. We might best conceive of literature, then, as aesthetic communication, be it oral or written. This section explores some of the performance practices and aesthetic texts of Western culture.

Greek and Roman Antiquity

The singer enjoyed a long reign in Greek history. In about 750 B.C., Homer sang of events that took place around 1200 B.C. Not until the sixth century B.C., however, did another kind of performer, the rhapsode, emerge on the scene. The rhapsode differed from the singer in two important ways. First, the rhapsode, using a staff made of laurel or myrtle to mark time, recited rather than sang his tales. Second, he memorized a written script instead of composing during performance. The rhapsodes, known as the *Homeridai* (meaning, literally, "sons of Homer"), established a fixed, written version of Homer's tales. Audiences learned these tales so well that it was possible at festivals and contests to require one rhapsode to continue the story where another rhapsode had ended.[8] Festivals and contests, remarkably popular in Greek culture, gave rhapsodes an opportunity to display their talents. Successful rhapsodes were influential and cherished members of their culture —so much so that Plato, the famous Greek philosopher, worried about their influence within his ideal republic. His final decision to ban them from his ideal state represents, more than anything else, an acknowledgment of their potential power.

Read Homer's description of the shield of Achilleus in Appendix A (p. 171). Based upon the description, characterize Greek life. How is the singer portrayed on the shield? Given that members of the Greek

PROBE 2

culture would view the shield itself as a work of art, articulate the artistic values the shield reflects.

The literary achievements of ancient Greece are indeed incredible: Homer's epics; Hesiod's didactic poetry in *Works and Days* and *Theogony;* the histories of Herodotus and Thucydides; the great dramas of Aeschylus, Sophocles, Euripides, and Aristophanes; and the considerable insights of Plato and Aristotle. These achievements, although written, were products of a culture that believed in the power of the spoken word. The spoken word also held power in ancient Rome.

Like the latter stages of classical Greece, Roman culture (ca. third century B.C.–fifth century A.D.) enjoyed a high level of literacy. Writing, however, still was meant to be read aloud. Reading aloud was so common, in fact, St. Augustine thought it worthy of comment in his *Confessions* (vi. 3) that he discovered Ambrose, the bishop of Milan, reading silently. People expected to read aloud in part because of how writers arranged their words. Writers used minimal punctuation, did not mark word divisions, and did not note changes of speaker with precision. Oral reading, then, was a way to help clarify meaning.[9]

Frequently, readings took place in the home for a small group of friends who served as critics. Festivals and contests continued to draw large crowds. The critics of such events often heard and praised texts that were highly didactic and moralistic, a literature that reflected the practicality and order of Roman society as well as Roman interest in rhetorical principles. The writer, the public speaker, and the performer could find advice in such works as Quintilian's *Institutio Oratoria*, Horace's "The Art of Poetry," Cicero's *De inventione* and *De oratore*, and Longinus' *On the Sublime*. A consistent theme of these works is reflected in Horace's dictate that poetry "instruct and delight." Perhaps the one Roman writer who did more to instruct and delight than anyone else was Virgil, whose epic poem the *Aeneid* was twelve years in the making and never finished to his satisfaction. Yet the *Aeneid* stands as a masterful chronicle of the rich history of Rome.

Medieval Age

The medieval period (ca. 450–1450) continued a rich performance tradition. The clergy recognized and exploited performance as a powerful tool for spreading the word of Christianity to a primarily illiterate population. The clergy carefully orchestrated church services as theatrical events to involve and entrance the churchgoer. It is not surprising that from this religious tradition, passion and nativity plays emerged. Prior to such events, however, the reading of the Bible aloud in church was common practice. The clergy received instruction in the effective delivery of sermons and biblical readings. The Benedictine Rule, a treatise on appropriate religious practice, offered specific guidelines for readers and listeners. In general, readers were to speak with humility in a clear and serious tone, while listeners were to maintain silence. Even when reading to themselves during their private time, the clergy were to observe the Benedictine Rule. Reading alone, then, was done not silently but out loud.

Although the performance practices of the Church held considerable power and influence, the medieval audience was familiar with other types of performance events. The jongleurs and the troubadours of southern France were professional performers who glorified heroic life and courtly love in verse, often singing of love in rather earthy terms. In Anglo-Saxon England, such performers were called scops and gleemen; later, they were known as minstrels. Usually accompanying themselves with a harp, minstrels probably composed such literary texts as *Widsith, Doer's Lament*, and *Beowulf.* Just as important, each of these texts offers a picture of the minstrels' performance work. A modern translation of *Beowulf*, for example, offers these two descriptions of the minstrel's work:

> One of the king's distinguished thanes, whose mind was full of lays and who remembered many old traditions, composed a new poem, in properly linked words. Skillfully he began to treat Beowulf's venture, and successfully he uttered an apt tale, varying his words.[10]

> There was song and music before the Danish King; the harp was touched, many a tale was told, and Hrothgar's minstrel recited a lay to entertain them along the mead-bench.[11]

In large mead halls, then, minstrels praised members of the court and told pagan stories from their Germanic past in a loud, engaging theatrical style. Some minstrels roamed the country to perform for ready audiences, whereas others were permanently connected to a court. Minstrels, like all performers since ancient Greece, served important cultural functions, as educators, historians, publishers, inspirational or religious guides, and, of course, entertainers.

Entertaining an audience through performance was not restricted to professional minstrels. Geoffrey Chaucer's *Canterbury Tales*, for instance, pictures a company of travelers engaged in the art of storytelling. It was quite common in Chaucer's day for travelers to ease the tedium of a journey by telling stories. The traveler who told the best tale would often receive a prize from the other travelers:

Each one of you shall help to make things slip
By telling two stories on the outward trip
To Canterbury, that's what I intend,
And, on the homeward way to journey's end
Another two, tales from the days of old;
And then the man whose story is best told,
That is to say who gives the fullest measure
Of good morality and general pleasure,
He shall be given a supper, paid by all.[12]

Renaissance

The Renaissance, meaning, literally, "rebirth" or "renewal," spread slowly across Europe. In Italy the Renaissance period dates from as early as the mid-1300s, with Dante's *Divine Comedy* and Boccaccio's *Decameron*. In English history, however, the Renaissance is usually dated from 1450 to 1660. Impelling Renaissance culture was a focus on the possibilities of human achievement. In keeping with a growing sense of nationalism, the people of the Renaissance boasted of their exploration of new lands and their scientific discoveries, struggled with questions of religious and political reform, and prided themselves with their artistic accomplishments. The literary works of William Shakespeare, John Donne, John Milton, and many others testify to the sophistication and quality of Renaissance art.

Perhaps the most important development in the Renaissance was the increasing use of the movable-type press, a technology that helped make native languages legitimate vehicles for artistic expression. Throughout the Middle Ages, Latin had been the privileged language. Increasingly, though, Renaissance artists turned to their everyday language for the creation of literary works. Writers also set the criteria for a number of different poetic forms, including the fourteen-line sonnet.

Latin, however, was still familiar to the educated. In the growing number of universities during the period, students received schooling in the classics, particularly the rhetorical principles of Quintilian and Cicero. It was common practice for students to recite publicly memorized selections from classical literature. The connection between rhetorical and poetic principles remained close. Even with print becoming more and more a part of cultural life, speech was still central in the Renaissance — so much so that many written texts of the period acknowledge a listening audience with such phrases as "listen to my words" and "hear my song." To the extent that poetic works were meant to be heard, rhetorical principles of composition and delivery influenced literary practice.

Public performers could consult a number of books designed to help with their presentations, including the first systematic treatment of gesture in

John Bulwer's *Chirologia* and *Chironomia*. Bulwer's specific rules, for example, included thirty-two cautions for the speaker:

> Caution X: To raise the *Hand* about the Eye, or to let it fall beneath the
> Breast, or to fetch it down from the Head to the lower belly, are ac-
> counted vicious misdemeanors in the Hand: yet the masters of this
> faculty doe grant a toleration sometimes to raise the Hand above the
> Head, for the better expressing of a just indignation, or when we call
> God. . . . [13]

Writers even gave the art of conversation serious attention. They recom-
mended guidelines for appropriate performance behaviors for telling
stories, jokes, and proverbs and for quoting passages from literary works.[14]

Neo-Classical Period

The neo-classical era (1660 – 1800) was the first to draw clear distinctions between delivery and composition. While in previous times some writers did
not perform their work, the link between these activities was intricately
bound. Writers often composed for the ear, not the eye. In the neo-classical
era, writing for the silent reader became common practice. More and more
people learned to read. With the coming of English dictionaries and the birth
of journalism, language became standardized, as conventions for spelling
and pronunciation were established and grammatical rules were set. This
was the Age of Reason, philosophically informed and richly skeptical.

The neo-classical era sought its truth in nature, a nature that was ordered
and rule-governed. The artist, whether writer or performer, was to observe
nature and, through artistic techniques and wit, improve upon the natural
order. Alexander Pope's *Essay on Criticism* perhaps captures this notion
best: "True wit is nature to advantage dressed/What oft was thought, but
ne'er so well expressed." In the Age of Reason, balance, restraint, and control emerged as literary values. It was an age that relished the satire of Jonathan Swift and appreciated John Dryden's dictate that the well-made play be
unified by time, place, and action.

An interest in the natural order was also the preoccupation of the best-
known performers of the day—the elocutionists. As print became increasingly available, oral skills began to erode. The work of the elocutionists was
in part a response to a need for effective delivery in religious, political, and
educational contexts. They unanimously believed that the effective performer should follow nature. Considerably less agreement existed, however,
on how to achieve that goal. Controversy centered on such issues as whether
performers should memorize their material or read from a manuscript,
whether performers should imitate others or find their own "natural" way,

whether instructors should first teach the reading of poetry or the reading of prose, whether performers should feel the emotions they were expressing, whether performers should mark their texts as a guideline or notational system for performance behaviors, and whether performers should plan their gestures or allow gestures to flow "naturally" from what was being said.

These concerns, many of which are still debated today, point to two different approaches to elocution. Following the leadership of John Walker, some believed that performers should follow nature by learning the rules of nature. Others, led by Thomas Sheridan, argued that performers should not rely upon prescriptive rules in their attempts to follow nature. Since both groups sought a natural style of delivery, the distinctions between approaches are somewhat misleading. Nevertheless, the different approaches suggest that the elocutionists had at their disposal a variety of techniques to pursue their goal. Most elocutionists freely borrowed performance techniques from their fellow practitioners.

The work of the elocutionists emerged at a time of increasing interest in the English language. People considered speaking and writing correctly to be essential skills for the educated person. In keeping with these concerns, the elocutionists helped establish standardized pronunciation, offered an impressive list of vocal and bodily performance techniques, and presented the first scientific examination of speech physiology.[15]

Romantic Era

Elocutionary practices continued throughout the romantic period (1800–1900). Particularly influential in the United States were Dr. James Rush and François Delsarte. Rush's *The Philosophy of the Human Voice* (1827) systematically described the characteristics of vocal behavior. His aim was to provide speakers with specific procedures for achieving the orotund vocal quality he felt was most natural and appropriate for public speech. In identifying physiological and behavioral dimensions of the voice, he generated an extensive vocabulary. His discussion of vocal pitch, force, quality, time, and abruptness continues to inform contemporary performance practice.[16]

Delsarte's work, as translated for an American audience by his student, Steele MacKaye, offered an integrated approach to the use of gestures in performance. More than anything else, Delsarte's system is a theological philosophy based in Catholicism. For Delsarte, each aspect of human spiritual and organic nature can be understood in terms of a trinity. The human body, for example, contains three dynamic mechanisms for expression—gestures from the vital zone (torso), the intellectual zone (head), and the moral zone (face). The direction of movement is classified as normal (about the center), concentric (toward the center), and eccentric (away from center). Neglecting much of what he had to say about human spiritual nature, the American elocutionists of the time found in Delsarte an appealing system for teaching performative gestures. The rigidity of the system, however, sometimes led to prescriptive rules and highly artificial performance behaviors.[17] Ironically, the elocutionists of both the eighteenth and nineteenth centuries, in their search for a natural performance style, generated models that often had just the opposite effect.

The writers of the day perhaps best captured the romantic spirit, so much so that many scholars mark the beginning of the romantic period with the 1798 publication of William Wordsworth and Samuel Taylor Coleridge's *Lyrical Ballads*. In the preface to the second edition of this volume (1800), Wordsworth rejects neo-classical values in favor of a creative, spontaneous poetics based in the poet's imaginative powers. For Wordsworth, the union of the creative and the imaginative transforms reality into spiritual experience. The poet's emotional engagement, creativity, and imaginative freedom allow the poem to be "a spontaneous overflow of powerful feeling recollected in tranquillity." For the romantic writer, individual expression is the central critical value. In England, poets such as William Blake, Percy Bysshe Shelley, John Keats, and Gerard Manley Hopkins and novelists such as Charles Dickens, William Makepeace Thackeray, and George Eliot reflected this romantic spirit. An American romantic tradition also took root, led by Emily Dickinson, Walt Whitman, Edgar Allan Poe, Nathaniel Hawthorne, Herman Melville, and many other writers.

By the end of the century, romantic literary influences, as well as the development of psychology and Darwinian evolution theory, began to affect elocutionary performance practices. Elocution gave way to expression. The shift from elocution to expression as a disciplinary label reflected an increased attention to the process of performance rather than a perfected technical display, a greater emphasis on personal self-improvement and education, and a more general concern with understanding authorial intent.

Teachers such as S. S. Curry, Charles Wesley Emerson, and Leland Powers, to name just three, opened schools of expression. Such schools offered a variety of courses and pedagogical approaches for the developing performer. In general, the schools aimed to enrich their students through the study of uplifting literature and to provide their students voice and body training so that they might achieve effective expression of thought and feeling. *Werner's Magazine*, the first journal devoted solely to communication, offered a forum for teachers of expression. First published in 1879, *Werner's* began as a magazine for stutterers, although it also contained discussions of the speech arts. By 1902, when it ended publication, theoretical and practical articles on vocal and bodily expression filled the magazine. Professional performers and lecturers also found an eager audience through the Lyceum and Chautauqua circuits. These performance outlets are perhaps best seen as moral entertainment centers. Their aim was to bring democratic, religious, and cultural enrichment to the American public.

The schools of expression, *Werner's Magazine*, and the Lyceum and Chautauqua circuits did not, however, totally escape their elocutionary heritage. *Werner's*, for example, published accounts of Delsarte's system. Many of the schools of expression taught Delsarte's ideas. The style of many Chautauqua performers was more in keeping with the principles of elocution than the principles of expression. Yet each of these outlets for performance practice was central to the shift from elocution to expression, in that they gave performers an opportunity to discuss and explore alternative performance practices.

Twentieth Century

Shortly after the turn of the century, the speech arts found a home in colleges and universities. Speech emerged as a respectable discipline of study in its own right, in part through a rejection of its elocutionary past. By 1915, communication teachers began meeting annually in their own professional organization, the National Association of Academic Teachers of Public Speaking, now known as the Speech Communication Association. The term *expression*, however, had a rather short history. With the publication of S. H. Clark's *Interpretation of the Printed Page* (1915), the label oral interpretation gained favor.

Initially, the performance style associated with oral interpretation was the restrained, suggestive art of reading aloud. Reading aloud, usually from a manuscript and accompanied by minimal movement and few, if any, theatrical accoutrements, became the preferred performance style for those in the interpretation field. They argued that such a style, unlike realistic acting, allowed the audience to participate imaginatively in the literary experience. As early as 1922, Rollo Anson Tallcott in *The Art of Acting and Public Reading* offered a system for classifying the different ways of presenting various types of literature in order to "give the young platform artist a clearer conception of his field so that he will not encroach upon the actor's art in the name of public reading."[18] In short, oral interpretation developed its own aesthetic dictates and conventions.

Given a set performance style, many claimed, oral interpretation could profitably be viewed as a performing art with its own aesthetic principles. While this presentational style gave oral interpretation its distinctive character, many interpreters began to feel that not all texts could be adequately staged by a restrictive list of prescribed rules for performance. This feeling was strengthened in the early 1950s by an increasing interest in group performance. Group performance, typically referred to in oral interpretation circles as Readers Theatre and Chamber Theatre, encouraged interpreters to experiment with a variety of theatrical styles. Thus, group performance also provided an impetus for breaking from the earlier performance aesthetic. Today, few scholars attempt to define the field based upon a particular performance style. Instead, most celebrate the variety of performance styles available for research and performance purposes.

Oral interpretation has been defined not only as a performing art, but also as a communicative act. This is not surprising, since interpretation teachers have typically been housed within departments of communication. The view of interpretation as a communicative act has relied upon a range of communication theories, from simple stimulus-response models to more-complex transactional perspectives. Underlying this conception of oral interpretation is the belief that performing literature is a communicative act similar to other forms of public speech.

The view of oral interpretation as a method of literary study, however, has had the greatest influence on twentieth-century thought. This pervasive conception of interpretation insists on the close relationship between textual study and performance. Much of twentieth-century interpretation scholarship focuses upon the intricate connection between performance practice and literary criticism. Understanding literary texts, rather than learning specific performance techniques, is the fundamental goal of this perspective. The relationship between textual understanding and performance unfolds in two primary ways. First, understanding emerges as a result of careful literary analysis. In this case, performance functions as a record or a demonstration of what the performer discovered through close textual scrutiny. Performers, working with a given system for analyzing texts, translate their insights into performance behaviors. Since the early 1960s, interpreters have most commonly used dramatism (see Chapter 4) as a critical method for analyzing texts. Second, understanding develops as a consequence of performance itself. This more-recent line of thought maintains that performance functions not as a finished product, but as a process or procedure for exploring texts. Through performance, the interpreter comes to understand the text. Performance, in this view, is a critical method for analyzing texts.

The views of oral interpretation as a performing art, a communicative act, and a method of literary study have informed most of the work in the field in the twentieth century. Each perspective is still rich and vital, opening out in a number of different directions, constantly changing, guiding research and practice.

As fully as possible, describe a performance by a singer, rhapsode, minstrel, elocutionist, and oral interpreter. Then compare and contrast these performers to the following contemporary performers.

PROBE 3

1. Rap musician
2. Storyteller
3. Actor in a television drama or film
4. Tour guide at a historical site

New Conceptions of Performance Practice

Currently, many scholars are calling for a new name for the field—a shift from "oral interpretation" to "performance studies." Expanding conceptions of texts, alternative roles for performers and audiences, and fresh definitions of performance have led many people to feel that the label performance studies is more in keeping with current practices and interests. Perhaps the first indication of new directions in the field was the publication of Elizabeth C. Fine and Jean Haskell Speer's 1977 article, "A New Look at Performance,"[19] which clearly established new agendas for those in oral interpretation. Since that time, considerably more research has reflected interests beyond the traditional scope of oral interpretation practice. More and more university programs and professional organizations are finding the name performance studies a more accurate label for their concerns. The field appears ready to embrace a new era—one that maintains its interest in literary texts but explores all forms of aesthetic speech and that views performance as an art and recognizes its communicative potential and function. It is this new era that is addressed in this textbook.

The history of performance studies outlined in the foregoing sections was restricted to an account of Western performance and literary practice. Moreover, it followed dominant cultures, beginning with Greece and ending with the United States. It should not be thought that performance practices ended when political power shifted from one culture to another. To offer a more complete history, however, is beyond our present purposes. A complete history of performance studies, one that takes into account performance practices across cultures and examines all forms of verbal art, has not yet emerged. Scholars have offered many insightful discussions that capture performance behaviors of a given moment in time, but no systematic treatment of performance studies has appeared. Performance studies scholars are just beginning to realize how the history of the field will be revised in light of alternative conceptions of performance.

Performance studies scholars will continue to explore the effects of shifting sensibilities as humans embrace alternative technologies. In a world of electronic media, scholars will not only trace the effects of writing and print but also the impact of current technologies on human consciousness and performance behavior. While continuing to examine performance practices in the Western tradition, performance studies histories will also focus upon performance practices in non-Western cultures.

The history of any field is always evolving and unstable. At best, history offers a limited perspective on the past that is guided by the historian's beliefs in what is valuable, is informed by what the historian takes as the scope of the study, and is limited by available information. No history is complete or without bias. History is an unending story, told from a point of view at a given moment in time. Nevertheless, the performance studies history described in this chapter should provide some access into the discipline, an entry into the world of performance. Each record of the past constitutes another thread in the field's historical web. This rich heritage invites participation.

Notes

1. M. T. Clanchy, *From Memory to Written Record: England, 1066–1307* (Cambridge: Cambridge University Press, 1979), 88–115.
2. Walter J. Ong, *Orality and Literacy: The Technologizing of the Word* (New York: Methuen, 1982), 7.
3. Marshall McLuhan, *The Gutenberg Galaxy* (Toronto: University of Toronto Press, 1962). Also see Elizabeth Eisenstein, *The Printing Press as an Agent of Change: Communications and Cultural Transformations in Early-Modern Europe*, 2 vols. (Cambridge: Cambridge University Press, 1979).
4. Richmond Lattimore, trans., *The Odyssey of Homer* (New York: Harper & Row, 1965), Book 8, lines 479–82.
5. Ibid., lines 521–23.
6. Albert B. Lord, *The Singer of Tales* (New York: Atheneum, 1974), 4–5.
7. Ibid., 4.
8. Eugene Bahn and Margaret L. Bahn, *A History of Oral Interpretation* (Minneapolis: Burgess, 1970), 11.
9. L. D. Reynolds and N. G. Wilson, *Scribes and Scholars: A Guide to the Transmission of Greek and Latin Literature*, 2nd ed. (Oxford: Clarendon Press, 1974), 4–5.
10. Constance B. Hieatt, trans., *Beowulf and Other Old English Poems* (Indianapolis: Odyssey, 1967), 40.
11. Ibid., 44.
12. Geoffrey Chaucer, *The Canterbury Tales*, trans. Neville Coghill (New York: Penguin, 1987), 40–41.
13. As quoted in Mary Margaret Robb, *Oral Interpretation of Literature in American Colleges and Universities*, rev. ed. (New York: Johnson, 1968), 37.
14. Diane Bornstein, "Performing Oral Discourse as a Form of Sociability During the Renaissance," in *Performance of Literature in Historical Perspectives*, ed. David W. Thompson (Lanham, MD: University Press of America, 1983), 211–22.
15. Frederick W. Haberman, "English Sources of American Elocution," in *History of*

Speech Education in America, ed. Karl R. Wallace (New York: Appleton-Century-Crofts, 1954), 105–26.

16. For excellent discussions of Rush's work, see Mary Susan Strine, "Performance Theory as Science: The Formative Impact of Dr. James Rush's *The Philosophy of the Human Voice*," in *Performance of Literature in Historical Perspectives*, ed. David W. Thompson (Lanham, MD: University Press of America, 1983), 509–28; and Mary Margaret Robb, "Dr. James Rush," in *Oral Interpretation of Literature in American Colleges and Universities*, rev. ed. (New York: Johnson, 1968), 81–102.

17. For excellent discussions of Delsarte's work, see Leland H. Roloff and John C. Hollwitz, "Performance and the Body: Gilbert Austin and François Delsarte," in *Performance of Literature in Historical Perspectives*, ed. David W. Thompson (Lanham, MD: University Press of America, 1983), 477–96; and Mary Margaret Robb, "The Delsarte System," in *Oral Interpretation of Literature in American Colleges and Universities*, rev. ed. (New York: Johnson, 1968), 142–52.

18. Rollo Anson Tallcott, *The Art of Acting and Public Reading* (Indianapolis: Bobbs-Merrill, 1922), iv.

19. Elizabeth C. Fine and Jean Haskel Speer, "A New Look at Performance." *Communication Monographs* 44(1977): 374–89.

Suggested Readings

Bahn, Eugene, and Margaret L. Bahn. *A History of Oral Interpretation*. Minneapolis: Burgess, 1970.

Brockett, Oscar G. *History of the Theatre*, 5th ed. Boston: Allyn & Bacon, 1987.

Chaytor, H. J. *From Script to Print*. Cambridge, England: Heffer, 1945.

Conquergood, Dwight. "Boasting in Anglo-Saxon England: Performance and the Heroic Ethos." *Literature in Performance* 1 (April 1981): 24–35.

Crouch, Isabel M., and Gordon R. Owen, eds. *Proceedings of Seminar/Conference on Oral Traditions*. Las Cruces: New Mexico State University, 1983.

Eisenstein, Elizabeth. *The Printing Press as an Agent of Change: Communications and Cultural Transformations in Early-Modern Europe*, 2 vols. Cambridge: Cambridge University Press, 1979.

Gellrich, Jesse M. *The Idea of the Book in the Middle Ages: Language Theory, Mythology, and Fiction*. Ithaca, NY: Cornell University Press, 1985.

Hollwitz, John C. "Steele MacKaye and the Origins of Performer Training in America." *Literature in Performance* 2 (November 1981): 50–55.

Hudson, Lee. "Between Singer and Rhapsode." *Literature in Performance* 1 (November 1980): 33–44.

Johnson, Gertrude, ed. *Studies in the Art of Interpretation*. New York: Appleton-Century, 1940.

Lentz, Tony M. "The Rhapsode Revisited: Notes Regarding Their Divine Inspiration, Success and Recognition." *Literature in Performance* 1 (November 1980): 45–50.

Lord, Albert B. *The Singer of Tales*. New York: Atheneum, 1974.

McLuhan, Marshall. *The Gutenberg Galaxy*. Toronto: University of Toronto Press, 1962.

Ong, Walter J. *The Presence of the Word.* New York: Clarion, 1970.

Ong, Walter J. *Orality and Literacy: The Technologizing of the Word.* New York: Methuen, 1982.

Pattison, Robert. *On Literacy: The Politics of the Word from Homer to the Age of Rock.* Oxford: Oxford University Press, 1982.

Phillips, Gerald M., and Julia T. Wood, eds. *Speech Communication: Essays to Commemorate the 75th Anniversary of the Speech Communication Association.* Carbondale: Southern Illinois University Press, 1990.

Reynolds, L. D., and N. G. Wilson. *Scribes and Scholars: A Guide to the Transmission of Greek and Latin Literature*, 2nd ed. Oxford: Clarendon Press, 1974.

Robb, Mary Margaret. *Oral Interpretation of Literature in American Colleges and Universities*, rev. ed. New York: Johnson, 1968.

Taft-Kaufman, Jill. "Oral Interpretation: Twentieth-Century Theory and Practice." In *Speech Communication in the 20th Century*, edited by Thomas W. Benson, 157–83. Carbondale: Southern Illinois University Press, 1985.

Thompson, David W., ed. *Performance of Literature in Historical Perspectives.* Lanham, MD: University Press of America, 1983.

Vallin, Marlene Boyd. "Mark Twain, Platform Artist: A Nineteenth-Century Preview of Twentieth-Century Performance Theory." *Text and Performance Quarterly* 9 (1989): 322–33.

Wallace, Karl R., ed. *History of Speech Education in America.* New York: Appleton-Century-Crofts, 1954.

Wimsatt, William, and Cleanth Brooks. *Literary Criticism: A Short History.* Chicago: University of Chicago Press, 1957.

Work, William, and Robert C. Jeffrey, eds. *The Past Is Prologue: A 75th Anniversary Publication of the Speech Communication Association.* Annandale, VA: Speech Communication Association, 1989.

PART II

✧ ✧

Exploring the Aesthetic Communication of Others

CHAPTER 4

The Dramatistic Approach

P|art I provided a framework for understanding performance studies. Part II focuses on helping performers explore aesthetic texts. Chapter 4 offers a procedure, the dramatistic approach, for analyzing the aesthetic communication of others. Chapter 5 describes how the performer's voice and body are basic tools for presenting and knowing the aesthetic texts of others. Chapter 6 argues that empathy is a fundamental skill for investigating others.

We briefly touched upon the dramatistic approach in Chapter 1. Now, our aim is to examine in some detail the dimensions of dramatism. This chapter looks at the basic assumptions informing the approach and explores several central questions of the method. It then focuses upon the speakers and types of aesthetic communication, before ending by offering some notes for working with dramatism.

Fundamental Assumptions of Dramatism

The dramatistic approach rests upon two central assumptions, the first being that the life/drama analogy offers a way of explaining human behavior. Dramatism assumes that thinking about life in dramatistic terms provides rich insights into the nature of human action. Human action is distinct from mere motion in that it is purposeful. Unlike the motions of a growing plant or a tree swinging in the breeze, human action is motivated action. Humans have a capacity for making choices, decisions, and commitments. Such a capacity is fundamentally dramatic, since each choice, decision, or commitment is potentially in conflict with its alternatives. Motivated human action, then, implies conflict, and conflict implies drama. All human behaviors are actions based in conflict and dramatic in nature.

The second assumption is that to understand human action requires a vocabulary or method for seeing behavior in its dramatic nature. In general, we can describe human action with reference to basic theatrical terms — as we did when we followed Eric through his day in Chapter 1. Many scholars, however, believe that a more systematic procedure is desirable. Following Kenneth Burke, they rely upon five fundamental concepts, known as the pentad, as a basis for a dramatistic explanation.[1] The pentad, comprising the elements of agent, purpose, scene, act, and agency, offers a flexible model for analyzing human action.

Before we turn to a description of the dramatistic method, one additional point is worth making. Many performance studies practitioners find dramatism a particularly appealing critical method for analyzing aesthetic texts because dramatism looks at aesthetic texts with a language that is both highly familiar and easily translated into performance behaviors. Many ways of analyzing aesthetic texts exist, but dramatism offers a particularly powerful vocabulary that performers can rely upon to understand texts and to guide performance choices. By analyzing aesthetic texts in dramatistic terms, performers discover specific clues for their presentations. A dramatistic explanation appears in terms that performers can comfortably employ in their efforts to stage texts. A particularly rich example of how dramatism is highly compatible with performers' interests is the notion that all texts have speakers. Such an idea encourages performers to see all texts as utterances, as communicative acts. In keeping with the spirit of this idea, we shall use the words *utterance* and *text* as synonyms.

The Pentad

Each dimension of the pentad corresponds to a fundamental question that can be asked of all human action:

Agent	Who?
Purpose	Why?
Scene	Where? When? To Whom?
Act	What?
Agency	How?

When applied to aesthetic communication, these questions lead to some general answers. A speaker or speakers (Who?) with an aesthetic intent or motive (Why?) in an aesthetic context (Where? When? To Whom?) present aesthetic communication (What?) in an aesthetic manner (How?). Such broad claims, however, say very little about the nature of any particular aesthetic act. For dramatism to be a useful analytic tool, we need a much more detailed account. To obtain such an account, we can ask a number of subquestions:

Who is speaking? (Agent)
1. What *physical characteristics* does the speaker possess? Tall? Strong?

Handsome? etc. How does the speaker dress? How does the speaker's body move? How does the speaker's voice sound?

2. What are the speaker's *demographic characteristics*? Age? Sex? Education? Religion? Race? Nationality? Social Status? etc.
3. What *attitudes* does the speaker have? Toward self? The audience? The subject? Do the speaker's attitudes change?
4. What *psychological characteristics* does the speaker possess? What is the speaker's disposition? Personality? Morality? Is the speaker likable?

Why is the speaker speaking? (Purpose)

1. What *motivates* the speaker to speak? To entertain? To persuade? To inform? To understand? etc.
2. What *cultural values* guide the speaker's utterance? Aesthetic conventions? Political agenda? Ethical concerns? etc.

Where and when is the speaker speaking? (Scene)

1. In what *performative context* does the speaker speak? Social? Literary? Theatrical? Does the speaker recognize the context as aesthetic?
2. In what *historical setting* does the speaker speak? Does the speaker speak from a particular time period? Romantic period? Vietnam era? Roaring twenties? etc. Does the speaker speak from a specific place? The South? Soviet Union? Bronx? etc.
3. In what specific *physical location* and *temporal dimension* does the speaker speak? Is the speaker on the porch? At a desk? In a theatre? In a bar? etc. Is the speaker speaking during the day? At night? During what time of year? Does the speaker speak in the past, present, or future? Is there a progression of time or a shift in physical location during the speaker's utterance?

To whom is the speaker speaking? (Scene)

1. To what *audience* is the speaker speaking? Self? A specific other? A general audience? Does the audience change during the speaker's utterance?
2. What is the speaker's *relationship to the audience*? Intimate? Friendly? Distant? Condescending? etc.
3. What *affect* does the audience have on the speaker? Physical? Psychological?

What is the speaker saying? (Act)

1. What does the speaker *mean*? What is the general sense or theme? What is the specific meaning of each word, phrase, and sentence?
2. What is the speaker *doing* when speaking? Driving a car? Having a drink? Scratching the head? Fixing clothes? etc.

How is the speaker speaking? (Agency)

1. Is the speaker speaking through *oral* or *written language*?
2. In what *mode* is the speaker speaking? Lyric? Dramatic? Epic?
3. In what *style* is the speaker speaking? What are the qualities of the speaker's language? Formal or informal? Concrete or abstract? Simple or complex? etc. What language devices does the speaker employ? Metaphor? Oxymoron? Personification? etc.
4. In what *structure* is the speaker speaking? How does the speaker organize the utterance? What form does the speaker use? Sonnet? Novel? Folktale? Ritual? Conversation? etc. What is the speaker's point of view? How does the speaker use sentence length, punctuation, and rhythm?

Some of the concepts used in these questions may not be familiar. In forthcoming chapters we shall examine these ideas in detail. For now, it is important to recognize the complexity and richness of the dramatistic approach and to start thinking in dramatistic terms.

Three central points should be kept in mind when working with the dramatistic method. First, the list of questions is suggestive, not exhaustive. With a given aesthetic act, some additional questions may seem more appropriate and some of the questions posed above may appear irrelevant. Common sense is a prerequisite to using dramatism wisely. The aesthetic act itself should guide decisions as to which questions are the most fruitful to pursue. In seeking to understand a particular text, a performer will gain little by spending considerable time speculating about unimportant aspects of that text. The dramatistic questions lead performers to what they *might* find, not to what they *must* find.

Second, the questions do not stand in isolation. The answer to one question informs the answer to another. An agent's purpose may influence scene, scene may affect agency, agency may mold act, and so on. People, for example, typically alter their talk (agency and act) as they move from one situation to another (scene). They may deem certain language appropriate for a party but inappropriate during a religious service. Each dimension of the pentad is interrelated; each dimension builds upon the others. A complete dramatistic explanation, then, depends not only upon answering the relevant dramatistic questions, but also upon recognizing how each answer influences all other answers.

Third, after looking at the relevant questions and their interrelationships, the task of pulling the analysis together remains. The dramatistic pentad allows performers to generate considerable information. As performers go about their analysis work, they find many details. Performers have to make sense of the bits and pieces they find. Often, performers discover a number of reasonable answers to the questions they ask. Some answers may even be contradictory to others. This is just to say that an aesthetic text may support a number of legitimate interpretations. Performers, then, should work to recognize the many ways a text might be understood before they pursue a particular interpretation for performance.

PROBE 1

To understand more fully how the pentad works, identify a specific communication event from your own life. Using the basic dramatistic questions, examine this experience.

1. Which questions seem the most relevant for understanding the event?
2. How do the questions interrelate? In other words, how was your communication affected by the scene you were in? In what ways was your purpose determined by who you are? How did your manner of speaking affect your audience? What other interrelationships help explain the communication event? Describe.

For a sample dramatistic analysis of an aesthetic text, see Appendix B, page 229.

The Speakers of Aesthetic Communication

Before initiating a dramatistic analysis, we should consider the various speakers that are involved in an aesthetic event. We can identify four distinct speakers: creators, personae, performers, and audiences. It may seem strange to think of all of these figures as speakers, but each plays a communicative role in an aesthetic event. Their utterances, whether written or oral, are communication acts open for interpretation. We can even see an audience's nonverbal response as a meaningful message, an act of communication in the ongoing aesthetic transaction. Figure 4.1 on page 52 specifies these speakers in dramatistic terms.

Creators are responsible for producing aesthetic acts. They compose, in written or oral form, a creative utterance, an aesthetic text. Their utterances are particularly expressive. In the ongoing flow of language, their texts stands out as new, fresh. Their original inventions are personal acts, emerging from their imaginative powers. Their creations unfold as private acts of the mind's making, whether evoked within the intimacy of one's room or on

The Speakers of Aesthetic Communication

Agents	Purpose	Scene	Agency
Creator	To compose	Within aesthetic world of personal and social action	Through an imaginative frame
Persona	To utter	Within aesthetic world of literary action	Through a linguistic frame
Performer	To present	Within aesthetic world of performative action	Through a theatrical frame
Audience	To respond	Within aesthetic world of personal and social action	Through a critical frame

FIGURE 4.1

a stage. Creators exist, then, in solitary or public scenes. The most familiar image of a creator of aesthetic texts is that of the writer, working in isolation. But creators may compose in a public arena, perhaps relying upon the audience to help in the composition. The minister who calls upon the congregation to provide an ''Amen,'' for example, is engaged in a public act of group composition.

We form impressions of creators in two fundamental ways. First, we may know a given creator personally, may have heard about a creator from friends and teachers, or may have read a creator's biography, if one exists. In such cases, we develop some sense of a creator as a person, a living being with a specific history and psychology. Second, our perception of a creator may stem from an encounter with the creator's work. Creators make strategic aesthetic choices, structuring their texts in particular ways. Observing a creator's aesthetic choices, we form a picture of the kind of person who would compose such an utterance. Each creator, then, has an implied self, the self that emerges from the creator's work. This self is typically referred to as an implied author.[2]

Personae exist only within aesthetic texts. They are the speakers the creators use to express what they want to say. Personae speak the words their creators permit. Personae perpetually utter the specific language given to them by their creators. They are the creators' constructions, set and fixed within linguistic structures, repeating the same words again and again. They only speak in a literary or aesthetic world. Creators and their personae may have much in common (e.g., attitudes, historical circumstances, style of speaking), or they may share very little. A writer, for example, might create a persona who holds some attitudes that the writer finds quite objectionable in order to mock such beliefs. Such is often the case when creators work with irony and satire. Irony and satire frequently depend upon the audience's awareness that differences exist between creators and their personae. John Betjeman's poem "In Westminster Abbey" presents a persona who shares none of Betjeman's values. When, for instance, the persona says,

> *Gracious Lord, oh bomb the Germans.*
> *Spare their women for Thy Sake,*
> *And if that is not too easy*
> *We will pardon Thy Mistake.*
> *But, gracious Lord, whate'er shall be,*
> *Don't let anyone bomb me.*

we know that Betjeman is inviting us to laugh with him at the persona's hypocrisy. Regardless of the degree of similarity, creators and personae are conceptually distinct. Personae live within their own aesthetic contexts, always a part of their creators' texts.

PROBE 2

Read an aesthetic text by one of your favorite authors. Search for and read a good biography of the creator (author) of the selection. You might find a biographical sketch by looking for a book on your creator (author) or by reference to such general sources as

> *Chambers' Biographical Dictionary: The Great of All Nations and All Times*, rev. ed. New York: St. Martin's Press, 1962.
> *Current Biography.* New York: Wilson, 1940 to date.

or to such literary biographies as

> Browning, David C. *Everyman's Dictionary of Literary Biography.* New York: Dutton, 1960.
> *Contemporary Authors: The International Bio-Bibliographical Guide to Current Authors and Their Works.* Detroit: Gale Research Company, 1962 to date.
> Kunitz, Stanley J., and Howard Haycraft. *Twentieth Century Authors.* New York: Wilson, 1942.

Then, answer the following questions:

1. What do the creator/author and the persona have in common? Demographic characteristics? Attitudes toward audience? Motivation for speaking? etc.
2. What differences, if any, do you find between the creator/author and the persona in the aesthetic text you selected?
3. What differences, if any, do you find between the real-life author and the implied author of the text you picked?

After working with one of your favorite authors, turn to the selections in Appendix A, page 169.

1. Read several selections looking for cases in which the persona and implied author appear similar and for instances in which the persona and implied author seem quite distinct.
2. Read Jorge Luis Borges' essay "Borges and I" in Appendix A (p. 175). Examine the relationship between "Borges the person" and "Borges the writer" described in the essay. Describe the persona and implied author of the selection. How do all these speakers compare with one another?

Earlier, we saw how all communicative acts are performative, how all humans are performing creatures acting on a social stage. Given such a claim, it follows that *performers* produce all communication. We also noted that this conception of the term *performer* breaks from typical associations of the word. As indicated, we are using *performer* in the more familiar and specific sense, to refer to a speaker who presents aesthetic texts within a theatrical frame. While performers may be the creators of the texts they present, typically performers are the speakers of others' communicative acts. They perform what others have already uttered. In this sense, a performer's behavior is at least twice behaved — once by the original speaker and once by the performer.[3] As a general rule, performers stage personae. Their task is to translate the utterances of personae into theatrical terms. In their efforts to present personae, many performers have found the dramatistic method a highly productive scheme. Performers, by asking the dramatistic questions of personae, come to understand the speakers they are to portray.

Audiences respond to performers' actions. Their responses, whether verbal or nonverbal, are communicative acts that contribute to aesthetic events. Audiences participate in social and personal scenes. They are members of an aesthetic community who view theatrical presentations. They bring to each aesthetic event their knowledge of theatrical conventions. They recognize what performers expect of them and know what they expect of performers. Likewise, they bring their own critical frameworks for making judgments of good and bad. On one end of the continuum, their evaluative schemes may be based simply on personal likes and dislikes. On the other end, their assessments may be informed by a highly sophisticated critical model designed to discriminate among performance events.

PROBE 3

Think of the last theatrical event you attended. What expectations did you have? What expectations did the event have for your own behavior? How did your presence contribute to the aesthetic event? How did you evaluate the event? What was the basis of your evaluation?

As a simple summary, we can say that creators compose personae who are staged by performers and responded to by audiences. Performers, given their usual task of presenting personae, generally start their analysis work by asking the dramatistic questions of the speakers within aesthetic texts. To obtain a full grasp of the entire aesthetic event, however, performers should apply the dramatistic pentad to all the speakers involved in the aesthetic act. Performers may be particularly motivated to examine other speakers when they feel their given dramatistic analysis of a persona proves to be an insufficient basis for their performance choices. Knowing something about a persona's creator or recognizing how an audience may contribute to the aesthetic act, for example, may provide the performer with a better understanding of the persona's utterance. Most often, then, performers look to other speakers in order to discover more about the personae they are to present.

Separating creators, personae, performers, and audiences offers some clarity and direction for the performers' analytic work, but it may also obscure some of the complexity of aesthetic events. Probe 4 explores this complexity.

PROBE 4

Listed below are four different discussion topics that point to the complexity of aesthetic events.

1. Make a case that each speaker (creator, persona, performer, audience member) can be seen in some ways as playing the roles of the other speakers: that is, demonstrate how creators can also be seen as personae, performers, and audience mem-

bers; how personae can also be seen as creators, performers, and audience members; how performers can also be seen as creators, personae, and audience members; and how audience members can also be seen as creators, performers, and personae.

2. Identify and describe a theatrical event in which a performer is not engaged in the staging of *another's* communicative act.

3. Discuss whether it is possible to have an aesthetic event without the presence of an audience.

4. Assume that a performer has faithfully presented a persona within a theatrical frame. To whom, then, is the audience responding? The creator? The persona? The performer? Themselves? A combination of all of the speakers in the event? Make a case for your answer.

The Aesthetic Communication of Speakers

In Chapter 2, we identified several ways of defining aesthetic communication and noted that this book restricts the definition of aesthetic communication to written or oral texts and to artistic performances. In general, an aesthetic text is a creative utterance that is available for the performer's presentation. Usually, the aesthetic texts that performers encounter are written, recorded utterances, but they may also be passed on orally from one generation to another or may emerge spontaneously in oral composition. Performers from literate cultures typically work from written texts, even if the texts originated within oral contexts. A performer who wishes to present an oral text may find that an essential first step is to translate the oral utterance into written form. This allows for a more detailed study and analysis of the text than a transitory oral text permits.

We can classify aesthetic communication, whether written or oral, in a number of ways. The most familiar categories for organizing traditional literary works are poetry, prose, and drama. These categories, however, do not offer performers much help in their efforts to stage texts. Another, more useful, scheme for classifying aesthetic communication is based upon the speaker's relationship to the audience. This way of looking at aesthetic communication arranges aesthetic acts according to mode. The modes of aesthetic communication are lyric, dramatic, and epic. Figure 4.2 demonstrates in dramatistic terms how each mode specifies a particular relationship between a speaker and an audience.

The Aesthetic Communication of Speakers

Modes of Aesthetic Communication	Agent	Act	Scene
Lyric	Single speaker	Personal action	Speaking alone to an audience
Dramatic	Two or more speakers	Interpersonal interaction	Speaking to each other
Epic	Two or more speakers	Combination of personal action and interpersonal interaction	One speaking alone to an audience and two or more speaking to each other

FIGURE 4.2

Aesthetic communication in the lyric mode is a personal utterance, an expression of an individual speaker's private realization or discovery. The lyric mode often seems to insist on the presence of an "I." Even when the speaker is speaking about others, the speaker's individual consciousness is keenly felt. The lyric utterance frequently carries a sense of intimacy and urgency. Expressive of an individual self, the lyric voice speaks in isolation and seems to yearn for response. Perhaps the lyric speaker seeks a self-response, standing as an audience for oneself. Or the speaker may be addressing a particular other, disclosing to a specific audience. Or finally, the speaker may be talking to a general audience, sharing thoughts and feelings with whoever will listen.

Aesthetic communication in the dramatic mode is a shared conversation between two or more speakers. Such interpersonal interaction is a private act, an exchange between participants. To engage in interaction demands another's presence, a partner, a company of voices. In the dramatic mode, audiences stand outside the speakers' interactions. They function primarily as witnesses to the exchange, allowed to listen but not to enter into the conversation. Many artistic performances are in the dramatic mode. Many rituals and modern staged plays, for example, rely upon a number of speakers who interact among themselves.

Aesthetic communication in the epic mode unfolds as story. Combining the qualities of the lyric and dramatic modes, a tale emerges in which a storyteller speaks directly to an audience and through other speakers who appear to speak for themselves. Thus, storytellers have something to tell and to show. As they tell their tales, a complex web of voices is heard, at times speaking in the "here and now," at other times conversing in the "there and then." Most often, speakers of the epic mode are constantly shifting from telling about an event to showing the private interactions between characters. A simple hypothetical exchange helps illustrate the point:

> She said laughing, "This is going too far."
> "Do you think we should stop?" her mother giggled.

Here, the speaker tells the audience directly, "She said laughing" and "her mother giggled." The speaker also shows the audience what the daughter and mother actually said. The mother/daughter exchange occurred in a time and place that is distinct from the speaker's "here and now" telling.

PROBE 5   To explore the various modes to a greater event, address the following:

1. Most often, poetry is in the lyric mode, plays are in the dramatic mode, and prose fiction (short stories and novels) are in the epic mode. Exceptions, however, can easily be found. As you listen to various aesthetic texts throughout the term, make a list of examples in which these typical relationships do not hold true.
2. Carnival barkers, auctioneers, and tour guides, to select just three examples, usually speak in the lyric mode. Attend or recall an event with one of these speakers and analyze whether the speaker performed in a lyric, dramatic, or epic mode.

As suggested, part of the appeal of thinking of aesthetic communication in modal terms is that modes point to speaker/audience relationships. This provides performers some clear guidelines for presenting the scenes in which personae exist. Figure 4.3 outlines the possibilities. When speakers address themselves, their scenes are closed. In such situations, speakers appear to be reflecting, thinking to themselves. Diary writers, for example, typically record their own experiences and thoughts for themselves. Likewise, a poem may have a persona who seems to come to some private realization, a personal insight, uttered for that persona's behalf. The performer who wants to evoke a closed, reflective scene on stage would avoid direct eye contact with the viewing audience. Most likely, the performer would stage the scene to give the appearance that the viewing audience was looking in through an imaginary fourth wall, hearing the speaker think aloud. The viewing audience sees the performer, but the performer gives the impression of

Speaker/Audience Relationships

Speaker's Audience	Relationship to Viewing Audience	Nature of the Communicative Act
Self	Closed	Reflective
Specific Other	Closed	Conversational
General Audience	Open	Presentational

FIGURE 4.3

not seeing the audience, since the viewing audience is not a part of the scene that the performer is trying to enact.

Scenes are also closed to the viewing audience when speakers are interacting with specific others. In this case, speakers engage specific others in direct conversation; two or more people are talking, carrying on some communicative exchange. Of course, conversations display considerable range, from intimate disclosure to furious argument. The key here is that a speaker is privately conversing with at least one other specified speaker. This situation is commonly found in love poetry. The title of Elizabeth Barrett Browning's poem "How Do I Love Thee?" identifies a particular other, "Thee," whom the persona is addressing. A similar context is suggested in the opening lines of "To His Coy Mistress" by Andrew Marvell: "Had we but World enough, and time,/This coyness, Lady, were no crime." What is clear in these poems is that each persona is articulating love for a specific other — a particular, not a general, audience. We also frequently encounter closed, conversational scenes in such forms as plays, initiation rites, and verbal dueling.

Solo performers who wish to stage closed, conversational scenes usually avoid direct contact with the viewing audience. Their intent is to show that the interaction is just between the personae in the text. Moreover, performers of closed, conversational scenes face the difficult problem of creating two or more personae. Characterization, a topic of discussion in Chapters 5 and 6, is perhaps the best method performers can use to distinguish between personae. Performers can also call upon the conventions of focus to differentiate characters. Focus, simply defined as where a performer chooses to look during a performance, allows a performer to visualize one persona while portraying another. In situations in which one persona is addressing a specific other who does not respond verbally, performers may elect to create the specific other by focusing upon a particular location on- or off-stage and by speaking to that location as if interacting with a real person. In cases in which two or more personae are verbally responding to each other, performers may decide to let each persona see the other persona(e) in a specific location.

Some scenes are open, or presentational, in nature. In such scenes speakers directly address a general audience, inviting all listeners to consider what they have to say. No one in particular is identified as the specific audience for such utterances. Instead, speakers present their thoughts to all who are willing to listen. This is often the case with speeches, sermons, essays, and stories. Speakers of such aesthetic acts, of course, may tailor their utterances for a particular occasion or may reflect their given historical circumstances, but they seem to design their discourse for anyone at that time and place. Other speakers do not point explicitly to a given time and place; they seem to transcend their initial contexts to address a universal audience. Performers of presentational scenes usually speak to the viewing audience directly. Performers assume that the audience is universal or that the viewing audience will accept the role of the audience for whom the author originally created the utterance.

Speakers' scenes, then, are closed when no direct interaction occurs between the speakers and the viewing audience. They are open when speakers address the attending audience directly. Most often, a speaker is in the lyric mode when reflecting privately and in the dramatic mode when conversing with another specified speaker. Speakers are in the epic mode when one speaker openly addresses a general audience and the other speakers speak with themselves.

Some Final Notes for the Performer

The task for performers is twofold: (1) to understand the speakers they find in aesthetic texts and (2) to translate that understanding into theatrical behaviors. The dramatistic method, as suggested, helps accomplish this task. It sets an agenda for viewing aesthetic texts. It guides performers' ways of seeing and grasping aesthetic acts. Yet, even when armed with the dramatistic method, all performers bring into play their own backgrounds and experiences for understanding the communication of others. While the dramatistic method is likely to generate certain interpretations of aesthetic acts, each individual's way of making sense of others' communication will lead to interpretive differences. Thus, interpretations of aesthetic texts are products of both the formal method one adopts to view texts and the everyday schemes people have for making sense of their world. We should also remember that people do not live in isolation. They are members of a social world that in part defines them. People come to share similar ways of seeing the world. Part of learning a language is learning how people within one's social community use language in particular ways. All interpretations of texts, then, depend upon three factors: membership within a particular social community, the unique interpretive processes of each individual, and the critical model

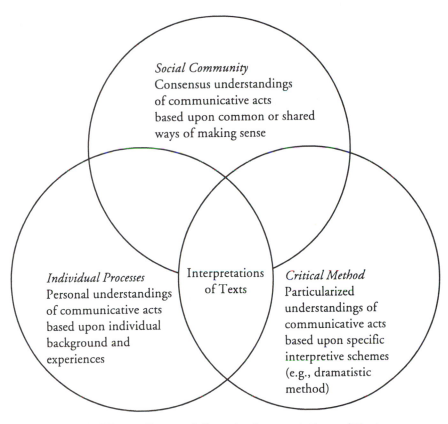

FIGURE 4.4   Factors Influencing Interpretations of Texts

one employs to examine aesthetic acts. Figure 4.4 identifies the factors that influence interpretations of texts.

Dramatism is likely to open up a number of different interpretations of any aesthetic text. With some texts, dramatism may offer a substantial amount of information that all careful readers would agree upon. With other texts, agreement among careful readers may be more difficult to find. In either case, performers must select which insights to stage. Performances are best seen as instances of preferred choices. A performer, for example, may discover through a dramatistic analysis that the persona in a particular text may be seen in a variety of possible scenes. In such a case, the performer would be wise to elect one scene to present, since to do otherwise could easily lead to audience confusion. Each performance, then, is only one possible rendering of a text. Texts yield a multiplicity of dramatistic explanations. Ideally, performers select a single, logically consistent dramatistic reading, honoring that which is textually certain. The obligation of performers is to feature the known over the speculative, the indisputable over the possible.[4] To present one legitimate reading of an aesthetic text is no minor affair. It stands as a descriptive account recording the performer's engagement with the aesthetic act of another.

Dramatism, however, is not the only analytic tool at the performer's disposal. Performance itself will provide additional clues into aesthetic texts. Using dramatism as a beginning point allows performers to initiate their explorations of aesthetic texts through the means of performance. Learning from performance is the subject of Chapter 5.

Notes

1. See Kenneth Burke, *A Grammar of Motives* (New York: Prentice-Hall, 1945).
2. See Wayne C. Booth, *The Rhetoric of Fiction*, 2nd ed. (Chicago: University of Chicago Press, 1983).
3. For an excellent discussion of the concept of twice-behaved behavior, see Richard Schechner, *Between Theatre & Anthropology* (Philadelphia: University of Pennsylvania Press, 1985).
4. For a fuller discussion of this point, see Beverly Whitaker Long, "Evaluating Performed Literature," in *Studies in Interpretation*, vol. 2, ed. Esther M. Doyle and Virginia Hastings Floyd (Amsterdam: Editions Rodopi N. V., 1977), 267–82.

Suggested Readings

Altieri, Charles. *Act and Quality: A Theory of Literary Meaning and Humanistic Understanding.* Amherst: University of Massachusetts Press, 1981.

Burke, Kenneth. *A Grammar of Motives.* New York: Prentice-Hall, 1945.

Burke, Kenneth. *Language as Symbolic Action.* Berkeley: University of California Press, 1966.

Campbell, Paul N. *The Speaking and the Speakers of Literature.* Belmont, CA: Dickenson, 1967.

Curry, S. S. *Imagination and Dramatic Instinct.* Boston: The Expression Company, 1896.

Geiger, Don. *The Sound, Sense, and Performance of Literature.* Glenview, IL: Scott, Foresman, 1963.

Geiger, Don. *The Dramatic Impulse in Modern Poetics.* Baton Rouge: Louisiana State University Press, 1967.

Gronbeck, Bruce E. "Dramaturgical Theory and Criticism: The State of the Art (or Science?)." *Western Speech Journal* 44(1980): 315–30.

Gudas, Fabian. "Dramatism and Modern Theories of Interpretation." In *Performance of Literature in Historical Perspectives*, edited by David W. Thompson, 589–627. Lanham, MD: University Press of America, 1983.

Gudas, Fabian. "The Vitality of Dramatism." *Literature in Performance* 3 (April 1983): 1–12.

Maclay, Joanna H., and Thomas O. Sloan. *Interpretation: An Approach to the Study of Literature*. New York: Random House, 1972.

Mattingly, Althea Smith, and Wilma H. Grimes. *Interpretation: Writer, Reader, Audience*, 2nd ed. Belmont, CA: Wadsworth, 1970.

Sloan, Thomas O., ed. *The Oral Study of Literature*. New York: Random House, 1966.

Thompson, David W., and Virginia Fredricks. *Oral Interpretation of Fiction: A Dramatistic Approach*, 2nd ed. Minneapolis: Burgess, 1967.

Yordon, Judy E. *Roles in Interpretation*, 2nd ed. Dubuque, IA: Wm. C. Brown, 1989.

CHAPTER 5

The Voice and Body as Analytic Tools

C hapter 4 presented the dramatistic method as a way of exploring aesthetic texts. Based upon dramatistic accounts of aesthetic texts, performers start their inquiry into the world of others. This chapter focuses upon the voice and body as instruments for examining the aesthetic texts of others. We shall see how the performer's voice and body are fundamental tools for generating understanding and for presenting aesthetic performances. The insights based upon a dramatistic analysis combined with the discoveries from vocal and bodily work lead the performer toward a truly knowledgeable stance. And only in knowing the other can the performer speak with authority.

Exploring Others through Voice and Body

Performing others means letting others live through one's own voice and body. As performers take on others through their voices and bodies, they question and reflect upon what they hear and feel. Their voices suggest what sounds right. Their bodies tell what seems valid. Performers are continually asking, "As I attempt to stage the persona, what are my vocal and physical behaviors telling me about the persona?" The procedure is one of trial and error, always referring back to what is known, always adding more information. A dialogue is set in motion. The process is a constant act of probing, speculating, discovering. It is a dialogue of experimentation. Some hypotheses appear true, others false. Those that appear true may be set and rehearsed with an eye toward a public presentation. Those that seem false are rejected as potential performance choices. But even the discarded is instructive: it tells the performer what characteristics the persona does not have. Knowing the inappropriate behaviors for the persona is often as important as knowing the appropriate. We can break down the procedure for exploring personae through voice and body to a five-step process: playing, testing, choosing, re-peating, and presenting.

Playing is the first step in the procedure. Ideally, performers start their vocal and bodily work with a playful attitude. A playful attitude suggests that performers are open, ready to respond. It allows them to wonder, ''What if?'' Guided by their dramatistic analyses, performers consider the full range of what is possible. One behavior triggers another. The playful stance invites performers to try out intuitions, to discover new ideas, to release inhibitions. A performer, for example, might try saying the aesthetic text with an accent, might explore moving toward the audience on a particular line, or might con-sider stressing a given word. With each playful act, performers store what is learned. At this point, though, they reject little or nothing. Playing calls for an open, receptive mind.

Playing, however, is not random. Performers rely upon their dramatistic understanding to guide their playful behavior. Performers play in keeping with the spirit of their texts: in other words, they remain sensitive to their texts during the process, maintaining a genuine regard for their personae. Playing may well reinforce or lead to revision of dramatistic beliefs. Through vocal and physical play, performers move into the world of others, learning more and more as they go and, perhaps, revising their dramatistic insights. By vocally and physically playing in the world of personae, performers enrich their understanding of what it means to be others.

During *testing*, the next step in the vocal and bodily exploratory process, performers probe their initial understandings of aesthetic texts. The testing process questions what performers think about their texts following drama-tistic analyses and vocal and bodily play. Vocal and physical playing gives performers an initial feel for aesthetic texts. In the testing stage, performers seek corroboration of their earlier insights. Once again, performers consider the validity of their first beliefs by being responsive to their vocal and physi-cal behavior. Performers accumulate evidence about others through vocal and physical experimentation. By using their voices and bodies to investi-gate aesthetic texts, they develop arguments based upon their own experi-ence. They form impressions as a result of their sensitivity to their own vocal and bodily clues. A performer, for example, may have discovered through a dramatistic analysis of Robert Browning's poem ''My Last Duchess'' that the persona may be primarily focused either upon the subject or upon the audi-ence in the opening lines: ''That's my last Duchess painted on the wall,/ Looking as if she were alive.'' During the testing stage, the performer would examine both options to determine if they are valid ways of understanding the persona's opening comments. The performer tests these possibilities by trying on the appropriate behaviors and then by listening to voice and body, sensing whether the vocal and physical actions feel right. Perhaps both op-tions will seem equally workable; perhaps the performer's voice and body will seem to favor one option over the other.

By exploring aesthetic texts through a dramatistic lens and by generating insights from vocal and bodily testing, performers become increasingly knowledgeable. Both dramatistic analyses and the vocal/bodily tests appear as witnesses willing to testify. Each may offer somewhat different versions of a given aesthetic text. Like judges, performers consider what each witness has to say to find out what they can know for sure. In the end, performers will ideally have a number of claims they can present with confidence. The aesthetic text always remains the constant center of attention. That is not to say, however, that performers' interpretations are not filtered through their own perspectives. As we saw in Chapter 4, understanding is a consequence of one's adopted analytic methods, individual experiences and background, and cultural membership. The combination of these factors will, in part, keep any two performances from appearing exactly alike. Nevertheless, performers by the end of the testing stage have developed a substantial case for the claims they are willing to support.

Choosing is the third step in the analytic process. Choices are made only after performers have vocally and bodily tested the full range of performance possibilities. Testing tells performers what options are supportable. Choosing is selecting from these valid options the ones that the performers are considering for presentation. With choice comes commitment. Performers begin to articulate visions. By trying on particular vocal and physical behaviors, performers find directions, interpretations to pursue. Performers now ask, "By choosing to present the persona with these particular vocal and bodily traits, what am I saying and learning about the persona?" Performers recognize that each choice is likely to influence other choices. Deciding to use a pounding vocal rhythm, for example, may encourage a performer to adopt some broad and repetitive physical gestures.

Two fundamental issues face performers at this point: (1) Are all choices consistent with one another? and (2) Are some choices more aesthetically appealing than others? The first issue obligates performers to question if all choices join into a coherent explanation. Suppose, for instance, that a performer chooses to place a Southern persona in the Deep South. To be consistent with the choice of scene, the performer might adopt a Southern accent. In essence, the performer ensures that all vocal and bodily choices work together. In some cases, a performer's voice and body may discover contradictory impulses. What sounds right to the ear may seem in tension with what feels right to the body. A quick, glib verbal style, for example, may feel at odds with a heavy, lethargic body. In such instances, performers must decide if the contradictory behavior is appropriate action for the persona. In listening to what their voices and bodies teach, performers should select between contradictory information or should find a reason for contradictory information to exist.

Picking the most aesthetically pleasing option, the second issue noted above, is an ongoing performance challenge that depends upon performers' technical skills and creative powers. Often performers elect not to attempt behaviors that they cannot execute in a convincing manner. Performers may avoid taking on a given accent, for instance, if they have not mastered the necessary vocal dimensions of the accent. The more performers can do, the more options are available for their textual explorations. Vocal and physical skills, learned over time, allow performers to choose what is possible. Creativity helps performers to find what has not been found before. We should remember, however, that creativity flows not just from inspiration or innate talent, but, much more, from hard work. Perspiration, not inspiration, accounts for creativity.

Repeating is the fourth step in the vocal and bodily procedure. Only through extensive vocal and bodily repetition can performers feel completely confident in their choices. Repetition permits performers to set and to refine vocal and physical choices. By repeating over and over the vocal and physical acts of the personae, performers achieve a depth of understanding. Performers become increasingly comfortable in being others. They learn what it means to make another's speech one's own. They find nuances; they uncover subtleties. Such behaviors as a raised eyebrow, an extended pause, the fixing of a tie, or a falling inflection may become powerful and telling moments. Fine discriminations only suggest themselves after intense and rigorous rehearsal sessions in which performers stay alive to what their voices and bodies are saying. With each repetition, performers bring the energy of a first encounter, sensing points of connection, questioning moments of unease, and trusting their own vocal and bodily discoveries. Performers are not ready for public presentation until they are fully at ease in taking on the voice and body of others. To perform a persona is to speak the persona's words and to move in the persona's body as if the persona's language and physical actions were one's own.

Presenting, the last step in using the voice and body as analytic tools, provides performers feedback on their rehearsed choices. This step requires performers to be sensitive to audience members' reactions in aesthetic acts as well as to their own vocal and bodily behaviors. Following public presentations, performers remember how audiences respond to their vocal and bodily behaviors. The line that a performer was sure would receive a laugh may be met with silence. The subtle gesture that a performer was confident would highlight a significant point in the persona's speech may be missed by the audience. In more general terms, a performer may learn that the audience refuses to accept certain vocal and bodily behaviors as valid or appropriate actions of the persona. Such feedback should drive the performer back to the persona's aesthetic act. In a classroom setting, the performer and the audience can openly discuss their similar or different understandings of the persona. In many other theatrical contexts, however, this option is not available to the performer, who must then rely upon sensitivity to the audience's public reaction during the presentation. The performer, however, must remain somewhat cautious when speculating about audience response. Simply observing audience behavior may not provide a valid indication of what audience members are thinking and feeling.

Performers also receive information from their own vocal and physical behaviors during public presentations. Under the demands of public presentation, performers may produce vocal and bodily behaviors that they have never experienced before. Even when performers rehearse extensively, new behaviors often emerge in front of audiences. This phenomenon gives performers yet another chance to reflect upon what their vocal and bodily behaviors are suggesting. Feedback, whether from audience members or from listening to voice and body, offers performers an opportunity to rethink, to try again to enter into the world of another, to call upon voice and body as instruments of exploration. Thus, a public presentation is best seen not as an end product, but as part of the continual process of exploring the aesthetic text of another.

PROBE 1

Complete a dramatistic analysis of the aesthetic text for your next performance. Then explore the aesthetic text following the playing, testing, choosing, repeating, and presenting steps. Keep a careful record of what you are learning about the aesthetic text at each point in the process. Make sure to describe your vocal and bodily discoveries in detail. Compare and contrast the insights you gained from your vocal and bodily exploration with the discoveries you made from the dramatistic analysis. How did these two methods for examining aesthetic texts inform each other?

Dimensions of the Voice

We have seen in general terms what is involved in using the voice and body as a method for exploring the aesthetic texts of others. This section outlines the dimensions of the voice that the performer can call upon when analyzing aesthetic texts. The vocal features of oral speech, sometimes referred to as paralanguage, not only aid communication, but also serve performers in their exploration of others. This section is not designed to train the "good speaking voice." It does not offer rules, advance programs for vocal improvement, or dictate standard vocal behaviors. Many sources are available for such purposes.[1] Instead, this section simply identifies the vocal behaviors that performers can use in their examination of personae. The assumption is that most individuals possess a voice that is sufficiently flexible to adapt to a wide variety of communicative demands. The different vocal behavior displayed by the vast majority of people when attending a funeral and when watching a sporting event supports such a claim. In everyday communication, most people demonstrate a wider range of vocal behavior than is typically asked of public performers. The discussion, then, identifies three fundamental vocal tools at the performer's disposal: clarity, variety, and quality.

Vocal clarity refers to issues of articulation and pronunciation, both of which deal with the formation of the sounds of spoken language. We can define articulation as the intelligibility of speech and pronunciation as the correctness of speech. Thus, a performer could clearly articulate the mispronunciation of a word or could pronounce a word accurately with poor articulation. Poor articulation is often a result of what is called lazy speech. In such cases, the articulators — the lips, teeth, tongue, and hard and soft palate—are not doing their work. They fail to shape properly the size and opening of the oral cavity. In other cases, poor articulation may be an intentional act, as when people mumble under their breath or when Little Leaguers offer their baseball patter. Pronunciation is a question of acceptable standards. What is acceptable in one region of the country, however, may not be acceptable in another. Regional preferences and the dictionary determine permissible pronunciations. Errors in pronunciation are usually a result of vowel or consonant omissions ("comin" for "coming"), additions ("idear" for "idea"), substitutions ("wader" for "water"), inversions ("interduce" for "introduce"), and misplaced accents ("ce´ment" for ce-ment´").

Vocal variety is primarily a matter of pitch, volume, and tempo. Pitch is the frequency of a vibration. In human physiology, the vocal folds vibrate as air pushes through. The rate or speed of the vibration determines the vocal pitch: the greater the number of vibrations per second, the higher the pitch. In general, males have a lower pitch than females, because the longer and thicker male vocal folds average fewer vibrations per second than do the shorter and thinner female vocal folds. The tension of the vocal folds also influences pitch: the greater the tension, the higher the pitch. The tension resulting from fear or excitement, for instance, might lead to a higher pitch than one would normally use. Even under normal circumstances, not all people speak at a pitch best suited to them. Habitual pitch is the range in which a voice typically operates. Optimum pitch, on the other hand, is the range in which a voice operates with the greatest ease. An individual's habitual and optimum pitches may or may not be the same. When an individual's optimum and habitual pitches are at variance, vocal flexibility and responsiveness may be restricted. People can find their optimum pitch by singing a vowel from the lowest to the highest point that can be reached without strain. On the keys of a piano, they should then locate those points and find the mid-range. Optimum pitch is usually about two notes below this middle point.

People rely on pitch to a remarkable degree to communicate what they want to say. People speak within a predominant key or tone as well as vary vocal inflection in order to express themselves. Speakers often use higher keys in communicating such attitudes as excitement, delight, and fear and lower keys in expressing such feelings as despair, reverence, and tranquility. People also alter vocal inflection in order to communicate. Vocal inflection, the upward and downward movement of the voice within or between words, is often the most important characteristic of meaningful speech. For example, people usually mark a question with a rising inflection and a statement of fact with a falling inflection. They create different meanings when saying the same word with different inflections. The word *really* might serve as an easy example. Voicing it with an upward inflection, people may suggest wonder or surprise at what someone else has said. Saying it with a downward inflection, they may indicate that they are adamant about their position. People, however, do not always vary their pitch. At times, they may speak in a monotone, saying a succession of sounds in one unchanging key. When speaking with a repetitive, unvaried pitch, they typically appear less expressive. The monotone voice often seems wearisome and tedious. Without variety, it lacks vitality.

Vocal vitality also comes from changes in volume or intensity. Volume is the amplitude of sound waves, the force or intensity used when speaking. Ideally, speakers should have sufficient carrying power or projection to reach their listeners. Projection is a consequence of how an individual controls the flow of breath through the vocal folds. People need adequate breath support for sufficient volume. In most circumstances, people try to speak loudly enough to be easily heard. When they fail to do so, listeners often feel frustrated — so much so that listeners may simply stop paying attention to them or, in more extreme cases, may avoid future conversations with them. Just as speaking too softly can have a negative impact on communication, so can speaking too loudly. Seldom, if ever, do listeners want to feel that someone is shouting or yelling at them. Altering volume within acceptable ranges, however, can help speakers communicate. By varying volume, speakers provide stress, intensifying meaning.

Vocal variety is also achieved by changing the rate or tempo of speaking. Tempo is the rate of speed at which sounds are produced. Ordinarily, people speak at a rate of 120 – 150 words per minute. Within this overall rate, people might count upon pausing and phrasing to help communicate their ideas. Speakers might use pausing and phrasing as vocal punctuation, indicating word relationships and establishing emphasis. Speakers also rely upon pausing and phrasing to produce rhythm, to build suspense, to reinforce meaning, and to generate comedy. Comedy, for example, often depends upon the effective use of the pause. Before delivering a punch line, speakers may pause, take a beat. In doing so, they may increase the comic impact.

Vocal quality is what allows people to discriminate one voice from an-

To work with vocal variety, try the following exercises: **PROBE 2**

1. Say the sentence "He ate the cake" to suggest the following meanings:

Questioning	Pleased
Disgust	Anger
Puzzlement	Surprise
Disappointment	Amused

2. Say the sentence "Let's go home" as if
   a. You are looking forward to being home.
   b. You really don't want to go home.
   c. You have serious business at home.
   d. You dislike your home.
   e. You want to go but the person you're speaking to does not.
   f. The person you're speaking to wants to go but you do not.
3. Repeat the vowels (a, e, i, o, u) ten times, accelerating your pace as you go.
4. Count to twenty, increasing your volume as you go.
5. Say the sentence "I found my favorite shoes" five times, stressing a different word each time. Describe the changes in meaning.
6. Mark a selection from Appendix A (p. 169) by placing a slash (/) for each meaningful unit of thought (phrase or sentence). Underline the words that merit stress. Repeat the exercise by identifying different units of thought and words worthy of stress.

other. Just as people can tell the difference between two musical instruments that strike the same note, people can specify the uniqueness of two human voices that have the same pitch. Vocal quality is what makes people feel that some voices are more pleasing than others. People tend to associate a resonant, interesting, effortless, melodic, or rich voice with a pleasing quality. On the other hand, people often hear a nasal, breathy, thin, strident, harsh, or hoarse voice as an unpleasing quality. Performers have long manipulated vocal quality in attempts to create characters. Hollywood, in particular, has fostered the unfortunate stereotypes that gangsters speak with a strident, harsh quality, that "sexy" women possess a breathy quality, and that weak men have a thin quality. Presenting such vocal stereotypes on stage, of course, is far from the ideal. Such broad and usually false characterizations fail to take into account the unique qualities of the other.

Performers can rely upon each of the vocal dimensions identified above to explore personae. Manipulating vocal clarity, variety, and quality allows performers to discover aspects of personae's aesthetic acts. Experimenting with various volume levels, for example, may offer some insight into a persona's temperament. We should remember that people form impressions of others, in part, based upon their vocal clarity, variety, and quality. Listeners make judgments, sometimes correctly and sometimes not, of others' sex, age, health, and status from hearing their voices. Likewise, they make assessments of others' personalities. They may decide, for instance, that an individual is shy since the person speaks softly, that an individual is dull or dumb since the person talks slowly, that an individual is kind since the person has a warm and resonant vocal quality, and so on. Clearly, the speakers' vocal dimensions carry important communicative functions. When working with the voice, then, performers should remain sensitive to how their vocal experiments may alter their own and others' impressions of personae. The power of the voice as an exploratory tool, however, depends upon the flexibility of the vocal instrument. The more performers can do with their voices, the more they are likely to discover about personae. The same can be said about performers' bodies, the subject of the next section.

PROBE 3

This probe is designed to guide you through an analysis of your vocal behavior. Tell a 3- to 5-minute story. As you do so, make a tape recording of your voice. Listen to the recording with a classmate and together answer the following questions.

Articulation

1. Was your articulation clear?
2. What words, if any, did you slur or mumble?

Pronunciation

1. Was your pronunciation correct? Any omissions, additions, substitutions, inversions, or misplaced accents?
2. In what ways, if any, did your pronunciation reflect your regional background?

Pitch

1. Was your habitual pitch level too high? Too low? Appropriate?

2. What variations in pitch did you use? How were these variations related to the sense of what you were saying?

Volume

1. Was your volume level too loud? Too soft? Appropriate?
2. What variations in volume did you use? How were these variations related to the sense of what you were saying?

Tempo

1. Was your rate too slow? Too fast? Appropriate?
2. What variations in rate did you use? How were these variations related to the sense of what you were saying?

Quality

1. Was your quality pleasing? Unpleasing?
2. Was your quality nasal, breathy, thin, strident, harsh, or hoarse? If so, was the quality related to the sense of what you were saying?

Having answered the above questions, how would you rate your vocal behavior? Are there aspects of your voice that you would like to change? If so, why? Does your voice display the range needed to explore the aesthetic texts of others?

Dimensions of the Body

Performers' voices do not operate in isolation. Voice is intricately connected to body. People rely upon both the verbal and the nonverbal behavior of others to make sense of what they say. The verbal informs the nonverbal, and the nonverbal informs the verbal. Occasionally, the verbal and the nonverbal behavior of a speaker seem contradictory. In such cases, people tend to believe the nonverbal behavior over the verbal. This implies that bodily action plays a powerful communicative role—so much so that some have argued that "one cannot not communicate." This double negative calls attention to the fact that everyone's physical presence is open to interpretation by others.

People take into account a number of factors as they make interpretations of others' nonverbal behavior, including the others' culture, context, demographics, and subject matter. Nonverbal communication is culturally learned, bound by context, and affected by the speaker's demographic features and subject matter. People make sense of others' nonverbal actions by considering such factors. People, for instance, would probably perceive a young adult who was having difficulty getting up from a chair as having some injury or illness, but they would see an elderly person who was displaying the same difficulty as acting appropriately for that age.

Performers begin their bodily examination of personae by recognizing how these factors (culture, context, demographics, and subject matter) might guide personae's actions. Often performers discover that a considerable amount of nonverbal behavior is fairly predictable. They also find, however, that playing against the expected may lead to some rich insights. Trying on physical adroitness in the portrayal of a ninety-year-old and breaching rules for appropriate nonverbal behavior in a given situation are instances of breaking expectations that may be quite informative. In addition, performers have a number of other physical dimensions they can call upon to investigate personae: kinesics, sign language, proxemics, object language, and tactile communication.

Kinesics is the study of gestures, movements, postures, and facial expressions. People rely upon kinesic behavior for four primary communicative purposes. First, speakers use kinesic behavior to illustrate what they are saying verbally. Through the use of gestures, people may reinforce or emphasize their ideas. In discussing the softness of a fabric, for example, a speaker might rub fingers together or stroke the air; both gestures underline what the speaker wants to say. Second, speakers depend upon kinesic behavior to convey emotions. Facial expressions are particularly powerful for communicating feelings. Research in this area has discovered twenty-three distinct eyebrow positions that indicate different meanings to people. Showing emotions nonverbally is sometimes called affect display. Such affect displays as happiness, surprise, fear, and anger appear universal; others are culturally specific. Rules for appropriate eye contact, for instance, vary from one culture to the next. In the United States, people tend to prefer eye contact when speaking, but they often feel that prolonged eye contact with a stranger or an acquaintance is unacceptable. Third, speakers employ kinesic behavior to regulate the speaking of others. For example, speakers may indicate through their eyes whether or not they are finished speaking, or they may suggest by a simple hand gesture when they want some feedback from their listeners. Likewise, listeners may signal nonverbally that they want speakers to elaborate, to repeat, to stop, and so on. Finally, speakers call upon kinesic behavior to serve personal needs. Scratching an itch, fixing disheveled clothes, and alleviating nervousness or boredom by such actions as clicking a ballpoint pen or twisting a paper clip are some common examples.

Sign language comprises the nonverbal behaviors that serve as word substitutions. The *V* for "victory," the circling of the first finger and the thumb for "OK," and the first finger placed over the lips for "quiet" are familiar examples. At times, sign language may be quite elaborate. The police, for instance, rely upon several signs in directing traffic. Much more complex is the American Sign Language system for the hearing-impaired.

Proxemics is the study of relational and environmental space. In general, the degree of intimacy people share with one another will determine the amount of space they maintain between each other. In intimate relationships, the distance between individuals when speaking varies from direct physical contact to about 18 inches. Even in intimate relationships, people feel a need to guard their space. People have a zone of comfort, an invisible bubble that they protect. They stake out their territory and become uncomfortable or defensive if uninvited guests violate their space. With friends, they usually establish greater distance than with intimates — a personal distance of 1½ – 4 feet. With more formal relationships, such as worker-supervisor or student-teacher, people typically assume a social distance of about 4 – 12 feet. In public contexts, they may insist upon distances well beyond 12 feet. The unspoken rules of appropriate distance to maintain when speaking with others are quite powerful. Failure to follow the rules is likely to generate a negative response. Imagine, for example, how people might react if someone, upon entering a crowded elevator, failed to turn around and face the door. Or consider how people might respond if a stranger sat right next to them when plenty of other space was available. Such flagrant violations of nonverbal rules may make people resentful or even hostile.[2]

The environments in which people find themselves will also influence their behavior. Some environments insist upon considerable formality; others invite relaxation; still others call for alertness. People, often unconsciously, react in keeping with the signals that environments send. When possible, people arrange the space under their control to create the kind of atmosphere they desire. For example, they may use space to establish their status. In general, the more space they have under their command, the greater their status. They may signal their position within an organization by their office size. Likewise, they may suggest their status by the quality and placement of their furniture.

Object language is a question of personal display. How people choose to dress, to fix their hair, to ornament their bodies, and to arrange belongings are some of the ways in which people manipulate physical objects as they present themselves to others. Borrowing some terms from theatrical practice, we could say that object language is the study of property and costume management. It is the props people elect to use and the costumes they choose to wear. Object language is highly influential in the formation of first impressions. To a large degree, people make decisions about others' attractiveness based upon their object language. The number of "dress for success" articles in popular magazines suggests that people are becoming increasingly aware of the impact of object language on their professional relationships.

Tactile communication focuses upon how people touch themselves, others, and physical objects. For the most part, people restrict their touching of others to sexual encounters, moments of consolation or support, and incidences of physical aggression. Touching, as we all know, is a powerful communicative act. The many common sayings in the English language associated with touch suggest just how powerful it is: we should be thick-skinned; we should handle people with care; we should avoid rubbing them the wrong way. Even a national telephone company urges us to "reach out and touch someone." We see the power of touch most clearly by noting that infants who are not touched become ill and sometimes die.[3]

All of the nonverbal variables specified above may come into play when presenting personae. In their process of exploration, performers try on various nonverbal behaviors to see what they can discover about personae. The performer's body functions as a critical tool, sensitive to any information the body acknowledges. The performer holds this information up against insights gained from vocal work and dramatistic analysis. The challenge for the performer is to be physically alive to others, to accept others through one's own presence and to let others speak through one's own body. Standing in for another requires bodily engagement.

PROBE 4

This probe leads you through an analysis of your bodily behavior. Answer all questions as honestly as you can.

Kinesics

If videotape is available, record yourself in a 5- to 10-minute conversation with a friend. Watch the tape carefully. If videotape is not accessible, watch your kinesic behavior in a full-length mirror as you tell a long joke or recite a familiar poem or story. Address the following questions:

1. How would you describe your gestures, movements, postures, and facial expressions? Was your kinesic behavior highly repetitive?
2. Were your gestures, movements, postures, and facial expressions in keeping with what you were saying?
3. Were your kinesic actions typical of your behavior?

Sign Language

Think about the physical actions you use as word substitutes. List as many as possible. Which ones would have universal recognition? Regional recognition? Local or private recognition?

Proxemics

Imagine yourself in the following contexts:

Church	Doctor's office
Movie theatre	Court
Classroom	Library
Political rally	Grocery store
Park	Home

Perform in as much detail as possible your probable proxemic behavior if you were speaking with a close friend in each of these contexts. Then act out your probable proxemic behavior if you were talking with a stranger in each of these contexts. Compare.

Object Language

Answer the following questions:

1. For the various contexts listed under proxemics, how would you typically dress? Would you wear makeup? Jewelry? If so, specify.
2. What image do you project by the object language you use?

Tactile Communication

Think about your touching behavior. Address the following questions:

1. Do you tend to touch the objects around you or tend to keep your hands to yourself?
2. Would you describe yourself as someone who frequently notices the feel of objects?

How would you rate your overall nonverbal behavior? Are there any aspects of your nonverbal actions that you would like to change? Is your body a flexible tool for exploring the aesthetic texts of others?

Working with the Voice and Body

The first section of this chapter outlined the general exploration process of playing, testing, choosing, repeating, and presenting. The second and third sections identified specific vocal and bodily dimensions that performers rely upon for their analytic work. This section provides some concrete advice on how performers might pursue their vocal and bodily inquiry when playing, testing, choosing, repeating, and presenting.

Playing first requires that performers get ready to encounter another by freeing or releasing the self. Three primary factors are generally responsible for blocking performers' readiness: inhibitions, tensions, and communication apprehension. People may be inhibited about a great number of things —expressing particular words or attitudes, doing certain physical actions, showing emotions in public, and so on. A student performer, for example, once selected for performance a poem that she discovered through analysis reflected a theological position with which she did not agree. The student felt that she could not perform the work given her religious convictions. Joke telling is another, more familiar, instance in which performers' inhibitions may color the performance act. It is not uncommon to see someone in telling a ''dirty'' joke demonstrate a reluctance to say certain words.

Each performer must decide which behaviors would be a genuine sacrifice of personal beliefs and integrity. A performer may have legitimate reasons for not wanting to present another. On the other hand, performers know that they cannot demand that all others share their own perspectives. Performers recognize that to stage others is only to stand in for them for the duration of the presentation. By doing so, performers can study others. They can learn what they feel is worth keeping from others. Based upon a genuine dialogue, performers can make that judgment in confidence that they have treated others fairly.

Tension appears to be a product of modern living. Few escape the pressures of everyday life. Unfortunately, tension often finds its way into one's voice and body. When it does so, the voice and body become limited, less flexible. It is to the performer's advantage, then, to release vocal and physical tensions. Probe 5 offers two relaxation exercises for reducing unwanted tension.

PROBE 5   Try the following exercises to release vocal and physical tension.

Progressive Relaxation[4]

Progressive relaxation works by tensing and relaxing your muscles in a particular order. After sitting straight in a comfortable chair, complete the following steps:

1. Tense your right hand and forearm. Hold for 5 – 10 seconds, then slowly release.
2. Tense your right biceps. Hold for 5 – 10 seconds, then slowly release.
3. Repeat steps 1 and 2 with your left hand, forearm, and biceps.
4. Tense your forehead. Hold for 5 – 10 seconds, then slowly release.
5. Tense your nose, tops of cheeks, and upper lip. Hold for 5 – 10 seconds, then slowly release.
6. Tense your mouth, jaw, and lower cheeks. Hold for 5 – 10 seconds, then slowly release.
7. Tense your chin and throat. Hold for 5 – 10 seconds, then slowly release.
8. Tense your chest, stomach, and back. Hold for 5 – 10 seconds, then slowly release.
9. Tense your right upper leg. Hold for 5 – 10 seconds, then slowly release.
10. Tense your right lower leg. Hold for 5 – 10 seconds, then slowly release.
11. Tense your right foot and toes. Hold for 5 – 10 seconds, then slowly release.
12. Repeat steps 9, 10, and 11 with your left upper leg, lower leg, and foot and toes.

Rag Doll

Drop your head forward to your chest and roll it slowly around, first to the right, then to the left, keeping your shoulders in a steady position. Feel the weight of your head as it moves from one position to another. After your neck feels free of tension, let your body drop over from the waist like a rag doll. Swing your body slightly from side to side, allowing your head to dangle. Gently bounce your head and arms by rocking from the waist. Slowly lift your body to an upright position while saying "Ahhh" in a continuous quiet tone.

A performer's tension may also result from apprehension about performing for an audience. Sometimes referred to as stage fright, communication apprehension can have crippling effects on a performer's work. Performers expect some degree of nervousness and realize that it is in fact beneficial. It is the body's way of getting ready to perform. That is why Leland Roloff prefers the term *presentational energy* to *stage fright*.[5] The difficulty arises when the performer's apprehension takes control. At such times, the performer's focus is typically upon the ability of the self to perform effectively rather than upon the aesthetic text of another. Perhaps the most useful strategy for controlling apprehension is to think about what the persona is saying rather than to evaluate how a performance might be progressing. During performance, then, the best question to ask is not "How am I doing?" but "What is the persona doing?" Feeling well prepared, doing relaxation exercises, practicing in front of friends before giving public presentations, and rehearsing in the space designated for the public performance are also helpful strategies for reducing apprehension. Performers seek the steps that work best for them. Their goal is to use their apprehension productively by channeling their energies toward the presentation of others.

Perhaps no strategy is more useful than doing voice and body warm-ups to release tension and apprehension. Vocal and bodily warm-ups take a variety of forms. Saying tongue twisters, varying pitch level, and changing vocal rate are some simple exercises that help energize and focus the voice. Physical exercises designed to loosen muscles and to tune coordination are beneficial for getting the body ready and directed. Just like an athlete, a performer would be unwise to participate without doing warm-ups. Warm-ups also aid concentration. When performers take warm-ups seriously, they can block out concerns from daily life and keep the task at hand clearly in mind. They can set their energies on the other; they can give their full commitment to the other.

Testing demands keen observation. Observation is a question of being attuned to the world as well as being sensitive to one's own vocal and bodily explorations. Performers are constantly observing others — noting how they walk, listening to how they sound, hearing how they sound, and so on. By studying human actions regularly, performers develop an awareness of the range of ways people go about their daily lives. Performers can use such observations as a catalogue of potential actions for presentation.

PROBE 6   Go to some public place (i.e., mall, busy street, student center) where you can unobtrusively watch people walk. Watch at least three different people very carefully, noting their pace, body movements, feet and arm positions, and so on. Consider where they seem to carry the weight of their bodies. Observe if they seem to lead from a particular part of their bodies. After studying these people as closely as you can, try performing their walks for your class.

Observing one's own voice and body while staging others, however, is in some ways a more difficult task. The senses are taking in a considerable amount of information. As performers take on others, the sound of the voice and the feel of the body are continuous sensations. So much information is coming in that to record every vocal and bodily clue is in fact extremely difficult. Performers, then, need to work much like the scientist who systematically selects and isolates variables for examination. If the voice and body are to be instructive analytic tools, performers must place each vocal and bodily action under a magnifying glass. Only by detailed attention to specific vocal and bodily behaviors can performers begin to understand what their voices and bodies are saying about personae. The investigation of such minute variables as the pronunciation of a single word, the quickness of a particular gesture, or the weight of a specific prop guides the performer's inquiry.

More often than not, performers focus their study on those vocal and bodily aspects that feel suspect. Suspicion often arises intuitively, as a sensation that a particular action is just not right. Such intuitive insights are frequently informed by our kinesthetic sense. Kinesthesia is the sensory experience of physical actions. Walking in a neighborhood where one feels safe, for instance, produces a different kinesthetic sense than does walking in a place where one feels unsafe. Usually, when feeling safe, the body relaxes; when feeling unsafe, the body tenses. Kinesthesia, then, is how actions feel. The kinesthetic sense tells performers when bodily movements and tensions seem in keeping with the attitudes of their personae. In staging an angry speaker, for example, the performer would examine how anger feels by acting out that attitude physically and reflecting upon bodily sensations.

Video and tape recordings can also aid the performer's observations. Recordings allow performers to focus upon themselves and to consider objectively their own behavior. Working in front of a mirror can serve a similar function. The risk in using these strategies is that some performers become highly self-conscious after seeing and hearing themselves. If this becomes a problem, the performer should avoid the techniques. We should remember, though, that most people experience some surprise when first hearing and seeing recordings of themselves.

As performers observe their own behaviors over time, they may become aware of their own personal style, a kind of personal signature that appears each time they perform. At times, performers may be locked into their style, unable to break from their set ways of staging others. In such cases, performers should work to expand their vocal and physical range. To develop full vocal and bodily range requires systematic and extended training over a number of years. Although such training is beyond present purposes, Probe 7 offers two simple physical exercises that can help performers break nonverbal habits.

PROBE 7   To break set, physical habits, try the following:

1. Right-handed people tend to gesture from the right side and left-handed people from the left. Try to embody a persona by using your opposite orientation.
2. Giving yourself an imaginary physical absurdity can also aid you in breaking nonverbal habits. Assume that a persona you are attempting to perform has one of the following physical absurdities.
   a. A 3-foot-long horn in the center of the forehead
   b. Feet that weigh 100 pounds
   c. Ten-inch fingernails
   d. Hands and arms made of eggshells
   e. A nose that hangs below the chin
   How did taking on a physical absurdity change your nonverbal behavior? In what ways were the changes in your behavior instructive?

Choosing requires a coordination of vocal and bodily actions. To do so, performers follow three essential steps: (1) moving from insight to behavior and from behavior to insight, (2) finding the motivation for vocal and bodily behavior, and (3) translating another's aesthetic act to a theatrical context. The performer's first step in coordinating vocal and bodily behavior involves the interplay between understanding and doing. Performers may discover a number of insights about personae through their analytic work but may be unable to present behaviors in keeping with what they know. On the other hand, performers may find that they are doing specific behaviors that seem appropriate to the persona but may not be able to articulate why. In either case, the performers are lacking an essential component of the performance dynamic. Ideally, understanding leads to doing, and doing leads to understanding. Yet performers know that this ideal will not always be met. When performers recognize that particular behaviors are beyond their capacities, they develop alternative performance strategies. This is not to imply that performers should never try to expand their technical skills; of course they should. But performers need to realize what actions would be a reasonable stretch. If performers know what behaviors to work on, they can develop their skills in a systematic way. They often learn what skills they need through their encounters with personae who demand certain vocal or bodily behavior for portrayal. Being unable to present these behaviors specifies for performers the technical skills they should develop.

When performers sense that their behaviors are in some undefined way capturing essential qualities of personae, they trust their intuitions in the hope that through the performance process, things will become clear. Performers often come to understand why an action felt right only after an extended time doing the behavior. Performers slowly learn to identify or label the meaning of their actions. But sometimes, performers never quite know why a particular action seemed to work. In such cases, performers can either accept that they cannot name it or examine it until they can.

The second step in coordinating vocal and bodily actions involves the question of motivation. All actions are motivated, designed to achieve some end. All vocal and bodily behaviors arise from some purpose, whether acknowledged or not. Thus, performers seek vocal and bodily actions that are consistent with the personae's attempts to reach their goals. A persona may close a door, for example, in order to stop a draft, to gain privacy, or to shut out an intruder. In each case, a reason motivates the action. The key for the performer is to recognize that performing is a process of engaging in purposeful action, not portraying specific emotions. Emotions result from actions. Performers, then, search for what motivates each particular vocal and bodily behavior. The focus is on what the persona might be doing, rather than on what the persona might be feeling.

The third step in coordinating vocal and bodily behavior involves the translation of an aesthetic text from one communicative context to another. Performers find aesthetic acts in a variety of contexts — on the page, in informal conversations, at public speaking events, in church rituals, and so on. The performer's task is to bring these aesthetic acts to the stage. In doing so, the performer may have to alter the persona's original vocal and bodily behavior to suit the demands of a theatrical context. Performers give an aesthetic text spoken in intimacy, for instance, sufficient volume for an audience to hear. Performers restrict the aesthetic text that emerged while hiking through the woods to the theatrical space. As a general principle, the performer should find some behavioral equivalency that captures the essence of the original utterance.

Repeating allows performers to set vocal and bodily behavior. To set behavior requires memorization and practice. A performer memorizes the other's utterance in order to achieve a genuine commitment to the other. By knowing the other's precise words, the performer learns about the other in an intimate way. Memorization forces attention to detail, demands that time be spent with the other, and insists that the other is valued. Memorization calls for an engaged mind. Memorizing is not difficult, but it does require time and effort.

PROBE 8   To help with memorization, try the following strategies.

1. Repeat the text, one part at a time, until you can get all the way through it. If you forget a part, start over. Make sure you work out loud, since giving voice to the text will help you remember it. Once you have decided where you will move in your presentation, say the text as you go through your blocking. Associating lines with physical space will help memorization.
2. Tape-record your piece. Listen to it as you get dressed in the morning, fall asleep at night, drive to school, etc. Stop the tape and repeat what you can.
3. Carry a copy of the piece with you at all times. Whenever you have a few moments throughout the day, take it out and memorize. You will be surprised by how much you can remember by this strategy.

Memorization, however, is not sufficient for setting vocal and bodily behavior. Once an aesthetic text is memorized, the performer embarks upon a period of seemingly endless drills, repeating and repeating the aesthetic text until able to speak the other's precise words as if they were the performer's own. Performers need time to develop insights into another, to gain intimacy with another, and to become comfortable in speaking for another. No substitutes exist for rehearsing until voice and body are knowledgeably and behaviorally set. Experienced performers typically require approximately 3 hours of rehearsal time for each minute of performance. Less-experienced performers need considerably more time if they are to master their performance choices.

Presenting occurs after performers have released, responded to, coordinated, and set their vocal and bodily behavior. Public performance is an offering. Performers present reasoned vocal and bodily actions on behalf of another; they speak for and to others. Their goal is to make their offering with respect, humility, and intelligence. Their right to stand in for others is earned through diligent and dedicated work. Their voices and bodies appear on stage in celebration of dialogic engagement. They remain open, receptive to a continuing exchange. They have initiated a process of exploration — a process filled with more questions than answers, a process of joyful encounter.

Vocal and bodily exploration combined with dramatistic analysis places the performer in a privileged position to speak for others. Considerable care and intensive work allows the performer to speak with some authority. By playing, testing, choosing, repeating, and presenting, the performer comes to know and learns to stage others. Such an effort is pursued in the name of the other, in the spirit of discovery, and in the earnest desire for a dialogic engagement.

Notes

1. For example, see Kenneth C. Crannell, *Voice and Articulation*, 2nd ed. (Belmont, CA: Wadsworth, 1991); Kristin Linklater, *Freeing the Natural Voice* (New York: Drama Book Specialists, 1976); Arthur Lessac, *The Use and Training of the Human Voice* (New York: Drama Book Specialists, 1967); and Lynne K. Wells, *The Articulate Voice* (Scottsdale, AZ: Gorsuch Scarisbrick, 1989).
2. For an extended discussion of intimate, personal, social, and public distances, see Edward T. Hall, *The Hidden Dimension* (Garden City, NY: Anchor Books, 1969).
3. Ashley Montagu, *Touching: The Human Significance of the Skin* (New York: Harper & Row, 1978), 35.
4. This exercise is based upon Edmund Jacobson's model of relaxation techniques. See Edmund Jacobson, *Progressive Relaxation*, 2nd ed. (Chicago: University of Chicago Press, 1938).
5. Leland H. Roloff. *The Perception and Evocation of Literature* (Glenview, IL: Scott, Foresman, 1973), 104–107.

Suggested Readings

Benedetti, Robert. *The Actor at Work*, 3rd ed. Englewood Cliffs, NJ: Prentice-Hall, 1981.

Birdwhistell, Ray L. *Kinesics and Context: Essays on Body Motion Communication.* Philadelphia: University of Pennsylvania Press, 1970.

Crannell, Kenneth C. *Voice and Articulation*, 2nd ed. Belmont, CA: Wadsworth, 1991.

Fisher, Hilda B. *Improving Voice and Articulation*, 2nd ed. Boston: Houghton Mifflin, 1975.

Fisher, Seymour. *Body Consciousness: You Are What You Feel.* Englewood Cliffs, NJ: Prentice-Hall, 1973.

Geiger, Don. "Poetic Realizing as Knowing." *Quarterly Journal of Speech* 59(1973): 311–18.

Hall, Edward T. *The Silent Language.* New York: Doubleday, 1959.

Hall, Edward T. *The Hidden Dimension.* Garden City, NY: Anchor Books, 1969.

Henley, Nancy M. *Body Politics: Power, Sex, and Nonverbal Communication.* Englewood Cliffs, NJ: Prentice-Hall, 1977.

Hershey, Lewis. "The Performance of Literature as Argument." *Southern Speech Communication Journal* 53(1988): 259–78.

King, Nancy R. *A Movement Approach to Acting.* Englewood Cliffs, NJ: Prentice-Hall, 1981.

Knapp, Mark. *Nonverbal Communication in Human Interaction*, 2nd ed. New York: Holt, Rinehart & Winston, 1980.

Lessac, Arthur. *The Use and Training of the Human Voice*. New York: Drama Book Specialists, 1967.

Linklater, Kristin. *Freeing the Natural Voice*. New York: Drama Book Specialists, 1976.

Lurie, Alison. *The Language of Clothes*. New York: Vintage, 1983.

Machlin, Evangeline. *Speech for the Stage*. New York: Theatre Arts Books, 1966.

Malandro, Loretta A., and Larry Baker. *Nonverbal Communication*. Reading, MA: Addison-Wesley, 1983.

Montagu, Ashley. *Touching: The Human Significance of the Skin*. New York: Harper & Row, 1978.

O'Brien, Jill L. "Performance as Criticism: Discoveries and Documentation Through Enactment." *Communication Studies* 40(1989): 189–201.

Park-Fuller, Linda, and Tillie Olsen. "Understanding What We Know: *Yonnondio: From the Thirties*." *Literature in Performance* 4(1983): 65–77.

Penrod, James. *Movement for the Performing Artist*. Palo Alto, CA: National Press Books, 1974.

Spolin, Viola. *Improvisation for the Theater*. Evanston, IL: Northwestern University Press, 1963.

Taylor, Jacqueline. "Documenting Performance Knowledge: Two Narrative Techniques in Grace Paley's Fiction." *Southern Speech Communication Journal* 53(1987): 65–79.

Wells, Lynne K. *The Articulate Voice*. Scottsdale, AZ: Gorsuch Scarisbrick, 1989.

CHAPTER 6

Empathy: The Understanding and Sharing of Feelings

T he preceding two chapters outline procedures for exploring the aesthetic texts of others. We have yet to mention, however, one fundamental tool at the performer's disposal. That tool is empathy, whose part in the inquiry process is so essential that it merits a chapter unto itself. After defining empathy, this chapter describes the empathic process in detail, giving particular attention to the point of view of others, the identification of one individual with another, and the adoption of another's feelings. The chapter ends by noting how performers might rely upon their empathic skills in the development of personae for presentation.

Empathy Defined

In many ways, dramatistic analysis and vocal and bodily exploration require empathic skills. Both methods call upon performers to take into account the perspectives of others. Both methods encourage performers to live in the world of others. Performers may enrich their dialogic engagement with aesthetic texts, however, by thinking of empathy as a distinct procedure. By combining the insights generated from dramatistic analysis and voice and body work with empathic understanding, performers can achieve a full encounter with aesthetic texts.

To establish empathy as a separate method, we need a clear definition of the term. People typically conceive of empathy as a process of feeling with another, of putting oneself in another's shoes. In general, people see empathy as a way in which individuals share feelings with others. The familiar expression "I know just how you feel" is a way of telling others that their feelings are understood and felt. These common associations are in keeping with how we shall define empathy here. Empathy, however, is such a complex phenomenon that considerable definitional precision is required if we are truly to understand it. We can state a formal definition as follows: *Empathy is a qualitative process in which individuals understand and share the feelings of others.* Each aspect of this definition requires explanation.

To suggest that empathy is a *qualitative process* is to recognize that (1) empathic skills develop over time and (2) empathic responses reflect degrees of understanding and sharing with another. As people mature into adulthood, they develop the ability to take into account the perspectives of others. In general terms, the developmental movement is from self-centered, egocentric to other-oriented, perspectivistic thought. Small children cannot differentiate between their own and others' points of view. They simply do not separate their own and others' ways of seeing and feeling. As they grow older, children recognize alternative perspectives, but they fail to see how differences in point of view might call for various communication strategies. Most six-year-olds, for example, acknowledge that a person who is smiling is more likely to return a ball that went into that person's yard than is a person who is frowning. But they typically would ask both people for the ball in the same manner. As children continue to develop, however, they gain the capacity to take into account the diverse perspectives of others for their communicative efforts.[1] By adulthood, people have the skill to structure their messages in keeping with their understandings of others' points of view. In fact, most adults become so sophisticated that they can engage a process of spiraling perspectives: "I think that you think that I think. . . ."[2] Yet, having the ability does not mean that people will elect to use that skill. For many communicative situations and tasks, people do not need or want to take into account the perspectives of others. This explains, in part, the differences in degrees of understanding and sharing of feelings.

The degree to which individuals understand and share the feelings of others is also a question of accuracy. Some empathic responses reflect the other's state of mind more precisely than do others. When people respond to the expression "I know just how you feel" with "No you don't," they are denying the empathic claim. In short, they refuse to accept that the other has an accurate sense of their feelings. Perhaps, given the differences in individual experiences, it is impossible to duplicate another's feelings completely. Yet people do believe at times that others have fully understood and shared in their feelings. Accurate empathy, then, may be a mutually authorized act. In such cases, the empathizer and the other accept that they have engaged in an understanding and sharing of feelings. Each authorizes the other's claim of an empathic response.

Not all situations, however, allow for mutual authorization. When a person claims to have empathized with a character in a novel, for instance, neither the character nor anyone else usually is present to authorize the claim. In such situations, people may turn to authorities beyond the immediate communication transaction for validation of their empathic responses. For example, people may seek the comments of literary, television, or film critics in part to check the adequacy of their own reactions. When people read a review of an event after viewing it, they are often measuring their own empathic responses against the reviewer's. At other times, people are quite content to trust their own judgment. Instead of seeking authorization, they simply assume that they understand and share in others' feelings. This is not surprising since people are often quite aware when they have genuinely felt with another.

Think of a situation in which you felt that you had engaged in an empathic transaction. Describe the experience in as much detail as possible.

PROBE 1

1. What feelings were shared and understood?
2. How did you react to sharing and understanding the feelings of another?
3. What specifically made you feel that you had empathized? Was the empathic transaction mutually authorized? If so, how? Did you look beyond the transaction for authorization? If so, to whom? Why? Did you simply trust your own belief that you had empathized? What, if anything, made you feel confident in this assessment?

Understanding another's feelings, the next aspect of the definition, is a fundamental component of an empathic reaction. Empathy depends upon the empathizer's awareness of the other's feelings. To empathize, a person must be able to perceive or recognize the other's state of feeling. Simply sharing feelings with another without having some understanding of those feelings falls short of a genuine empathic response. The empathizer must know not only what the other's feeling are, but also the reasons, causes, and context informing the other's feelings. Assume, for example, that two friends, Alice and Jennifer, are engaged in conversation. Alice is depressed because she knows that she is flunking out of school. Jennifer takes on Alice's depression, but she believes that Alice's feelings are a result of failing an important test. Both individuals are sharing the same feeling; but by not understanding the reason for Alice's depression, Jennifer misses an essential aspect of Alice's mental state. It would be unlikely in such a case that Alice would see Jennifer as empathic. Understanding, then, involves both recognition and analysis of the other's feelings.

Sharing another's feelings, the last dimension of the definition, implies an emotional communion between two people. To share in the feelings of another is to take on the other's emotional state, to live in the other's affective world, to breathe in the other's cry. Such a profound engagement may lead to shared physiological responses. The participants may shed tears in unison; they may feel pain together; they may offer joyous smiles in mutual celebration.

Performers call upon their empathic skills in their explorations of others. They know that to understand without sharing and to share without understanding are insufficient analytic positions. They strive for a full encounter. They want to feel confident that a true understanding and sharing of feelings has transpired. Such an engagement is indeed complex. The next section describes the basic steps involved in an empathic response.

The Empathic Process

Sharing and understanding the feelings of another is a highly sophisticated mental process. People call into play their intellectual and emotional capacities. They must be willing to engage in a genuine dialogue with another. In short, to empathize requires energy and commitment. Achieving such an empathic state is a difficult task that demands that the individual work through three fundamental steps: recognition, convergence, and adoption.

Recognition

Recognizing the other's feelings initiates the empathic process. The individual must understand as fully as possible what the other is experiencing emotionally and why the other feels that way. This claim reduces to the formula "the other feels . . . because . . ." At this point, the individual is working toward a clear perception of the other but has not joined in the other's feeling state. Knowing what another is thinking and feeling is in part a question of understanding the other's point of view.[3] Point of view is the perspective from which an utterance unfolds. It is a speaker's angle of vision or communicative stance, reflected in language. All communication has a speaker who selects and shapes what others can see and hear. Listeners, in determining a speaker's point of view, are restricted to what the speaker chooses to say. Like a camera that focuses upon certain things in a particular order, a speaker controls what listeners may take in. Listeners see through speakers' eyes. They allow speakers' perspectives to color events.

On the most fundamental level, a speaker's point of view may emerge in first, second, or third person. First-person texts, characterized by the use of *I* or *we*, tend to personalize, to insist on the presence of the speaker. First-person utterances generally have the effect of drawing listeners' attention to the speaker. We can identify a second-person text by the use of *you*. In some cases, it seems to bring the listening audience into dialogue. It openly invites participation, calling on the audience to become a central part of the utterance. The effect of such second-person texts often rests upon the listeners' willingness to accept the speaker's rendering or positioning of them. In other cases, second-person speech seems to encourage the listening audience to observe the relationship between the speaker and a specified other.[4] In third-person speech, defined by the use of *he*, *she*, or *they*, the speaker often seems to disappear. The speaker usually seems intent on focusing listeners' attention on another person or subject. While we can find some exceptions to these general tendencies, they suggest how the choice of speaking in first, second, or third person may create a broad sense of the speaker's relationship to the audience.

We can obtain a more specific sense of speakers by looking at a number of other dimensions of point of view. Speakers will appear more or less *credible* and more or less *objective*. Credible speakers are believable; their communication seems accurate. Listeners tend to accept their version of "what really happened." Utterances lacking credibility generally lead listeners to wonder about the "true" version and to reflect upon the reasons for the dubious statements. In short, credible speakers seem trustworthy. Objective speakers suppress their biases. Like traditional news accounts, the facts dominate their reports. No report, however, is totally objective. The mere fact that someone has specified something to say suggests some subjectivity. Objectivity allows listeners to receive, to the extent that objectivity is possible, an unbiased account. Hearing objective speech, listeners may form their own opinions and judgments. Subjectivity pulls listeners' attention to the personal views of the speaker.

The opening lines of Ernest Hemingway's short story "The Killers" establishes an objective and credible stance: "The door of Henry's lunchroom opened and two men came in. They sat down at the counter." Here, the speaker appears to stick to an unbiased report of what actually took place. The speaker seems trustworthy, a credible source of information. Archibald Marshall's story "The Ancient Roman" creates quite a different effect when the speaker begins: "Once there was an Ancient Roman, and he lived in a Roman villa with a pavement and wore a toga and sandals and all those things and he talked Latin quite easily, and he was a Senator and very important." In this case, the narrator's rambling and immature style raises questions of credibility. The narrator's speech is also highly colored by personal views. As these examples suggest, credibility and objectivity often function together. Highly subjective utterances, however, may appear extremely credible, just as highly objective communication may seem quite unbelievable.

Another dimension of point of view is *privilege*. Privileged speakers have the power to see into the minds of those they are discussing. They tell of others' thoughts, not based upon speculation or inference, but by a godlike ability to know what is inside others' minds. That is why such speakers are sometimes referred to as omniscient. The opening of Gail Godwin's "A Sorrowful Woman," for example, displays the speaker's godlike ability to see what the main character is feeling and thinking: "One winter evening she looked at them: the husband durable, receptive, gentle: the child a tender golden three. The sight of them made her so sad she did not want to see them ever again." Listeners may question how privileged speakers know what they know, but, most often, they accept the speakers' abilities to see into the minds of others as a common technique that speakers might use when telling stories. In short, privilege is a convention of storytelling. Privileged speakers, then, show listeners what others think; they open up the minds of others for listeners' consideration.

Speakers will also seem more or less *characterized* and *central* to their utterances. Characterized speakers are fully developed, multidimensional people. Their communication provides considerable evidence about who they are. After hearing their speech, listeners sense that they have encountered complete personalities. Central speakers assume a place in the forefront of their utterances. Their personal presence is essential to the tale they tell. The narrator, Sister, in Eudora Welty's "Why I Live at the P.O." is fully characterized and central in her tale. Even in the initial paragraph of Sister's story, listeners begin to see a clear character who places herself in the middle of her tale:

> I was getting along fine with Mama, Papa-Daddy and Uncle Ronda until my sister Stella-Rondo just separated from her husband and came back home again. Mr. Whitaker! Of course I went with Mr. Whitaker first, when he first appeared here in China Grove, taking "Pose Yourself" photos, and Stella-Rondo broke us up. Told him I was one-sided. Bigger on one side than the other, which is a deliberate, calculated falsehood: I'm the same. Stella-Rondo is exactly twelve months to the day younger than I am and for that reason she's spoiled.

The recognition step of the empathic process, then, involves understanding the intricate dimensions of a speaker's point of view. Such an understanding allows for insights into how texts unfold. Perhaps more importantly, various points of view are likely to have certain effects on listeners. Recognition of the potential effects of speakers' points of view permits listeners to see how language guides their perceptions. How speakers decide to structure their utterances controls empathic responses. Speakers set the boundaries by shaping texts in particular ways. Regardless of whether listeners respond positively or negatively, their task is to understand through careful analysis the perspectives of speakers.

The following two exercises are designed to increase your understanding of point of view.

First, Second, and Third Person

Write a short description of some humorous incident from your life, first in first person, then in second person, and finally in third person.

1. Which version strikes you as the most humorous? Why?
2. Which persona appears the most credible? Objective? Characterized? Central? Explain why.
3. Is any persona privileged? If so, with what effect?

Changing Speakers

Tell a traditional fairy tale, such as "Little Red Riding Hood" or "The Three Little Pigs," from the point of view of each of the characters in the tale. For example, "Little Red Riding Hood" would be told from the points of view of Little Red Riding Hood, Little Red Riding Hood's mother, the wolf, the grandmother, and the hunter. Then answer the following questions.

1. How did changing the speaker alter the point of view of the story?
2. What details were included in one version of the tale that were not in others? Identify the information that each speaker is aware of that the others are not.
3. Whose story is the most credible? Why?

Convergence

In this step in the empathic process, a listener and speaker come together. They form a union or bond. The speaker becomes a part of the listener's affective world. The listeners take in the speaker on an emotional level. Moving beyond a distanced recognition of the speaker's point of view, the listener merges with the speaker. Based upon the speaker's utterance, listeners tap and pull into play their own feelings. Emotions begin to correspond—

anger elicits anger, happiness elicits happiness, and so on. Convergence, then, is an act of identifying with the other's emotive state. Identification is a result of projective or adjustive mental processes.

With projective identification, listeners rely upon themselves as a basis for feeling with another. Listeners ask, "How would *I* feel if *I* were in the other's situation?" Thus, the listeners' own experiences dominate the nature of their responses. This conception parallels Constantin Stanislavski's notion of the "magic if." Stanislavski advises performers to imagine what they would do *if* confronted with the same "given circumstances" as a character they are attempting to portray. Performers, using the "magic if," project themselves into a character's likely emotional state and actions.[5] The assumption guiding projective identification is that people respond in similar ways when facing the same situation. Such identification occurs in the belief that the other's emotions would be in keeping with one's own.

Adjustive identification starts with an awareness of similarity of emotional states but takes into account others' views of their experiences. Instead of asking, "How would *I* feel if *I* . . . ," listeners perceive the given situation through the other's eyes. To do so, listeners adjust or accommodate their own thinking to the other's ways of seeing. This may require listeners to alter their own schemes for making sense of the world. In this sense, the other dominates the nature of the empathic encounter. Listeners, in acknowledging the unique ways in which the other makes experience meaningful, adapt to the other. Adjustive identification taps parallel feelings by giving the other control, by allowing the other to change how one sees, by accepting the other's unique sense of personal feelings.

Adoption

Once listeners have assimilated the other through projective identification or accommodated to the other through adjustive identification, they adopt the stance of the other. Convergence fostered an emotional union; adoption secures the merger. The other's feelings become firmly planted or solidified as one's own. A listener incorporates the other's way of seeing, making it a fixed dimension of the listener's own being. Security with another's perspective, however, may take several forms.

On the first level, listeners might adopt another's feelings based upon stereotypes. In this case, listeners see others in terms of how others view their social or cultural positions. The other's roles, status, and memberships may provide a basis for understanding. Adoptive stereotyping rests on a belief that by classifying people according to some category, we gain some understanding of them. Listeners assume, for example, that a fraternity man, politician, Greek, president, doctor, or student would feel a particular way because each of them is self-defined as that type of person. Although not the richest possible, such understandings should not be viewed negatively. People often explain their feelings by reference to the roles they play or the positions they hold. The actor John Ratzenberger, who portrays the character Cliff on the television program *Cheers*, extends this idea to comic extremes. Ratzenberger's Cliff understands himself first and foremost as a "mailman," and to empathize with Cliff is to recognize that his feelings often generate from this view of himself. To adopt another's feelings based upon a stereotypic image, however, may neglect important aspects of the other.

On the next level, listeners might adopt others' feelings based upon the others' conception of their dispositional traits. In this instance, listeners rely upon others' views of their personality characteristics or temperament as a key to others' emotional stance. Listeners believe, for instance, that kind, bitter, friendly, or nervous people would feel a certain way because they see themselves as people who act in keeping with such personality traits. Here again, listeners adopt the other's feelings by reference to a general category for understanding.

On the final level, the individualistic, listeners take into account the particular features of the other. They do not simply depend upon set categories for sharing and understanding the feelings of another. Instead, they recognize others' conception of their distinctive dimensions at the present moment. They see how others define themselves, including taking into consideration how others perceive their stereotypic and dispositional qualities. Listeners distinguish the other as a discrete and specific person on the assumption that all people, no matter how much they may have in common, are unique.[6]

The relationship between empathic convergence and adoption is described in Figure 6.1, page 96. The central question with the convergence stage is whether the self or the other dominates the nature of the experience. The primary issue with the adoptive step is the degree to which listeners take into account the unique dimensions of the other. As we have seen, the empathic process of recognition, convergence, and adoption is complex. We might consider a variety of responses as empathic. Perhaps the richest empathic encounter occurs, however, when listeners converge through adjustive identification and adopt others in terms of others' views of their individualistic features.

Empathy and Performance

Thus far, we have addressed the concept of empathy as a fundamental human ability. This section applies this information to the performer's task. We shall see how empathy may work as a tool of analysis when performers stage others.

The Relationship between Empathic Convergence and Adoption

	ADOPTION		
CONVERGENCE	Stereotypic	Dispositional	Individualistic
Projective Identification	Self-dominated experience in which the individual understands and shares the other's feelings based upon the other's social or cultural position	Self-dominated experience in which the individual understands and shares the other's feelings based upon the other's personality traits	Self-dominated experience in which the individual understands and shares the other's feelings based upon the other's unique features
Adjustive Identification	Other-dominated experience in which the individual understands and shares the other's feelings based upon the other's social or cultural position	Other-dominated experience in which the individual understands and shares the other's feelings based upon the other's personality traits	Other-dominated experience in which the individual understands and shares the other's feelings based upon the other's unique features

FIGURE 6.1

The performers' first obligation in using empathy as an investigative method is what we might call a process of imaginative entry. Here, performers move through the recognition, convergence, and adoption steps of the empathic process. Recognition calls for questioning, a process of careful scrutiny of the other's perspective. Convergence necessitates identification, adjusting oneself to the world of the other. Adoption demands that the other's unique qualities be incorporated, felt, taken on as one's own. Each step takes performers closer to others as they attempt to enter the others' worlds.

As performers proceed, they have an advantage that people in everyday communication typically do not. Performers repeatedly say, word for word, the specific speech of the others. Such an act allows performers a depth of understanding, an understanding much richer than if they would have just paraphrased what the other had said. To paraphrase is to reduce others. Saying the exact words of others in their unique form, in their complexity, in their style, in their intensity, helps performers to live in others, to share and understand worlds that are not their own. Such parroting functions as a procedure for coming, emotionally and intellectually, to know others. Performers, then, proceed through the empathic process aided by their exact verbalizations of the utterances of others. Such a procedure requires an imaginative leap into the worlds of others, a leap that is supported by the others' specific words.

The performers' second obligation is to move from an empathic response to behavioral action. Performers may share and understand the feelings of others, but their presentations may lack evidence of the fact. Performers not only must respond to others' feelings, but they also must translate that response into behavior. To do so, performers rely upon several clues that often emerge during the empathic process. One such clue is the performer's kinesthetic reactions during an empathic encounter. When a kinesthetic reaction accompanies an empathic response, performers can look to their own kinesthetic memories in their search for appropriate behaviors. Remembering and duplicating bodily sensations that emerged during an empathic encounter helps performers to move from empathic responses to behavioral action.

Performers also find a clue for appropriate behavior simply by recognizing how empathic responses may trigger empathic expressions. By empathizing when uttering the specific speech of another, performers often find that appropriate behaviors emerge naturally. The logic of this procedure unfolds in the following manner: (1) if performers have an empathic response to another, and (2) if, while empathizing, they utter the other's speech, then (3) often they will naturally find appropriate vocal and bodily behaviors. In empathizing with a persona's sad feelings, for example, a performer may discover that when saying the persona's words, the performer's voice and body will reflect sadness. An empathic response, then, may allow performers to discover vocal and bodily behaviors in keeping with the personae they are attempting to portray.

The performers' final obligation is to engage in a series of empathic responses. Each encounter performers have with another calls for a fresh empathic response. Each new response offers performers additional insights into others and provides performers with a productive stance for exploring others. In working with others' aesthetic texts, performers tap their empathic skills over and over, always seeking richer understandings and always willing to embrace others.

Performers should ask the following list of questions to guide their empathic work.

Imaginative Entry
1. What is the persona's point of view? Does the persona speak in the first, second, or third person?

2. To what extent is the persona credible? Objective? Is the persona privileged? To what extent is the persona characterized? Central?

3. How does the persona's point of view shape or control my response?

4. To what extent am I identifying with the persona? Am I understanding and sharing the persona's feelings?

5. To what extent am I projecting myself into the persona's position, letting my own experiences dominate the nature of the transaction? To what extent are my own experiences similar to those of the persona?

6. To what extent am I adjusting my own ways of seeing to those of the persona? How am I accommodating my ways of seeing to those of the persona?

7. To what extent am I adopting the persona into my world?

8. To what extent am I relying upon stereotypes, dispositional traits, and unique qualities in my adoption of the persona?

9. What have I learned about the persona by empathizing?

10. If it were possible, would the persona authorize my empathic claim?

Finding Behaviors and Responding Again

11. What clues for vocal and bodily behavior do my kinesthetic reactions to the persona provide?

12. What vocal and bodily behaviors are called into play when I utter the persona's speech while empathizing? Are these behaviors in keeping with the persona's behaviors?

13. To what extent am I empathizing with the persona each time I say the aesthetic text?

14. What different things am I learning each time I empathize with the persona?

Combining the information obtained by answering the above questions with the insights from dramatistic analysis and vocal and bodily work should provide performers with a rich understanding of the personae they are attempting to stage. At a minimum, a dialogic engagement with the aesthetic texts of others demands such analytic attention.

Notes

1. Jesse G. Delia and Ruth Anne Clark, "Cognitive Complexity, Social Perception and the Development of Listener-Adapted Communication in Six-, Eight-, Ten-, and Twelve-Year-Old Boys." *Communication Monographs* 44 (1977): 326–45.

2. The concept of a spiral of reciprocal perspectives is developed in R. D. Laing, H. Phillipson, and A. R. Lee, *Interpersonal Perception* (New York: Springer, 1966).

3. For more elaborate discussions of point of view, see Norman Friedman, *Form and Meaning in Fiction* (Athens: University of Georgia Press, 1975) and Wayne C.

Booth, *The Rhetoric of Fiction*, 2nd ed. (Chicago: University of Chicago Press, 1983).

4. For an excellent summary of the types of second-person address, see John Capecci, "Performing the Second-Person." *Text and Performance Quarterly* 9(1989): 42–52.

5. Constantin Stanislavski, *An Actor Prepares*, trans. Elizabeth Reynolds Hapgood (New York: Theatre Arts Books, 1952), 39–67.

6. For a scheme similar to the one outlined here, see Eugene A. Weinstein, "The Development of Interpersonal Competence," in *Handbook of Socialization Theory and Research*, ed. David A. Goslin (Chicago: Rand McNally, 1969), 753–75.

Suggested Readings

Bacon, Wallace A., and Robert S. Breen. *Literature as Experience*. New York: McGraw-Hill, 1959.

Bakhtin, M. M. *The Dialogic Imagination*. Translated by Caryl Emerson and Michael Holquist. Austin: University of Texas Press, 1981.

Booth, Wayne C. *The Rhetoric of Fiction*, 2nd ed. Chicago: University of Chicago Press, 1983.

Capecci, John. "Performing the Second-Person." *Text and Performance Quarterly* 9(1989): 42–52.

Horton, Joyce F. "The Response: A Discussion of Empathy." In *Perspectives on Oral Interpretation: Essays and Readings*, edited by John W. Gray, 65–86. Minneapolis: Burgess, 1968.

Howell, William S. *The Empathic Communicator*. Belmont, CA: Wadsworth, 1982.

Katz, Robert L. *Empathy: Its Nature and Uses*. Glencoe, IL: Free Press, 1963.

Laing, R. D., H. Phillipson, and A. R. Lee. *Interpersonal Perception*. New York: Springer, 1966.

Lanser, Susan S. *The Narrative Act: Point of View in Prose Fiction*. Princeton, NJ: Princeton University Press, 1981.

Lee, Vernon. "Empathy." In *Modern Book of Esthetics*, edited by Melvin R. Rader, 305–10. New York: Henry Holt, 1935.

Lipps, Theodore. "Empathy, Inner Imitation, and Sense Feelings." In *Modern Book of Esthetics*, edited by Melvin R. Rader, 295–301. New York: Henry Holt, 1935.

Parralla, Gilda C. "Projection and Adoption: Toward a Clarification of the Concept of Empathy." *Quarterly Journal of Speech* 57(1971): 204–13.

Pelias, Ronald J. "Empathy: Some Implications of Social Cognition Research for Interpretation Study." *Central States Speech Journal* 33(1983): 519–32.

Rubin, Louis D., Jr. *The Teller in the Tale*. Seattle: University of Washington Press, 1967.

Stanislavski, Constantin. *An Actor Prepares*. Translated by Elizabeth Reynolds Hapgood. New York: Theatre Arts Books, 1952.

Stewart, David. *Preface to Empathy*. New York: Philosophical Library, 1956.

PART III

The Nature of Aesthetic Texts in Aesthetic Transactions

CHAPTER 7

The Language of Aesthetic Texts in Aesthetic Transactions

C hapters 7 and 8 explore the nature of aesthetic texts in aesthetic transactions. Chapter 7 looks at the features typically associated with the language of aesthetic texts, and Chapter 8 examines the structural dimensions common to aesthetic utterances. These chapters, then, focus on aesthetic qualities, not only identifying the qualities we often find when encountering aesthetic texts, but also specifying the characteristics likely to be present in aesthetic transactions.

Chapter 7 first presents a variety of aesthetic textual forms, in an effort to identify the types of aesthetic texts before turning to their specific qualities. Next, the chapter argues that the participants within aesthetic transactions play specific roles and display degrees of involvement and competence. It further states that the language of aesthetic texts is both expressive and unified. Thus, the chapter isolates participants' involvement, competence, and roles as central to aesthetic transactions and the expressiveness and unity of language as basic qualities of aesthetic acts.

The Classification of Aesthetic Texts

As we saw in Chapter 4, we can classify aesthetic communication according to mode. The modal categories of lyric, dramatic, and epic point to the speaker's relationship to the audience. The lyric speaker is a single, private voice addressing the self, a specific other, or a general audience. Dramatic speakers engage in a closed conversation, a private interaction among two or more speakers. Epic speakers combine the dimensions of the lyric and dramatic modes, offering an utterance in which one speaker talks directly with an audience as well as showing two or more speakers in private conversation. The advantage of thinking in modal terms is that it allows performers to base performance choices upon their classification of aesthetic texts. Mode suggests how performers might understand speakers' relationships to their audiences.

One disadvantage of the modal scheme for classifying aesthetic texts, however, is that the categories may obscure more-familiar labels that are part of everyday vocabulary for understanding communicative acts. Often, understanding the communicative behavior of others is, in part, a process of recognizing the kind of utterance one is hearing. Such recognition guides listener response. Listeners know, for example, that a joke calls for laughter, that a sermon demands reverence, that a fairy tale requires entry into a make-believe world, and so on. The purpose here is to identify some of the common forms of aesthetic texts. Some of the terms will be familiar; others probably will not be. In either case, each classification or grouping of aesthetic texts specifies what is called a genre. Each genre is distinct, although some texts may fit into more than one category. The intent, then, is to establish standard schemes or labels for aesthetic texts.

To specify generic categories, however, is not to insist that all texts in that particular form are aesthetic. The utterance may or may not possess aesthetic qualities or elicit an aesthetic response. A letter from a bill collector, for instance, is seldom an aesthetic act, yet many letters are seen as aesthetic. With this in mind, we can identify three broad terms that help to organize the various forms of aesthetic texts: traditional literary forms, conversational forms, and ceremonial forms.

Traditional literary forms include poetry, prose fiction (short stories and novels), drama, letters, diaries, autobiographies, speeches, and essays. Probably, all would quickly agree that poetry, prose fiction, and drama are literary forms. Letters, diaries, autobiographies, and essays, however, enjoy less-universal agreement concerning their aesthetic status. Most would acknowledge that these forms permit literary works to emerge. Generally speaking, to claim that a text is literary is to argue that the text (1) appears in an established literary form and (2) meets generally accepted criteria for separating literary and nonliterary works. Criteria for such judgments are numerous. Although many competing arguments for separating literary from nonliterary works have been made, in recent years the tendency has been to blur the lines between literary and nonliterary texts.[1] Calling into question the distinctions between literary and nonliterary texts is in large part a result of recognizing similarities among many forms of communication. As we shall see in the next section, many conversational and ceremonial forms share the aesthetic qualities of traditional literary forms.

Aesthetic conversational forms emerge in everyday talk, in the ongoing flow of communication. They are an integral part of the speech environment. Speakers usually create these types of talk orally with the intent to engage others in a face-to-face communicative exchange. Speakers, however, often signal that they want others to listen before responding to their conversational texts. In other words, speakers typically take the floor while offering their texts. Conversational forms include such familiar types of communication as storytelling, verbal dueling (see Chapter 1), joke telling, toasts, fables, proverbs, tall tales, legends, myths, and fairy tales. Although often uttered by a single speaker, these oral forms typically fit into ongoing conversation. At a minimum, they call upon the participants to attend to each other. Such acts may be formal or informal, routine or special, passed from one generation to another or completely original.

A less familiar label, role speech, identifies another conversational form. With role speech, individuals adopt or take on a particular social character, complete with carefully developed scripts and, at times, quite elaborate costumes, props, even set and light designs. Much like actors, people who take on role speech present personae. However, their personae primarily serve a social or cultural function, an instrumental purpose. Usually, role speech is not designed for aesthetic ends. Most tour guides, auctioneers, flight attendants, carnival hawkers, and fortune tellers are speakers who present a persona for nonaesthetic purposes. In doing so, they usually adopt a definite performance style for their presentations, a style often in keeping with set performance conventions appropriate to their role. While such speakers may not see themselves as creating aesthetic texts, often their utterances carry aesthetic features.

We can apply another term, speech play, to those forms of talk in which speakers indicate, usually through tone, that listeners should hear their utterances as fun or playful. In such cases, speakers typically suggest that the primary purpose of their utterances is to entertain, to play a language game. Teasing, quoting real and imaginary dialogue, puns, transparent lies, mock threats, mimicking, and sound effects are a few examples of everyday talk that speakers often frame as speech play. Speakers code such playful conversational acts as performance, as aesthetic acts presented for listeners.[2]

Isolate your own or someone else's *role speech* and describe the utterance in as much detail as you can.

PROBE 1

1. To what extent was the talk scripted? Did it require the use of costume, props, or other theatrical devices?
2. Identify the performance expectations listeners would typically hold when encountering such speech.

List as many types of *speech play* as you can. Then respond to the following:

1. Describe the performance expectations listeners would typically hold when encountering such talk.

2. Reflect upon your own speech behavior. What communicative acts do you use that you would call speech play? Describe your own performance of these communicative acts.

Ceremonial forms are usually formal, solemn acts, marking a social, religious, or state occasion. At times, they function as rites of passage — a time set aside to acknowledge an individual's transition from one condition to another. For example, an individual may move from nonmembership to membership, from unmarried to married, or from childhood to adulthood. Ceremonial acts not only signal changes in status, but also reinforce the values of ceremonial participants. Ceremonies are often public displays of faith for cultural members. Common ceremonial forms include initiation rites (inaugurations, commencements), pledges/oaths, religious rituals (wedding, burial, baptism, communion, bar mitzvah, confirmation), chants (sports cheers, political slogans, magical incantations), and commemorations.

PROBE 2   Think of a ceremonial event you have attended. Describe in as much detail as possible the performance behaviors of the participants.

1. What participants spoke? How would you describe their talk? Was it planned? Spontaneous? What did the tone of their talk suggest? Etc.?
2. How was the event staged? What participants took center stage? How did the staging change during the event? Etc.?
3. Did the ceremony mark for any of the participants a change in status? What beliefs were endorsed or reinforced as a result of the ceremony?

The preceding list of types of aesthetic texts is not exhaustive. Nor are the categories rigid or exclusive; at times, the categories merge or overlap. The list, however, should serve as a firm beginning point in the performer's search for aesthetic texts to present. Depending upon the form, the performer may be more or less likely to discover aesthetic acts. Some forms more commonly carry aesthetic dimensions than do others. Since not all texts in these forms achieve aesthetic status, it may be helpful to identify the general qualities of the participants and language of aesthetic acts in aesthetic transactions.

The Participants and Language in Aesthetic Transactions

As noted in Chapter 2, aesthetic communication involves creativity and craft. On the broadest level, speakers of aesthetic communication offer creative acts emerging from their skillful work with craft. Thinking of aesthetic communication in this manner, however, may obscure part of its dynamic nature. Aesthetic communication implies a transaction. As such, it requires both a speaker and an attending audience. An aesthetic act is created by a speaker, but its life depends upon a careful listener. This section describes some of the defining characteristics of participants in aesthetic transactions, as well as the language of aesthetic texts.

Participants

In any aesthetic transaction, the participants (a speaker and an audience) are necessary to complete the process. The participants in the process reflect degrees of *engagement* and *competence* and take on *specified roles*. We shall discuss each of these dimensions in turn.

Engagement suggests that the participants take part in the aesthetic encounter. The participants are willing to enter the aesthetic exchange, are directly involved, are drawn in. The process calls upon their intellectual and emotional capacities. They share membership in the aesthetic world. Their presence is essential and felt. Engagement, however, operates in degrees. On the one hand, a participant may be totally engrossed, possessed, held within the aesthetic transaction. On the other hand, a participant may have only a peripheral interest, a detached or distanced stance. Engagement, then, requires that the participants give, at a minimum, some focused attention to the aesthetic event. To some degree, the speaker and the audience must come together, must become mutually connected through the aesthetic transaction.[3]

Participation in an aesthetic transaction, however, demands some competencies. The speaker carries the obligation to fashion an aesthetic form, to create an aesthetic text. The audience has the burden of response. Audiences must recognize what the speaker is asking of them. At times, speakers invite audiences to be careful listeners or observers. Their task in such cases is to respond with sensitivity to the subtle clues of the speakers' aesthetic utterances. At the very least, a sensitive response demands a knowledge of aesthetic conventions, the ability to recognize essential and significant details, and the capacity or willingness to become involved.

At other times, speakers require spectators to play an even more active role. Some aesthetic transactions may ask the audience to drop the listener stance and to adopt a speaking role. The structure of many riddles, for instance, solicits from the audience a statement of ignorance in order for the form to be completed. The proper response to "Why did the fireman wear red suspenders?" is "Why?" If the spectators answer the question, "To hold up his pants," they tell the joke but they breach the aesthetic form. Many aesthetic forms request that the audience accept a speaking part in the aesthetic transaction. Failure to do so may stifle or deny the aesthetic transaction.

The above example suggests that the roles between the speaker and the audience may at times become somewhat blurred. Nevertheless, speakers and audiences typically recognize in any aesthetic transaction what roles they are to play. The role of the speaker is to create; the role of the audience is to respond. Even in cases in which the audience members speak, their utterances are usually within set boundaries, offered in response to the original speaker's request. In such cases, audience members typically do not see themselves as creating: they are simply doing what the speaker asked them to do, merely helping the speaker along. Only when audience members feel that they have control over the direction of the aesthetic event are they likely to define themselves as speakers rather than as audience members. More often, speakers and audiences find considerable security in their respective roles. Knowing the roles they are to play specifies their obligations, guides their behavior, and helps make aesthetic transactions understandable.

PROBE 3   Describe in as much detail as possible the relationship between the speaker and the audience in each of the following situations.

1. A comedian working with a disruptive audience member.
2. A preacher calling upon the congregation for verbal support.
3. Johnny Carson asking audience members to play "Stump the Band."
4. The film *Rocky Horror Picture Show* encouraging or allowing audience members to engage in such collective actions as throwing toast and rice, flicking lighters, costuming as the characters in the film, making choral responses, and so on.

Do the roles between speakers and audience members in the above situations ever become blurred? How do the speakers guide audience members' behaviors? In each situation, what could an audience member do that would seem inappropriate?

Language

The language of aesthetic texts is often *expressive* and *unified*. Expressive language moves beyond pragmatic or instrumental concerns. It is not talk a speaker designs simply to achieve some practical end. Its literal, denotative sense is secondary to its evocative, connotative power. Expressive language avoids the ordinary, the cliché, the everyday. Striking in effect, it surprises, delights, enriches, moves, and compels listeners. In short, it commands attention and it is keenly felt. Its power arises from a reliance upon the sensuous, figurative, rhythmic, and reflexive.

Sensuous language appeals to the listeners' visual, auditory, tactile, olfactory, and gustatory senses. By inviting listeners to see, to hear, to touch, to smell, and to taste, sensuous language calls for immediate bodily involvement. To experience sensuous language, listeners must remain alive, ready to respond to utterances with their senses. Audience members crystallize images—they see pictures, hear sounds, feel textures, smell odors, taste substances. Listeners, then, depend upon their senses to bring to life the images they find in aesthetic texts.

Read Matthew Arnold's poem "Dover Beach."   **PROBE 4**

The sea is calm tonight
The tide is full, the moon lies fair
Upon the straits; on the French coast the light
Gleams and is gone; the cliffs of England stand,
Glimmering and vast, out in the tranquil bay.
Come to the window, sweet is the night air!
Only, from the long line of spray
Where the sea meets the moon-blanched land,
Listen! you hear the grating roar
Of pebbles which the waves draw back, and fling,
At their return, up the high strand,
Begin, and cease, and then again begin,
With tremulous cadence slow, and bring
The eternal note of sadness in.

Sophocles long ago
Heard it on the Aegean, and it brought
Into his mind the turbid ebb and flow
Of human misery; we
Find also in the sound a thought,
Hearing it by this distant northern sea.

The Sea of Faith
Was once, too, at the full, and round earth's shore
Lay like the folds of a bright girdle furled.
But now I only hear
Its melancholy, long withdrawing roar,
Retreating, to the breath
Of the night wind, down the vast edges drear
And naked shingles of the world.

Ah, love, let us be true
To one another! for the world, which seems
To lie before us like a land of dreams,
So various, so beautiful, so new,
Hath really neither joy, nor love, nor light,
Nor certitude, nor peace, nor help for pain;
And we are here as on a darkling plain,
Swept with confused alarms of struggle and flight,
Where ignorant armies clash by night.

Identify the sensory appeals in this poem, then ask:

1. What words, phrases, and lines appeal to more than one of the senses? Are there lines that do not seem to appeal to your senses?
2. To what extent did your own senses come alive in the reading of Arnold's poem? What images did you see, hear, feel, smell, and taste?
3. How might a performer benefit from a sensitivity to sensory appeals?
4. What is the relationship between the performer's sensory responses and the persona's sensory responses?

Expressive language also gains its power through the use of figures of speech—language devices that convey more than their literal sense. By moving beyond literal or direct statements, speakers fashion striking and memorable utterances. Literal language simply reports information. It appears one-dimensional, factual, concrete, expected. The best figurative language often is multidimensional, fictional, ambiguous, and initially unexpected. Not all figurative language, however, is engaging. Many figures from everyday speech have become clichés, dead. The statement "The evening is quiet as a mouse" is one example. Although more expressive than the literal claim that "the evening is quiet," the familiarity of the comparison weakens its power. Listeners no longer feel its richness; they no longer see it as evocative. The following comparison by William Wordsworth is quite another case: "It is a beauteous evening, calm and free, / The holy time is quiet as a nun / Breathless with adoration." These lines work on and into listeners, establishing a compelling image of quiet. The lines insist on the listeners' deepest response.

Figures of speech tend to work by comparison or association. Two common figures of speech are the simile and metaphor. A *simile* directly expresses a similarity between two objects, usually through the use of *like* or *as*. We fill our everyday talk with many familiar similes (e.g., "eats like a bird," "warm as toast," "drinks like a fish," "grows like a weed"). Richard Wilbur moves well beyond such clichés when he writes, "Mind in its purest play is like some bat / That beats about in caverns all alone." So does T. S. Eliot when he says, "The worlds revolve like ancient women / Gathering fuel in vacant lots." *Metaphors* also insist upon a comparison, but the comparison is implied rather than directly stated. Shakespeare's metaphor "merry larks are ploughmen's clocks" draws a connection between larks and clocks. When John Milton says, "Who best / Bear His mild yoke, they serve Him best," he describes God's mastership over the human animal. Similes and metaphors, then, suggest that two things enjoy a relationship, that they share a likeness or similarity. The speaker yokes together both things in the comparison, inviting listeners to consider how those things do and do not correspond to each other.

Many companies rely upon metaphoric expressions for their commercial advertisements. Identify the implied comparisons in each of the following slogans: **PROBE 5**

  "Reach out and touch someone" (AT&T)
  "Get a piece of the rock" (Prudential Insurance)
  "The good hands people" (Allstate Insurance)
  "For the best times in your life" (Kodak)
  "Oh, what a feeling" (Toyota)

Similes and metaphors are related to several other figures of speech: oxymoron, synecdoche, and metonymy. An *oxymoron* is a combination of contradictory or incongruous terms (e.g., silent speech, honest crook, icy hot, mute cry). Oxymorons create a reverberation between the incongruous terms. They often seem paradoxical. The terms seem self-contradictory, yet somehow true. For example, during the Vietnam war, many government officials believed that the United States was "fighting for peace." Those against the war were quick to recognize the incongruity of such a claim and to demand that the government officials explain how such an idea could be true. A *synecdoche* is figurative language that names a part of an object to designate the whole. To say "sail" for "ship," "hands" for "sailors," "wheels" for "car," or "rhyme" for "poem" is to use a dimension of the whole to signify its entirety. Closely associated with synecdoche is *metonymy*, which works by naming one object to identify another, closely related object. Using "bread" to stand for "food," "Washington" for "government," or "crown" for "king" are some familiar examples.

Figurative language can also function by suggesting more or less than it intends. *Hyperbole* works by overstatement or exaggeration. We often rely upon hyperbolic expressions in everyday talk: "I have a ton of homework," "I've told you a thousand times," and "I'm dying of thirst." Two less-familiar examples of hyperbolic speech come from the rural South: "That food looks so good that if you put it on my head, my tongue would beat my brains out trying to get to it" and "It was so windy, it blew the barbs off the wire fence." *Understatement* works by stating less than it indirectly suggests. With understatement, the speaker plays down the significance of the claim in order to demonstrate its importance. When Jonathan Swift remarks, "Last week I saw a woman flayed, and you would hardly believe how much it altered her person for the worse," he wants listeners to take the implied rather than the literal sense of the utterance.

Figurative language can also function by associations, encouraging listeners to reflect upon the connections being made. *Personification* associates human qualities with nonhuman entities, attributing human status to nonhuman organisms, abstract ideas, or inanimate objects. When John Milton says, for example, "The floods clap their hands," he is inviting listeners to see the floods as having the human capacity to clap hands. *Apostrophe* is a figure of speech in which the speaker directly addresses an absent person or an abstract idea as if physically present (e.g., William Wordsworth's "Milton! Thou shouldst be living at this hour;" the American spiritual, "Death, ain't you got no shame?"). *Allusions* are references to fictional or historical persons, things, or events. In Western cultures, many allusions come from the Bible and classical mythology. The effectiveness of an allusion rests upon a recognition and understanding of the reference. Unless the speaker and the listeners share the common knowledge of the reference, the allusion loses its power.

Figures of speech, then, invite listeners to make fresh connections, to see similarities in otherwise dissimilar things, to discover new relationships. Through comparisons and associations, figures of speech increase the evocative power of language. Figurative language subordinates literal sense in order to lead listeners into a rich and alive linguistic world.

We can further identify expressive language by its frequent reliance upon the rhythmic. In simple terms, repetition establishes rhythm, which is the result of a repeated pattern over time. Rhythm is so central to our daily lives, in fact, that one could assert that human life is a rhythmic life. From the rhythms of biological, historical, and psychological time to the mechanical "tick-tock" rhythm of clock time, the rhythmic pulse of existence catches all people. Expressive language, however, plays upon additional rhythms, manipulating time in other ways. The familiar "once upon a time" story opening calls upon listeners to enter into another time and place. In doing so, it requests that listeners exist above time. The story opening encourages listeners to escape from the rhythms of their everyday worlds and to become engaged in the rhythms of an aesthetic utterance. Sensitive listeners surrender to the request; they immerse themselves within the world of the aesthetic text, leaving behind the rhythms of daily life and letting the rhythms of the expressive language hold or capture them. The listeners feel the time of the aesthetic world. Once engaged within an aesthetic transaction, listeners sense the carefully constructed cadence of expressive language. They hear the beat of the poet's metered lines; they laugh as a result of the comedian's comic timing; they relish the storyteller's repeated theme. In short, speakers often structure their expressive language so as to captivate listeners through their use of rhythm.

In addition to its sensuous, figurative, and rhythmic qualities, expressive language is also reflexive. Reflexive utterances are those that turn back upon themselves. They are communication about communication. Only humans have the capacity to talk about talk. Such speech is a key characteristic of aesthetic texts, which invite listeners to look at themselves, to examine their own actions, to consider alternative behaviors. In this sense, each aesthetic text is offered as a hypothesis. Listeners test what speakers place before them to see if it appears true. As speakers hold up actions for examination, listeners question. Each aesthetic text is a probe, a comment on human behavior, an opportunity for self-reflection. Aesthetic texts provide people the opportunity of taking on alternative conceptions of themselves and others without risk. Seeing, for example, Shakespeare's Othello murder his wife in a fit of jealousy allows listeners to experience Othello's feelings and to explore the implications of such actions without suffering the consequences. Aesthetic texts, then, offer fresh visions of human existence, new perspectives for making sense of the world, and alternative behaviors for deliberation and possible adoption. Aesthetic texts are public offerings, actions held up for consideration.[4]

The language of aesthetic texts is not only expressive, but also unified. Unified simply means that each aesthetic text is a completed whole. All of its parts cohere, come together to form its entirety. The communicative task of speakers and listeners is to make the parts of each aesthetic text work together. Even when speakers require listeners to look beyond the immediate utterance to find unity, they tend to point in specific directions. When speakers want to parody a given subject, for instance, they select for the object of attack a subject they believe their listeners will know and include textual clues that help listeners recognize the referent. In this sense, unity is what speakers and listeners come to see as part of a given aesthetic act. Speakers often indicate to listeners how they intend their aesthetic texts to be unified by using three basic strategies: (1) framing them as complete communicative events, (2) embedding them in a world of conventional understandings, and (3) presenting them in a formulaic or set linguistic pattern.

At times, people may indicate literally how they want others to understand their utterances. Parents who say to their children, "I mean it this time," or teachers who claim, "This is the most important point for today," are asking listeners to see their statements a particular way. In short, such statements frame the relevant communicative act. It is as if speakers are placing brackets around what they particularly want listeners to hear. Such framing calls upon listeners to acknowledge the speakers' intents, to consider how the speakers see what they are saying. At other times, speakers may trust that the communicative context will help make their talk meaningful: that is, they depend upon the communicative context to provide the frame. Context may be sufficient to clue listeners into how they should understand speakers' utterances. We would see the statement "I would give a hundred dollars for that stereo system" quite differently if someone uttered it to a friend at home than if that same person said it publicly at an auction.

In a similar fashion, speakers use communicative statements and contextual features to frame their aesthetic acts. Listeners often anticipate an aesthetic act because the speaker has marked it as aesthetic. In everyday talk, people may draw attention to the fact that they intend to use language expressively, to offer an utterance that is distinct from other kinds of talk. "Have you heard the one about . . . ?" or "Let me tell you this story," are familiar examples of how people frame their talk by asking permission to engage in a particular kind of communicative act. Speakers can also mark aesthetic texts nonverbally. The cover of a book identifies the literary work contained within, organ music signals the beginning and end of many church services, and tapping a glass at a banquet indicates that a speech is about to start. Likewise, the context may help speakers frame their aesthetic texts. When sitting around a campfire, people may tell ghost stories; when attending a political rally, people may chant a campaign slogan. Framing, then, allows listeners to see what speakers want them to consider as part of the aesthetic act. Framing points to what speakers include within the frame. Speakers mark the beginning and ending of their aesthetic acts. They signal the opening and closing of their texts. When a speaker insufficiently frames an aesthetic text, listeners may become uneasy, thrown off balance. Poor framing may elicit such questions as, "Was that part of your story?" "Are you finished?" or "Why did you say that?" Each of these questions points to the listeners' struggle to find the dimensions that the speaker wants unified.[5]

Often, people recognize an aesthetic text as a completed whole because of set conventions for understanding communication. Based upon prior experiences and cultural norms, people come to view certain communicative acts as aesthetic. People learn that some types of talk serve aesthetic functions. They discover the traditional ways in which speakers present such utterances. Listeners generally expect speakers to follow the rules and conventions governing aesthetic texts. Understanding how speakers have offered aesthetic texts in the past guides listeners' present understanding and provides a basis for judging what constitutes the whole aesthetic act. For example, to present an aesthetic text in everyday conversations, people often feel obligated to ask permission of their listeners. The "Have you heard the one about . . . ?" and "Let me tell you this story" examples noted above are communicative acts that request the listeners' assent before going on. Such statements are conventional ways in which speakers might frame their aesthetic texts. A listener who responds, "Yes, I've heard that one" or "Please don't start into one of your stories," is denying the request. Following conventional rules, the requesting joke teller or storyteller most likely would not continue, and the potential aesthetic act would not occur. However, if a listener said, "No, I haven't" or "Tell me your story," then the speaker probably would proceed with the joke or the story. The rules of communication in this case would encourage the speaker to try to create an aesthetic text. Conventions also alert listeners when and where to expect aesthetic acts. People recognize that at certain times and places aesthetic acts are appropriate and likely to unfold. Such conventional understandings help listeners see aesthetic texts as unified.

We can also determine unity by recognizing a familiar linguistic pattern. People understand certain utterances as completed acts because they are aware of the established form or set formula upon which the speaker is relying. The structure of many aesthetic texts is highly predictable. Jokes typically have punch lines; most stories have plots that unfold; speeches often make a point. Listeners may depend upon their knowledge of literary traditions in anticipation of certain linguistic patterns. Sonnets have fourteen lines and possess a particular rhyme scheme. Likewise, listeners may carry certain grammatical expectations, leading them to assume, for example, that speakers will not finish talking until they have completed a sentence or until they have signaled the end of their turn to speak. Familiarity with such linguistic patterns helps listeners discover the unity of aesthetic texts.

Figure 7.1 (see p. 116) provides a model of the qualities of aesthetic texts in aesthetic transactions. This summary model suggests that in any aesthetic transaction, there are three fundamental and interrelated dimensions: the

Model of An Aesthetic Transaction

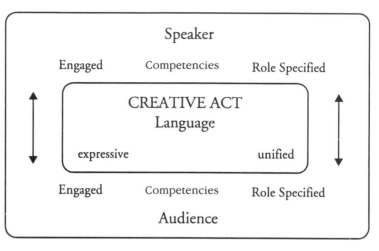

FIGURE 7.1

speaker, the audience, and the creative act. The speaker and the audience must participate in the event and display some degree of aesthetic competence. In doing so, they take on specific roles. We can best see the creative act as expressive and unified language. As an expressive act, it is sensuous, figurative, rhythmic, and reflexive. As a unified act, all of its parts function together. Listeners find unity in aesthetic texts, in part, because speakers frame them as aesthetic, because they rely upon conventional understandings, and because they use familiar linguistic patterns. We should remember that these characteristics are typical, not essential, qualities of aesthetic texts. We should also remember that all aesthetic texts exist within a cultural and historical context (see Chapter 1). The point in specifying such a list is to aid in our search for aesthetic texts and to provide some understanding of the fundamental dimensions we most likely will find in aesthetic transactions. In the next chapter, we shall turn to the common structural characteristics of aesthetic texts. Together, Chapters 7 and 8 should offer a solid grounding on which to pursue the study and performance of aesthetic texts.

Notes

1. Paul Hernadi, ed., *What Is Literature?* (Bloomington: Indiana University Press, 1978).
2. For an excellent discussion of "speech play," see Bryan K. Crow, "Conversational Performance and Performance of Conversation," *The Drama Review* 32(1988): 23–54.
3. For a more extensive discussion of this point, see Beverly Whitaker, "Edward Bul-

lough on 'Psychical Distance'," *Quarterly Journal of Speech* 54(1968): 373–82; and Daphna Ben Chaim, *Distance in the Theatre: The Aesthetics of Audience Response* (Ann Arbor, MI: UMI Research Press, 1984).

4. The concept of reflexivity is developed in Victor Turner, *The Anthropology of Performance* (New York: Performing Arts Journal Publications, 1987).

5. "Framing" receives extended development in Erving Goffman, *Frame Analysis* (New York: Harper Colophon, 1974).

Suggested Readings

Adorno, T. W. *Aesthetic Theory*. Translated by C. Lenhardt. London: Routledge & Kegan Paul, 1984.

Barricelli, Jean-Pierre, and Joseph Gibaldi, eds. *Interrelations of Literature*. New York: Modern Language Association of America, 1982.

Bateson, Gregory. *Steps to an Ecology of Mind*. New York: Ballantine, 1972.

Beardsley, Monroe C. *Aesthetics: Problems in the Philosophy of Criticism*. New York: Harcourt Brace & World, 1958.

Campbell, Paul N. "Performance: The Pursuit of Folly." *Speech Teacher* 20(1971):263–74.

Chaim, Daphna Ben. *Distance in the Theatre: The Aesthetics of Audience Response*. Ann Arbor, MI: UMI Research Press, 1984.

Cohen, Ted, and Paul Guyer, eds. *Essays in Kant's Aesthetics*. Chicago: University of Chicago Press, 1982.

Collingwood, R. G. *The Principles of Art*. London: Oxford University Press, 1958.

Crow, Bryan K. "Conversational Performance and the Performance of Conversation." *The Drama Review* 32(1988):23–54.

Fabian, Johannes. *Time and the Other: How Anthropology Makes Its Object*. New York: Columbia University Press, 1983.

Frye, Northrop. *Anatomy of Criticism*. Princeton, NJ: Princeton University Press, 1957.

Goffman, Erving. *Frame Analysis*. New York: Harper Colophon, 1974.

Grotowski, Jerzy. *Towards a Poor Theatre*. New York: Simon & Schuster, 1968.

Grugeon, Elizabeth, and Peter Walden, eds. *Literature and Learning*. London: The Open University, 1978.

Hauser, Arnold. *The Sociology of Art*. Translated by Kenneth J. Northcott. Chicago: University of Chicago Press, 1982.

Hernadi, Paul. *Beyond Genre: New Directions in Literary Classification*. Ithaca, NY: Cornell University Press, 1972.

Hernadi, Paul, ed. *What Is Literature?* Bloomington: Indiana University Press, 1978.

Ingarden, Roman. *The Cognition of the Literary Work of Art*. Translated by Ruth Ann Crowley and Kenneth R. Olson. Evanston, IL: Northwestern University Press, 1973.

Iser, Wolfgang. *The Act of Reading: A Theory of Aesthetic Response*. Baltimore: Johns Hopkins University Press, 1978.

Manfredi, John. *The Social Limits of Art*. Amherst: University of Massachusetts Press, 1982.

Perloff, Marjorie, ed. *Postmodern Genres*. Norman, OK: University of Oklahoma Press, 1989.

Pratt, Mary Louise. *Toward a Speech Act Theory of Literary Discourse*. Bloomington: Indiana University Press, 1977.

Richter, Peyton E., ed. *Perspectives in Aesthetics: Plato to Camus*. New York: Odyssey Press, 1967.

Whitaker, Beverly. "Edward Bullough on 'Psychical Distance,' " *Quarterly Journal of Speech* 54(1968):373–82.

Wreen, Michael J., and Donald M. Callen, eds. *The Aesthetic Point of View: Selected Essays of Monroe C. Beardsley*. Ithaca, NY: Cornell University Press, 1982.

CHAPTER 8

The Structures of Aesthetic Texts in Aesthetic Transactions

A fter examining the participants and language of aesthetic texts in aesthetic transactions, we now turn to the structures of aesthetic texts. Our purpose here is to explore the typical ways in which speakers organize and arrange their aesthetic utterances. We shall divide the discussion into two sections: "Structuring the Whole," which focuses upon the broad patterns that speakers might manipulate in the construction of their aesthetic texts; and "Structuring the Parts," which looks at the smaller details that might contribute to the structural whole.

Structuring the Whole

We have already said much about how speakers might structure aesthetic texts. In Chapter 7, we identified several types of aesthetic texts, including traditional literary forms, conversational forms, and ceremonial forms. One of the first decisions speakers might make concerns the kind of utterance they want to make. Such choices often guide the creation of aesthetic texts. Creating a poem, for example, calls upon the speaker to work with language in a different way than that involved in presenting a sermon. All aesthetic forms have developed over time a body of set conventions, distinct ways of molding different kinds of communication. In short, audiences recognize different types of utterances, in part, because generic expectations exist. Speakers, aware of such expectations, often structure their aesthetic texts in keeping with what audiences have come to anticipate. Speakers not only decide upon the form of their texts, but they also may take into account the point of view, forces in conflict, and sequence of their utterances. We shall examine each of these broad structural patterns.

119

Point of View

In Chapter 6, we saw that all communication carries a point of view—an angle of vision or stance from which it unfolds. We noted that speakers may appear more or less credible, objective, privileged, characterized, and central. Each of these terms helps clarify the speaker's relationship to the audience and subject. By recognizing a speaker's stance, the audience may enter or share in the speaker's vision. The audience comes to see what the speaker sees. Part of seeing what the speaker sees requires the audience to accept the utterance as given, to construct the speaker's stance in sympathy with the speaker. To understand point of view fully, however, requires another step. The task for the audience is also to recognize how the speaker's stance empowers one angle of vision while silencing others. In this sense, point of view is also a question of power.

Point of view unfolds through language. As we discovered in Chapter 7, the language of aesthetic texts is expressive. But it is also repressive. Language structures the way people think. People understand their world in keeping with their linguistic system. Language determines and solidifies cultural values. For example, Abraham Lincoln opened his famous Gettysburg address with the sentence, "Four score and seven years ago our fathers brought forth on this continent a new nation, conceived in liberty, and dedicated to the proposition that all men are created equal." The point of view articulated in this sentence is a familiar one. It reflects common, taken-for-granted cultural values. Uttered by a highly credible speaker, the claim is often seen as a self-evident cultural truth. Yet many people could question this accepted stance. Feminists could easily point out that the use of the masculine "fathers" and "men" to refer to all people, in essence, renders women invisible. It is as if only men had a part in the formation of the United States. The American Indian could just as easily react with genuine bitterness when hearing "brought forth on this continent a new nation." One could also call into question how the United States culture has come to understand "liberty" and "equality." Would all members of the United States culture feel that they enjoy "liberty" and "equality"? Are liberty and equality the prerogatives of only some members of the culture?

Lincoln's opening remark, then, articulates a viewpoint that some would applaud while others would question or reject. The sentence empowers some members of the culture while negating others. It reinforces the predominant cultural attitudes; it silences minority opinions. To see how a speaker's point of view is always an issue of empowering one stance at the expense of others, we can ask several basic questions:

1. How would other characters identified in the speaker's utterance alter what is said if they were speaking?
2. What points of view does the speaker's stance neglect?

3. What specific cultural values does the speaker's point of view include or carry?
4. How does the speaker's use of language reinforce conventional cultural values?

Thinking in this manner allows us to see how point of view is a fundamental structural dimension of all aesthetic texts. Point of view is not just a reflection of the speaker's angle of vision and language usage; it is also an indication of the cultural values the speaker explicitly or implicitly supports.

Read the opening line of Lincoln's Gettysburg address again: **PROBE 1**

> Four score and seven years ago our fathers brought forth on this continent a new nation, conceived in liberty, and dedicated to the proposition that all men are created equal.

Then perform the line as if you were

1. A person who completely accepts the truth of Lincoln's remark.
2. A feminist who is unhappy about Lincoln's use of sexist language.
3. An American Indian who feels that an Indian nation was destroyed.
4. A person who strongly believes that liberty and equality are the prerogatives of only some members of the United States culture.

Forces in Conflict

Speakers often structure their aesthetic texts around conflict. Conflict simply suggests that there are at least two forces pulling in opposite directions. The conflict may be between people, may emerge within a single individual, or may unfold between an individual and the environment. In general, speakers who structure their texts around conflict break their utterances into two basic parts: complication and resolution. Complication establishes the aspects of the conflict that create tension. During the complication phase of the utterance, the audience typically learns who is involved and why the conflict exists. During the resolution phase, the audience sees how the conflict is handled and what conclusions emerge. Of course, not all conflict ends in resolution. Some aesthetic texts offer only a description of the conflict.

PROBE 2   Read the poem "Preface to a Twenty Volume Suicide Note," by LeRoi Jones (Imamu Amiri Baraka).

> *Lately, I've become accustomed to the way*
> *The ground opens up and envelops me*
> *Each time I go out to walk the dog.*
> *Or the broad edged silly music the wind*
> *Makes when I run for a bus—*
>
> *Things have come to that.*
>
> *And now, each night I count the stars.*
> *And each night I get the same number.*
> *And when they will not come to be counted*
> *I count the holes they leave.*
>
> *Nobody sings anymore.*
>
> *And then last night, I tiptoed up*
> *To my daughter's room and heard her*
> *Talking to someone, and when I opened*
> *The door, there was no one there . . .*
> *Only she on her knees,*
> *Peeking into her own clasped hands.*

Describe the conflict in this poem:

1. What forces are working upon the speaker? Does the speaker describe who is involved and why the conflict exists?
2. Is the conflict resolved? Following the first and third stanzas, a single line seems to summarize the speaker's feelings. After the final stanza, however, the speaker offers no commentary on his daughter's behavior. How does this detail influence your understanding of whether the speaker resolves the conflict? Is it significant that the title of the poem indicates that a much longer work (twenty volumes) is to follow this utterance? Explain.

We can break down the simple complication/resolution pattern of conflict to a greater extent. The literary genre of drama in its traditional form often possesses six stages of conflict. In the first stage, *exposition*, the audience discovers who the characters are and what their relationships are. The situation becomes clear; motivations become evident. In short, the audience receives the necessary background to follow the subsequent action. The *challenge*, the second stage, puts into motion the conflicting forces. Characters take actions that disrupt the stability of the situation. This leads to the third stage, *rising action*. Here the characters confront heightened conflict as they pursue their distinct goals. In the *crisis*, the fourth stage, the characters reach a turning point, a moment that makes the resolution of the conflict inevitable. The *climax*, the fifth stage, is the culmination of all the elements of the conflict. The climax is the highest point of intensity in the drama. In the final stage, *resolution*, the drama relaxes into a new balance. The characters have played out all the elements of the conflict and the audience members feel that the conclusion satisfies their expectations. Clearly, not all literary dramas follow these stages. Moreover, there is considerable variety in how playwrights might manipulate these dimensions. Nevertheless, playwrights have often arranged conflict in their aesthetic texts in keeping with this structural pattern.[1]

Victor Turner, with his concept of social dramas, offers another detailed description of how conflict might evolve naturally in everyday events. According to Turner, a social drama is a process that allows a culture to challenge and examine its social and political practices. The social drama emerges in four developmental steps. In the first stage, there is a *breach* of some rule governing social life. This develops into the second phase, *crisis*. The crisis may split the community into competing coalitions. To avoid this, the community leaders engage in the third step, *redressive measures*, designed to find some remedy for the conflict. In the final stage, the conflict is either resolved through *reconciliation* or solidified by recognition of *permanent breach*.[2]

Closely related to these patterns of conflict are the concepts of plot and action. Action is the series of events or episodes that makes up the aesthetic text. Each incident is a distinct action. Yet action in itself seems insignificant or inconsequential. Action needs plot, which arranges or structures the action into meaningful relationships. Plot, the unifying principle of action, is the sense we make of the action. Essential to plot and action, however, is conflict. Conflict is the raw material or motivating force of plot and action. Without conflict, there is no action; without action, no plot.

The descriptions of literary dramas, social dramas, and plot and action show how speakers can structure conflict in quite complex ways. Conflict, by its nature, is dramatic. As opposing forces are pitted against one another, tension emerges. Speakers may work with that tension as the organizing principle of their aesthetic texts. Speakers, then, may use conflict in more or less complex ways to structure or pattern their aesthetic utterances.

Sequence

Speakers sequence all utterances: that is, they say one thing before another. Language moves in a linear progression. That progression, however, can take a number of forms. A few common sequencing patterns are perceptual, temporal/spatial, argumentative, and ritualistic.

A speaker who relies upon a perceptual sequencing offers a seemingly random report of what crosses the speaker's consciousness. It is as if the speaker utters whatever comes to mind. The listeners can only discover the logic that connects one thought by examining the speaker's working psyche. The audience often feels as if the speaker is presenting the utterance uncensored, finding what to say at the moment of speech. Frank O'Hara's "Poem," for example, employs perceptual patterning.

> *Lana Turner has collapsed!*
> *I was trotting along and suddenly*
> *it started raining and snowing*
> *and you said it was hailing*
> *but hailing hits you on the head*
> *hard so it was really snowing and*
> *raining and I was in such a hurry*
> *to meet you but the traffic*
> *was acting exactly like the sky*
> *and suddenly I see a headline*
> *LANA TURNER HAS COLLAPSED!*
> *there is no snow in Hollywood*
> *there is no rain in California*
> *I have been to lots of parties*
> *and acted perfectly disgraceful*
> *but I never actually collapsed*
> *oh Lana Turner we love you get up*

O'Hara offers the audience a glimpse of a mind spinning after learning Lana Turner collapsed. Thoughts bounce off of thoughts; ideas fly in a variety of directions. Perceptual sequencing, then, displays a mind in the process of thinking, of sharing whatever enters consciousness.

Temporal/spatial sequencing structures speech by using time or place. Speakers who employ temporal/spatial patterning indicate when or where they see what they do. All speakers communicate in the "here and now."

Speaking is a present-tense activity, located in the space speakers occupy. Speakers, however, may refer in their speech to the "there and then," another time and place. The simple sentence, "He went to the store," suggests that the speaker is referring to a past event, an action that occurred prior to the utterance. A speaker may describe a town, for instance, by moving systematically through the physical environment, noting details as they appear. Such temporal/spatial references can be the key structural principle that orders aesthetic texts.

Return to the LeRoi Jones poem presented in Probe 2. Notice the temporal references in lines 1, 7, and 12.

PROBE 3

1. To what extent are these temporal references an organizing principle for the poem?
2. Do the temporal references mark changes in the speaker's attitudes? If so, specify.
3. Try performing the poem by thinking of the temporal shifts as changes in the speaker's attitudes.

Speakers may also pattern aesthetic texts to move between the "here and now" and the "there and then." This commonly occurs in stories when the speaker offers quoted dialogue between characters. Eudora Welty opens her short story "Petrified Man" with the following paragraph.

"Reach in my purse and git me a cigarette without no powder in it if you kin, Mrs. Fletcher, honey," said Leota to her ten o'clock shampoo-and-set customer. "I don't like no perfumed cigarettes."

Here, Mrs. Fletcher and Leota exist in a different time and place from those of the speaker relating the tale. The speaker who says, "said Leota to her ten o'clock shampoo-and-set customer," is telling the story in the "here and now." The speaker shows Mrs. Fletcher and Leota talking in a distinct temporal/spatial world. They are speaking in the "there and then." In many stories, the temporal/spatial structure produces a movement between the "here and now" telling and the "there and then" showing.[3]

The temporal rhythm of many stories often results from the patterning of scene, summary, and description. Scene, usually offering the dialogue between two or more characters, moves at a normal conversational rate. Summary tends to accelerate time. The speaker may reduce events from an extended period of time in a variety of locations to a single utterance. The sentence "She spent the summer traveling Europe," for example, renders several months' travel to a number of places to a simple summary claim. Description presents a detailed picture of something or someone; it offers a close verbal inspection of a subject. Description seems to elongate or stop time. As the speaker pauses to scrutinize the intricacies of a subject, time appears to slow down or halt. Speakers often rely upon description to build suspense in their stories. Description allows speakers to hold off or delay the listeners' knowledge of the outcome of some event. Speakers, then, manipulate time by presenting scenes that move along at a regular conversational rate or by calling upon summary and description to speed up or slow down their tales. Working with scene, summary, and description, speakers can control the temporal rhythm of their utterances.[4]

Temporal/spatial sequencing, then, permits speakers to structure their communicative acts by relying upon direct references to time or place, by shifting between the "here and now" and "there and then," or by controlling temporal rhythm through the patterning of scene, summary, and description. Temporal/spatial patterns offer another way for speakers to order aesthetic texts.

Argumentative sequencing is a structural pattern speakers use to make a case. Making a case involves two fundamental steps. The first requires speakers to define the problem, to lay out the conditions that exist; the second demands that speakers articulate the implications or conclusions that follow from the given problem. In short, argumentative sequencing unfolds in an "if/then" pattern. Speakers using this type of sequencing seem to say, "If x exists, then y follows." They imply or explicitly state a logic. As the argument develops, speakers develop their cases by moving from concrete to abstract claims, from the known facts to the unknown questions, from exterior observations to interior insights, from specific details to general statements, or other such ways of building arguments. In each instance, it is as if speakers come to some discovery or realization. Through their arguments, they reach some understanding, a way of making sense of their subjects.

PROBE 4

Shakespearean sonnets typically rely upon an argumentative structure. In general, the first twelve lines articulate a problem and the final two lines resolve it. Read William Shakespeare's "Sonnet 130."

My mistress' eyes are nothing like the sun;
Coral is far more red than her lips' red;
If snow be white, why then her breasts are dun;
If hairs be wires, black wires grow on her head.
I have seen roses damasked, red and white,

But no such rose see I in her cheeks;
And in some perfumes is there more delight
Than in the breath that from my mistress reeks.
I love to hear her speak, yet well I know
That music hath a far more pleasing sound;
I grant I never saw a goddess go —
My mistress, when she walks, treads on the ground:
And yet, by heaven, I think my love as rare
As any she belied with false compare.

Answer the following questions.

1. How does the speaker describe his mistress in the first twelve lines of the poem?
2. What final claim does the speaker make in the last two lines?
3. How do the specific descriptions in the first twelve lines establish a foundation for the speaker's conclusion? What does the speaker realize?
4. What might this suggest for performance? Try performing the poem paying close attention to the structural turn of the final two lines.

Ritualistic sequencing often follows a predictable progression. Ritualistic patterns are conventional, expected arrangements developed over time, yet marked as distinct from everyday experience. Speakers who adopt ritualistic sequencing often structure their aesthetic texts with an allegiance to a fixed or set order. Changes in the stable pattern may evolve, but change is a slow and cautious process. The typical Protestant church service, for example, has a highly predictable ordering of events. Hymns are sung, the sermon given, the Bible reading presented, communion taken, and the offering plate passed in a specific and anticipated arrangement. The congregation knows the structure and expects it to be followed. In a similar manner, fraternal groups establish conventional ways of initiating new members. Typically, in order to obtain membership, the individual must first be accepted as a person worthy of consideration for membership. Then, the individual must learn the values and norms of the fraternity through some training program. Finally, the individual must participate in some ceremony that marks entry into membership. Each of these stages is likely to involve set, conventional patterns. Members design these ritualistic sequences to perpetuate the organization with members of its liking. The individual who resists the ritual procedures will probably not obtain membership.

Rituals, then, develop specific patterns — structures that the participants usually know well, expect, and recognize as special. Each ritual evolves its own structure; no two rituals are likely to have identical procedures. Ritualistic patterning finds its power in its predictability, its stability, its familiarity, its specialness. Each time participants perform a ritual, they find the meaning of the event becomes more deeply textured. The participants, by engaging in repeated structural patterns, reinforce their values and community identity.

PROBE 5   Identify a ritual (e.g., wedding, fraternity initiation, graduation ceremony) in which you were a participant. Describe in as much detail as possible the sequence of events. Then ask

1. What structural patterns do the participants repeat each time they perform the ritual?
2. What changes in the ritual would the participants feel are legitimate? What would the participants say could not be changed?
3. How does the structure mark the event as special?
4. What knowledge did the participants need to have for the ritual to take place?

Sequencing, whether perceptual, temporal/spatial, argumentative, or ritualistic, provides speakers a means for ordering their aesthetic texts. Speakers organize their utterances by relying upon familiar ways of understanding or structuring experience. While other means of arranging aesthetic texts exist, the sequencing patterns described above are typical strategies that speakers use to structure their aesthetic acts.

The broad structural patterns of point of view, forces in conflict, and sequence are some ways in which speakers commonly organize their aesthetic texts. Speakers may rely upon any one or any combination of these patterns in the creation of their aesthetic texts. The chosen pattern provides a stable structure ready to support other aesthetic dimensions. Thus, the broad patterns are general schemes that shape the smaller aesthetic details. In the next section, we shall look at the smaller details of aesthetic texts that speakers structure.

Structuring the Parts

Speakers compose aesthetic texts of many parts. Of particular significance, speakers work with audience, character, character speech, and sound and rhythm as parts of their aesthetic utterances. Each of these aspects of aesthetic texts functions within the shape of the aesthetic whole and contributes to its overall effect. This section focuses on how speakers may define their relationship to their audiences, develop character, display character speech, and manipulate sound and rhythm.

Audience

Speakers establish relationships with their audiences in three fundamental ways. First, they specify or imply to whom they are speaking. As we saw in Chapter 4, speakers may address themselves, specific others, or general audiences. When addressing themselves or specific others, speakers function within closed scenes. When speaking to general audiences, speakers exist within open scenes. Closed scenes invite the attending audience to overhear; open scenes encourage the attending audience to hear and, perhaps, to speak. Thus, the decision to address a particular audience—whether oneself, a specific other, or a general audience—shapes the speaker's relationship to the attending audience.

Second, speakers state or suggest attitudes toward their audiences. Speakers' views of their audiences may reflect considerable range, from positive to negative, from simplistic to complex, from friendly to hostile, and so on. Regardless, their attitudes toward their audiences are likely to color what they wish to say. Attitudes influence communication and, in doing so, set in motion a developing relationship between speakers and audiences.

PROBE 6

Imagine yourself giving a speech on a topic that is very important to you. Also assume that you present the speech on five different occasions. Your audience, however, changes each time you give the speech. On the various occasions, your audience is composed of people who you see as

1. Poorly informed on your selected topic.
2. Highly sophisticated, intelligent.
3. Cruel, nasty.
4. Stubborn, difficult to please.
5. Irresponsible, immature.

Given these attitudes, how would your speech change from one occasion to the next? How would your imagined attitudes alter what you would say? How would your behavior vary from one situation to the next?

Third, speaker/audience relationships may result from distinctions between the values of creators and those of their personae. *Reliability* is the term used to describe the relationship between a creator's and persona's attitudes and beliefs. Reliability indicates the degree to which the creator of a work and the persona in the work share the same values. In some instances, the beliefs and attitudes of the creator and persona appear similar. The persona seems to reflect the creator's viewpoint. In such cases, we would consider the persona reliable. With an unreliable persona, however, a distinction is drawn between the creator's own values and those of the persona. The creator fashions a persona who articulates values the creator rejects. This strategy allows creators to put on display values they may wish to mock, to ridicule, or to undercut. It is as if the creator is winking at the audience behind the persona's back. The creator and the audience share an understanding of which the persona is not aware. Working with unreliable personae, creators often seem to elicit intimate and covert relationships with their audiences.[5]

Character

We can broadly define a character as any person who exists within a speaker's aesthetic text. Characters are the personae who populate speakers' communicative acts. Speakers structure the listeners' impressions of characters by manipulating what characters do, what they say, and what other characters say about them. Speakers may provide information about characters' physical qualities, personalities, and motivations. When speakers offer limited amounts of information about characters, the characters usually appear flat, unidimensional, static, unchanging. This is often the case when a character simply serves a minor role within an aesthetic text. Flat, unidimensional characters, however, can also work for comic, ironic, or other purposes. Of course, not all characters appear static. Many seem just the opposite — round, multidimensional, dynamic, changing. Speakers, working with varying degrees of character dramatization, draw audience attention in certain directions. Generally speaking, the more fully dramatized a character, the more likely the character will pull audience focus. Thus, speakers encourage audiences to notice the characters they render most fully.

Character Speech

Speakers may structure their utterances by having characters speak. Audiences listen to what characters say. The audience reacts to characters, making judgments, based in part upon the speech the characters use. Their speech may be formal or informal, voiced in standard English or dialect, and so on. Often, their speech reflects their social position and interests. It also typically carries the illusion of naturalness, a suggestion that this is how a person would genuinely speak. Such considerations feed into how audiences form impressions of the characters they encounter. Speakers, then, may report the speech of characters. They may accomplish this through the use of direct and indirect discourse.

Direct discourse occurs when speakers present the exact utterance of a character, usually identified in writing by quotation marks. When not writing, speakers may use their voice and body to indicate the communication acts that they are quoting. For example, speakers might raise or lower their pitch or might make imaginary quotation marks in the air to signal when they are presenting another's speech. Indirect discourse is more complex. With indirect discourse speakers take on the perspective of a character and, at times, may adopt a character's speech style while continuing to assert their own presence. The speaker gives the audience the character's viewpoint and perhaps the character's diction. At the same time, the audience is reminded that the speaker is presenting the character. Notice the following two sentences:

Richard thought, ''I'll never do that again.''
Richard thought that he would never do that again.

In the first sentence, the speaker offers Richard's direct discourse, identified by quotation marks. In the second sentence, the speaker offers Richard's thought indirectly. The audience hears simultaneously the speaker's voice reporting what Richard thought and Richard's own declaration. Here is another example, from Gail Godwin's ''A Sorrowful Woman.''

One beautiful noon, she went out to look at her kitchen in the daylight. Things were changed. He had bought some new dish towels. Had the old ones worn out? The canisters seemed closer to the sink.

After telling us that the woman enters her kitchen following her long withdrawal from her family, the speaker reports the woman's perceptions and thoughts about her changed kitchen. The speaker gives a blend of voices—the speaker's own as well as the woman's.

Speakers may shift between direct and indirect discourse within the same tale. Notice the following excerpt from Doris Lessing's ''To Room Nineteen.''

She said to Matthew in their bedroom: "I think there must be something wrong with me."

And he said: "Surely not, Susan? You look marvellous — you're as lovely as ever."

She looked at the handsome blond man, with his clear, intelligent, blue-eyed face, and thought: Why is it I can't tell him? Why not? And she said: "I need to be alone more than I am."

At which he swung his slow blue gaze at her, and she saw what she had been dreading: Incredulity. Disbelief. And fear. An incredulous blue stare from a stranger who was her husband, as close to her as her own breath.

In this short encounter, the speaker uses direct discourse, with and without quotation marks, as well as indirect discourse. Through the use of direct discourse, the speaker tells the audience exactly what Matthew and Susan say to each other. The speaker also gives the audience access to Susan's direct thoughts: Why can't I tell him? Why not? In the final paragraph, the speaker relies upon indirect discourse, sharing Susan's perspective and diction in the telling of the tale. Starting with the word *incredulity* and stopping at the end of the paragraph, the speaker's presence is asserted while showing the audience Susan's viewpoint. The use of the *her* pronoun throughout suggests that the speaker is not simply reporting Susan's direct speech.

Speakers, then, structure character speech to provide telling details about the characters who populate their aesthetic texts. Character speech often is a key to how audiences understand the characters they encounter. By offering through direct and indirect discourse the speech of characters, speakers not only tell their audiences what they deem worthy of reporting, but also stir audiences to form impressions of the characters they present.

Sound and Rhythm

Speech unfolds in sound and rhythm. Audiences hear a voice and respond to its clarity, variety, and quality. They note accents, pauses, phrasing, and so on. They enjoy distinct sounds as well as the interplay of sounds. Speakers, aware of the potential power of sound and rhythm, may orchestrate their aesthetic texts with a sensitivity to individual word choices and sound patterns. They may select a word whose sound suggests its sense. Examples of such onomatopoetic word choices include *whiz, buzz, crash, bang, yakety-yak,* and *splat,* each of which offers some indication of its meaning by its sound. Speakers may also reinforce meaning by providing sound effects to accompany their actual words. Children frequently use sound effects in their imaginary games — monsters growl, cars screech, baby dolls cry, and horses trot.

Even in adult speech we may find the use of sound effects to amplify meaning. People who slap their hands together to suggest the sound of a crash or comics who depend upon sound effects within their routines are two familiar examples. In each of these instances, the speaker uses a sound instead of a word to suggest meaning.

The term *diction* refers to the specific word choices speakers make for their aesthetic texts. Words carry both a denotative and a connotative dimension. Dictionaries offer direct access to a word's denotative sense, its explicit meaning. Words, however, may connote quite different things to different people. Connotations are the cluster of implications or associations that accompany words. Connotations may be personal or universal. They may emerge from the usage of a word within a linguistic context. Most important, the connotations of words point to emotional colorations that speakers invite listeners to share. In addition to their denotative and connotative sense, words may seem formal or informal, familiar or unfamiliar, standard or colloquial, concrete or abstract. Opening a speech, for example, by saying, "Ladies and gentlemen, I want to thank you for joining me on this most important occasion," establishes a formal tone. The utterance uses standard English and seems quite familiar and concrete. A speaker would create a significantly different effect by saying, "OK, you guys. Let's get started. Thanks for coming. It's really important that you are here."

Speakers not only manipulate individual words and sounds in their aesthetic texts, but they also work with patterns of sound. Sound patterns emerge as a result of using assonance, consonance, alliteration, rhyme, and meter. Assonance is a pattern of sound in which vowel sounds (a, e, i, o, u) correspond. For example, "d*ee*p and f*ee*t" and "m*ai*d and r*ai*n" repeat vowel sounds and would be considered assonant. Consonance works by matching consonant sounds: e.g., "stro*k*e and luc*k*" and "be*d* and so*d*." Alliteration is a succession of similar consonant sounds, especially initial consonants. John Keats uses alliteration in his poem "Ode to a Nightingale" when he says, "*b*eaded *b*u*bb*les winking at the *b*rim." Words that rhyme, such as *night* and *light* and *master* and *faster*, also emerge from a repetition of sounds. In rhyming words, the identical or similar accented vowel sound is followed by identical succeeding sounds but different preceding sounds. Each of these sound devices functions to bind words together. By coupling words through sound, speakers produce emphasis on these words and establish a musical quality to their utterances. Perhaps the most musical of all utterances, however, are those that rely upon meter.

Meter, most often associated with poetry, relies upon the regular recurrence of accent. Metrical patterns emerge through the arrangement of stressed and unstressed syllables. There are four basic patterns in English verse: iambic (·/, unstressed-stressed), trochaic (/·, stressed-unstressed), anapestic (··/, unstressed-unstressed-stressed), and dactyllic (/··, stressed-unstressed-unstressed). Less common are the spondee (//, stressed-

stressed) and the pyrrhic (--, unstressed-unstressed). Each stress pattern constitutes a foot. We classify lines not only according to their stress pattern, but also by the number of feet they contain.

> 1 foot = monometer
> 2 feet = dimeter
> 3 feet = trimeter
> 4 feet = tetrameter
> 5 feet = pentameter
> 6 feet = hexameter
> 7 feet = heptameter
> 8 feet = octameter

Thus, we define every line of verse, first, by the type of feet it contains (iambic, trochaic, anapestic, or dactyllic) and, second, by the number of feet in the line. For example, the line

$$- \; / \quad - \; / \quad - \; / \quad - \; / \quad - \; /$$
When I / have fears / that I / may cease / to be

is iambic pentameter. It repeats the iambic unstressed-stressed pattern five times.

Scansion, the process of determining a poem's metrical pattern, is easier and more meaningful if a few general rules are followed. First, the individual word has no necessary relationship to the foot. To scan, for instance, "my mother thinks and thinks again," would require that we divide the two syllables in *mother* between two feet. The two syllables in *again*, however, we would consider one foot in this iambic tetrameter line:

$$- \; / \quad - \; / \quad - \; / \quad - \; /$$
my moth / er thinks / and thinks / a gain

Second, the meter cannot violate the natural accentuation of a word:

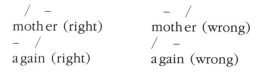

Third, key words are usually accented; less-important words are usually not. Two lines from Matthew Arnold's "Dover Beach" highlight this principle.

$$/ \quad - \quad - \quad / \quad - \quad / \quad - \quad /$$
Listen! / you hear / the gra / ting roar
$$- \quad / \quad - \quad / \quad - \quad / \quad - \quad / \quad - \quad /$$
Of peb / bles which / the waves / draw back, / and fling

In these iambic lines, no article (neither *the*), preposition (*of*), or conjunction (*and*) receives stress. Fourth, breaks in an established pattern take on particular significance. Variations from a pattern usually give added weight to what the speaker is saying. Notice the trochaic substitution in the first foot of the first of Arnold's lines quoted above. The substitution breaks the established iambic rhythm, intensifying the speaker's address to his audience. Finally, we should take the entire poem into account when determining meter. Often, the dominant pattern will repeat itself as the poem moves from line to line.

Scan William Butler Yeats's "The Second Coming."   **PROBE 7**

Turning and turning in the widening gyre
The falcon cannot hear the falconer;
Things fall apart; the center cannot hold;
Mere anarchy is loosed upon the world,
The blood-dimmed tide is loosed, and everywhere
The ceremony of innocence is drowned;
The best lack all conviction, while the worst
Are full of passionate intensity.

Surely some revelation is at hand;
Surely the Second Coming is at hand;
The Second Coming! Hardly are those words out
When a vast image out of Spiritus Mundi
Troubles my sight: somewhere in sands of the desert
A shape with a lion body and the head of a man,
A gaze blank and pitiless as the sun,
Is moving its slow thighs, while all about it
Reel shadows of the indignant desert birds.
The darkness drops again; but now I know
That twenty centuries of stony sleep
Were vexed to nightmare by a rocking cradle,
And what rough beast, its hour come round at last,
Slouches toward Bethlehem to be born?

Answer the following questions:

1. How would you classify Yeats's poem? What is the dominant metrical pattern?
2. Did you discover any variations in the established metrical pattern? If so, what is the significance of the variation(s)?
3. Read the poem aloud, voicing its metrical pattern. What effect does this reading produce? What insights into the poem does this reading provide?

Traditional meter is a highly organized, conventional scheme. Few modern poets, however, restrict themselves to such strict metrical patterns. Most modern poets discover or create their own structures as they work with their material. We typically call poems created in such a manner "free verse" or "organic." Free-verse poets structure their poems a number of different ways. They may manipulate either the number of stresses per line (accentual verse) or the number of syllables per line (syllabic verse). Instead of using both syllables and stresses, as in traditional metrics, poets may count either syllables or accents for their rhythmic effects. Poets may use their own breath as a guide for organizing their poems. Composing in this fashion, poets record the rhythm of their breathing in each poetic line. Poets may depend upon visual arrangement, structuring their poems typographically; in doing so, they may create rhythms or even literal pictures of their subjects. Poets may call upon syntax or grammar to pattern their lines. By placing words in a particular order, poets provide emphasis, guiding listeners to focus upon particular things in their poems. To say, "Smiling, he entered," pulls more attention to "smiling" than to say, "He entered smiling." Poets may rely upon lining or stanzas as structural devices. As poets shape their utterances, lines unfold that, in turn, develop into stanzas. Generally, stanzas bring together a body of associated ideas, connected by some unifying principle. Poets, then, work not only with words, but also with larger linguistic units to create the rhythm and form of their aesthetic texts.

As speakers orchestrate patterns of sound, they produce a rhythm, a felt pulse or beat. Rhythm emerges from a series of recurrences, a pattern of sounds that may accelerate or retard the pace of utterances. By manipulating stresses, playing with sound, indicating pauses, and working with phrasing, speakers pull their audiences into their aesthetic world. Speakers seduce their audiences by providing sounds that flow and breathe. Sound and rhythm, then, go hand-in-hand. Speakers may structure their texts to appeal to audiences' auditory sense, to engage their audiences in sound and rhythm.

Model of An Aesthetic Transaction

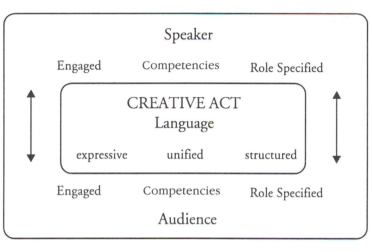

FIGURE 8.1

Much of what we have discovered in this chapter points to the individual style of a speaker. As we saw in the discussions on "Structuring the Whole" and "Structuring the Parts," speakers may orchestrate many elements in the creation of their utterances. As they do so, they place their personal stamp on their material. No two speakers will structure their communicative acts in exactly the same manner. Each speaker has a voice, a personal signature, a style. Style is ultimately a question of individuality asserting itself.

At this point, we can return to the model of an aesthetic transaction (Figure 7.1) presented at the end of Chapter 7. As a summary to this chapter, we can add a final dimension, structure, to the model (see Figure 8.1). Creative acts are structured acts. Speakers, by working with point of view, forces in conflict, and sequence, form their aesthetic texts. Speakers, by manipulating such elements as audience, character, character speech, and sound and rhythm, generate their aesthetic texts.

Notes

1. For discussions of dramatic structure, see Martin Esslin, *An Anatomy of Drama* (New York: Hill & Wang, 1977); and Robert W. Corrigan, ed., *The Making of Theatre: From Drama to Performance* (Glenview, IL: Scott, Foresman, 1981).
2. Victor Turner, *Dramas, Fields, and Metaphors: Symbolic Action in Human Society* (Ithaca, NY: Cornell University Press, 1974).
3. For a fuller discussion of this idea, see Joanna H. Maclay, "The Interpreter and Modern Fiction: Problems in Point of View and Structural Tensiveness," in *Studies*

in Interpretation, eds. Esther M. Doyle and Virginia Hastings Floyd (Amsterdam: Editions Rodopi NV, 1972), 155–70.

4. See Phyllis Bentley, *Some Observations on the Art of the Narrative* (New York: Macmillan, 1947).

5. See Wayne C. Booth, *The Rhetoric of Fiction*, 2nd ed. (Chicago: University of Chicago Press, 1983).

Suggested Readings

Bentley, Phyllis. *Some Observations on the Art of the Narrative.* New York: Macmillan, 1947.

Chatman, Seymour. *Story and Discourse: Narrative Structure in Fiction and Film.* Ithaca, NY: Cornell University Press, 1978.

Ciardi, John, and Miller Williams. *How Does A Poem Mean?*, 2nd ed. Boston: Houghton Mifflin, 1975.

Corrigan, Robert W., ed. *The Making of Theatre: From Drama to Performance.* Glenview, IL: Scott, Foresman, 1981.

Culler, Jonathan. *On Deconstruction: Theory and Criticism After Structuralism.* Ithaca, NY: Cornell University Press, 1982.

Dacey, Philip, and David Jauss, eds. *Strong Measures: Contemporary American Poetry in Traditional Forms.* New York: Harper & Row, 1986.

Eagleton, Terry. *Literary Theory.* Minneapolis: University of Minnesota Press, 1983.

Espinola, Judith. "The Nature, Function, and Performance of Indirect Discourse in Prose Fiction." *Speech Monographs* 41(1974):193–204.

Esslin, Martin. *An Anatomy of Drama.* New York: Hill & Wang, 1977.

Friedman, Norman. *Form and Meaning in Fiction.* Athens: University of Georgia Press, 1975.

Fussell, Paul Jr. *Poetic Meter and Poetic Form.* New York: Random House, 1965.

Kennedy, X. J. *An Introduction to Poetry*, 5th ed. Boston: Little, Brown, 1982.

Maclay, Joanna H. "The Interpreter and Modern Fiction: Problems in Point of View and Structural Tensiveness." In *Studies in Interpretation*, edited by Esther M. Doyle and Virginia Hastings Floyd, 155–70. Amsterdam: Editions Rodopi NV, 1972.

McAuley, James. *Versification: A Short Introduction.* East Lansing: Michigan State University Press, 1966.

Overstreet, Robert. "Preservation of Line Shape in the Performance of a Poem." *Southern Speech Communication Journal* 45(1980):268–81.

Preminger, Alex, ed. *Princeton Encyclopedia of Poetry and Poetics*, 2nd ed. Princeton, NJ: Princeton University Press, 1974.

Queneau, Raymond. *Exercises in Style.* Translated by Barbara Wright. New York: New Directions, 1981.

Scholes, Robert, and Robert Kellogg. *The Nature of Narrative.* Oxford: Oxford University Press, 1966.

Turco, Lewis. *The New Book of Forms: A Handbook of Poetics.* Hanover, NH: University Press of New England, 1986.

PART IV

✧ ✧

The Performative and Evaluative Roles of the Audience

CHAPTER 9

The Performative Role of the Audience

C hapter 9 looks at the audience in three primary ways. First, the chapter describes how we may consider performers to be audience members to their own aesthetic acts. Second, it outlines how we may see the attending audience members as performers. Third, it discusses the nature of audience participation and competence within an aesthetic transaction. Chapter 10 explores the evaluative role of the audience, first offering several frameworks for evaluation and some practical guidelines for performance criticism, then discussing particular problems facing the performer and the performance critic when confronted with an aesthetic text translated from the page to the stage. The chapter concludes by raising some ethical questions for performers and critics to consider. By the end of Part IV, then, we shall recognize how audience members may be active and creative participants within an aesthetic exchange and how they may make informed critical judgments of others' aesthetic acts.

As we have seen throughout this book, the audience in any aesthetic transaction plays an active role. Chapter 7 argued that if an aesthetic transaction is to occur, the audience members must participate in the transaction, possess some degree of competence, and recognize the role they are to play. The intent of this chapter is to develop these ideas more fully, as well as to explore some additional thoughts about audiences. Our first task, however, is to demonstrate how we may view performers as audience members to their own aesthetic acts.

The Performer as Audience

Although performers strive to become the characters they are portraying, they always remember that they are standing in for or presenting someone else. This simple, but necessary, awareness allows performers to maintain a sense of self and to reflect upon their performances as they perform. To forget that one was performing could lead to highly unfortunate results. Imagine the consequences if during a fight or murder scene, a performer believed that the staged actions were the same as everyday reality. In actuality, however, this seldom, if ever, occurs. Performers know they are performing no matter how real it may seem to them or to the attending audience. This recognition is indeed essential to performers, for it permits them to execute their performance choices, to assess their work, and to learn from their presentations. To accomplish such things requires that performers have some perspective on themselves. In short, they are audience members to their own performances. This, however, is a complex process involving, as suggested above, at least three fundamental components: executing, assessing, and learning.

Performers are often keenly aware of executing their performance choices. They know when they are to enter and exit, when they are to move, when they are to look at something on stage, and so on. Ideally, such behavioral choices have become automatic and natural as a result of extended rehearsals (see Chapter 5). But even when actions are automatic and natural, performers possess a clear sense of whether their actions are going according to plan. Such an awareness is greatly intensified when something occurs on stage that is not in keeping with planned choices. In such cases, performers may adapt to the contingencies at hand. They may recognize that they are not speaking loudly enough and alter their volume, they may sense that they must hold for a laugh that they did not anticipate, or they may realize that they must adjust what they intended to say because they have forgotten a line. As these examples suggest, there are times when performers are highly conscious of their executed choices. At other times, performers may only possess a vague sense that everything is proceeding as planned. In either case, awareness of their own performance behaviors allows performers to move forward, as well as to improvise or adjust to any circumstances that might arise at any given moment in the performance. This process suggests that performers are audience members who monitor and, at times, alter their aesthetic communication.

Performers are also audience members to their own performances when they assess their presentations. Performers may describe their own behavior and may evaluate its effectiveness. It is as if they can stand outside and look back at themselves, seeing themselves in the process of performance and making judgments about what they see. At times, such reflections during performance may become disabling. Upon deciding, for instance, that the delivery of a particular line was poorly done, a performer may become so focused upon that aspect of the performance that other performance problems arise. Centering upon how a presentation is proceeding can be crippling, particularly when the performer believes that it is not going well. On the other hand, performers often have at least some minimal sense of their behaviors and how well those behaviors are working. Ideally, such an awareness will not be at the forefront of their thinking during performance. To the extent that performers assess their performances, however, they are audience members to their own presentations.

Performers are always learning from their work. By staging others, performers may discover what it means to be someone else. What they come to know may remain intuitive, keenly felt but inexpressible. Or it may result in clearly articulated insights. Performances are trial experiences, allowing performers to feel and to see the consequences of particular behaviors. As performers present others, they try on possible scripts for their own lives. In doing so, they are engaged audience members, ready to learn what performance teaches.

Having a sense of executing, assessing, and learning is often more forcefully felt during rehearsal than during public performance. In rehearsal, performers are making decisions about their actions, reflecting upon the effectiveness of various choices, and experimenting with behaviors that may be quite removed from their own typical actions. Such processes require that performers assume the stance of an audience member in order to determine which performance behaviors they will take on. During public performance, however, the performers' audience role is usually less central to their thinking. Most performers believe that their best work occurs when they are ''in'' character, acting as if they are another. Too much attention on the act of performance itself may function against performers' engagement with others. Ideally, performers achieve a delicate balance of surrendering themselves to the characters they portray while holding on to a sense of themselves standing in for others.[1]

Think of one of your in-class performances. Describe in as much detail as possible the ways in which you were an audience to your own performance.

PROBE 1

1. Describe this presentation in terms of your awareness of executing, assessing, and learning from your performance choices. Specify any other ways in which you were a spectator to your own performance.
2. Did your consciousness of your audience role change as you went from rehearsal to public performance? Identify whatever differences existed in this regard between your rehearsals and your public performance.

3. Talk with another performer and determine how your experience of being an audience member to your own performance compares with the other's experience. Use the executing, assessing, and learning categories to help structure your discussion.

The Audience as Performer

Chapter 7 noted that an aesthetic transaction demands the presence of both a performer and an audience. Like the performer, the audience has a role to do—the role of spectator. Deciding to attend a theatrical event usually implies that one is willing to take on the role of audience member. In general terms, spectators know how to accomplish their role satisfactorily. Theatrical and social conventions dictate proper audience behaviors. Audience members know, for example, when they should speak, how they should dress, when they should laugh, and so on. By playing their role, audience members become a central aspect of the aesthetic event. They are public performers who contribute to the aesthetic dynamic. As they perform their role, speakers observe, respond to, and evaluate them. When speakers comment, "What a terrific audience we had tonight," they are applauding how well they believe the attending audience performed its role.[2] Speakers, then, attribute meaning and value to audience members' overt public behaviors. Likewise, audience members engage in the tasks of sense-maker and evaluator.

When audience members confront an aesthetic act, their first performative task is to make sense out of what they are seeing and hearing. We might ask, then, how audience members go about understanding aesthetic events. First, they count upon the fact that they possess the same linguistic system as speakers. Sharing a language is essential for the participants. Without this common ground, shared meaning is extremely limited. This point seems obvious when we remember or imagine an experience of seeing a foreign film without reading the subtitles. In such situations, we can gather some of what is going on, but much is lost. When listeners are fluent in the speaker's language, they can make sense of what they are hearing in part because of their previous experiences with that language. They expect that speakers will use language in predictable ways. They assume, for example, that speakers will follow grammatical rules, that speakers will use standard definitions of words, and so on. Such assumptions are a fundamental basis for their interpretations. Audience members depend upon a shared understanding of how language typically functions as they construct the meaning of events.

Second, audience members trust in the fact that utterances occur within situational and cultural contexts. The situational context may privilege certain meanings by encouraging listeners to associate an utterance with a specific circumstance. To ask if it is raining upon waking up in bed has a meaning quite different from asking the same question while standing in a heavy downpour. The cultural context may define specific meanings by leading listeners to focus upon the linguistic practices of a particular group or community. Sharing cultural membership allows people to understand their world in part by depending upon their common cultural interpretations. In the United States, for instance, people often associate the color white with purity. In some other cultures, however, white takes on significantly different connotations, including ''cowardly'' and ''sickly.'' The situational and cultural context of an utterance, then, helps listeners make sense of events.

Finally, each audience member depends upon individual perceptual tendencies in making sense of aesthetic acts. To a large extent, individual differences in perception emerge from differences in prior experiences, knowledge, and expectations. Obviously, no two people have the same life experiences. What is perhaps less obvious is that these experiences have a significant impact upon who people are and how they make sense of their world. Prior experiences also contribute to the knowledge level that individuals bring to any communicative exchange. The individual who has extensive experience with and knowledge of theatrical events is likely to see more in a given event than the less experienced and knowledgeable person. As theatrical experience and knowledge increase, people gain more schemes for processing theatrical events. What individuals expect to see also influences what they do see. Listeners, for instance, are more likely to laugh if they anticipate a comedy than if they expect a serious drama. Expectations, of course, may not be fulfilled, but they often guide at least initial impressions of events. Listeners, then, attempt to make sense of others by calling upon their prior experiences, knowledge, and expectations.

Sharing a linguistic system, recognizing the situational and cultural context and following perceptual tendencies will have a significant impact upon how audiences construct meaning. It would be misleading, however, to imply that audience members make sense of aesthetic events with only limited reference to them. Aesthetic utterances themselves play a large part in how listeners form meaning. One useful way to think about this is to view utterances as structures or frames guiding perception. Audience members fill in, complete, or put flesh upon utterances as they create meaning. Some texts require more filling in than others. In other words, some utterances demand more from listeners than others because they appear less explicit or self-evident. Audience members, then, are performers as they engage in their role of sense-maker. In this performative task, they rely upon the use of a familiar language, presented within a situational and cultural context. Moreover, their individual perceptions bend and are bent by the aesthetic events they confront.[3]

Playing the role of evaluator, audience members depend upon their own personal responses as well as the judgments of others. It is difficult to avoid making judgments after viewing an aesthetic act. The judgment may be as simple as "I liked it" or "I didn't like it," but typically people form some evaluation of the experience. They may give their own assessments high credence or may bow to the judgments of others. They may grant performers a voice in the assessment or believe that performers' opinions are invalid. They may turn to professional critics or deny the latter any authority. They may base their evaluations upon their attitudes toward a given performer or text. Some people enjoy seeing particular performers no matter what they are performing. Or they may avoid certain performers. They may only attend theatrical events that work with certain kinds of texts and, hence, may carry a positive expectancy into the performance. Whatever the case, people form opinions, deciding that some events are better than others. The next chapter discusses the evaluator role in much greater detail.

PROBE 2   Explore the following:

1. Explain why you might or might not share similar perceptions and evaluations of a given theatrical event. To help in this effort, think about a performance you saw in class that you perceived and evaluated differently than some of your classmates.
2. What preconceptions or expectations do you have for theatrical events? Be specific. Identify which are positive and which are negative. Isolate any that have changed during the semester.
3. Identify and describe an experience in which an audience member(s) influenced your impressions of a theatrical event.

In their sense-maker and evaluator roles, then, audience members are actively engaged in aesthetic transactions, performing an essential and collaborative part. Aesthetic meaning occurs at the point where the participants meet. It emerges from a union of speaker, creative act, and audience in an ongoing social process. Meaning is not something that the speaker has; meaning is something that is cocreated. Speakers and audience members are performers, creating and created by a mutually formative process.

Participation and Competence
within Aesthetic Transactions

Audience members, in playing an active, participatory role within aesthetic transactions, often find themselves deeply involved with aesthetic acts. They become fully engrossed in aesthetic worlds. This intimate relationship between audience members and aesthetic acts demands the audiences' concentrated energy, and, ultimately, fusion with aesthetic acts. In becoming fully engaged with aesthetic experiences, audience members may respond emotionally and intellectually. Even their bodies may sense and record the experiences before them. Absorbed in a given event, the self recedes into the background. The self, however, is not lost. Audience members recognize that the experience is aesthetic. In short, audience members move into aesthetic acts, letting themselves go with the events, but always knowing that the events are staged, fictive. Not all encounters with aesthetic acts, however, function in this manner.

In some circumstances, audience members may not become fully engaged with aesthetic communication. This may be a problem with the communicative act itself or a problem with the viewer. In the first case, a speaker may have structured the aesthetic act in such a poor fashion that it negates the possibility of aesthetic engagement. In the second case, an audience member may be so preoccupied with private matters that involvement is impossible. Or an audience member's negative attitudes or inadequate training may deny an aesthetic encounter. These descriptions (both ideal and otherwise) of audience members' relationships to aesthetic acts point to the various psychological stances audience members may experience with aesthetic events. The term that identifies this psychological relationship is *aesthetic distance*.[4]

How might audience members, then, assume the ideal psychological relationship or distance to aesthetic acts? We cannot give an easy answer to that question, since each aesthetic event is likely to call for slightly different behaviors. A few principles, however, seem to hold across all aesthetic acts. Audience members should give their focused attention to the event, remaining open and actively receptive. This may require that they free themselves from certain preconceptions and personal biases. It may demand that they take an imaginative leap into the aesthetic world, willingly suspending their own disbelief. It may necessitate that they hold their judgments in check, taking in the event before commenting upon it.

Audience members should also look to aesthetic events themselves as a guide for establishing an ideal psychological relationship. Some aesthetic acts seem to invite a deep emotional union between the self and the aesthetic world, as if the aesthetic acts pull the audience members within. Other aesthetic events seem to call for a more reflective stance, as if the aesthetic acts push away, so that the audience may comprehend. A preacher in a tent revival, for instance, typically asks the audience for a different psychological relationship from that asked by a satiric or witty essayist. In each case, the aesthetic act calls for a distinct psychological relationship. By questioning one's own stance toward aesthetic events, as well as by remaining sensitive to the demands of aesthetic acts, audience members place themselves in the best position to assume an ideal distance to aesthetic acts.

As implied above, a significant part of assuming an ideal stance toward aesthetic acts is adopting active listening behavior. Listening may seem such a natural part of everyday life that it hardly seems worthy of commentary. The truth of the matter, however, is that most people are rather poor listeners. Adults spend over half of their communication time listening, but they retain only about 20–25 percent of what they hear.[5] Part of the reason is that listeners are at times indifferent to what they are hearing. Effective listening requires work; it demands energy. It is an active process calling upon individuals to commit themselves fully to the interaction. Active listeners are physically and mentally alive. They are ready to respond emotionally and intellectually, ready to participate in the mutual construction of meaning. In short, they assume a supportive and receptive attitude.

PROBE 3   Think of a time when you genuinely wanted to understand what someone was saying. Describe your behavior in as much detail as you can.

1. How did your body respond during the encounter? Did you lean forward? Did you look intently at the person with whom you were talking? Did you offer much nonverbal feedback while the other person was talking? Etc?
2. What were you thinking about during the encounter? Were you more focused upon what the other person was saying than upon what you wanted to say?

Now think of an aesthetic communication event in which you were deeply involved. Compare and contrast this experience to the one you just described.

Good listening behavior is not only a question of assuming a productive attitude, but also a matter of employing effective listening skills. Three listening skills are particularly relevant to engaging aesthetic acts: empathy, selectivity, and neutrality. Empathic listening requires that audience members share and understand the feelings of the speaker. Empathic audience members will place themselves in the position of the other in order to feel as the other does, to share and understand the other's world. It is a process of emotionally giving of oneself. The focus is not only on what the other is saying, but also on how the other feels about what is being said. Selective listening demands that audience members perceive the essential dimensions of aesthetic acts. Selective audience members identify what is significant from the perspective of the speaker. They select from the entire aesthetic act what the speaker suggests is the most important, the most salient. Guided by their knowledge of theatrical and textual conventions as well as their sensitivity to the unique qualities of a given aesthetic event, they discover the essence of the aesthetic utterance. Neutral listening calls upon audience members to hold their judgments in check. Neutral audience members take in aesthetic acts before evaluating them. They block out any negative preconceptions and prejudices during the transaction. It is a process that takes speakers seriously and respectfully. Before judgment, audience members permit speakers to be heard. Through empathy, selectivity, and neutrality, audience members may escape the trap of their own rigid perspectives and inclinations. Ideally, they are in a dialogical relationship—engaged, giving of themselves and getting much in return.

Think of the last in-class performance you heard and describe your psychological relationship to the event.

PROBE 4

1. Would you describe your aesthetic distance as ideal? If so, what characterizes the ideal aesthetic distance?
2. Were there times during the performance when you felt your aesthetic distance was less than ideal? If so, what factors contributed to this?
3. Describe your listening behavior. To what extent did you empathize? Did you focus upon the most important aspects of the performance? To what extent did you remain neutral during the aesthetic transaction?

To give fully of oneself requires a reward, a reason for putting energy into the exchange. Throughout the long history of human behavior, people have received satisfaction from becoming engaged in aesthetic acts. Satisfaction or pleasure derives from the power of aesthetic acts to both delight and instruct. Aesthetic performance events delight by holding up human action for inspection. Performers, by presenting others, work not only on behalf of the speakers they portray, but also on behalf of the attending audience. Performers offer aesthetic worlds for audience response and consideration. As audience members identify with aesthetic worlds, they experience the pains and joys of human existence. In doing so, they may satisfy their psychological needs and may release their deeply felt emotions within a safe theatrical framework. Such a process is not without instructive value. Aesthetic events, by crystallizing human action, show audiences what people are and what they ought to be. In short, aesthetic acts are reflexive. They are possible histories of human action, teaching people about themselves. Audiences see what it means to be human. They discover patterns of human behavior, learn alternative ways of thinking and behaving, realize how to express what they could never say before. Such insights extend consciousness, allowing audiences to reflect upon their own experiences, to modify their own thoughts, and to alter their own actions. Ultimately, the reward of aesthetic encounters is a greater understanding of oneself and others.

In summary, we might describe competent participation in terms of an ideal three-step process. The first step requires audience members to become engaged, for engagement is essential if an aesthetic transaction is to take place. The performer and the audience must establish a dialogue. During this step, audience members assume a receptive and empathic stance: they strive to block out their personal biases and to hold their judgments in abeyance. The second step necessitates a sensitivity to the given aesthetic act, as well as a knowledge of theatrical and textual conventions. As the audience members form impressions, they must stay attuned to the dictates of the given aesthetic event. They focus upon the essential aesthetic qualities as they make sense of the event. Armed with a knowledge of traditional performance and linguistic forms, they recognize how the given aesthetic act is or is not in keeping with historical practices. The third step insists that spectators reflect upon the experience. Audience members are open, ready to examine their responses. They consider their own emotional reactions and the lessons such reactions might teach. In the end, they are enriched by their aesthetic encounter.

Notes

1. For a discussion of how performers see their work, see Toby Cole and Helen Krich Chinoy, eds., *Actors on Acting* (New York: Crown, 1957).
2. For a discussion of the interchange between performers and audiences, see Patti Peete Gillespie, "The Performing Audience," *Southern Speech Communication Journal* 46(1981):124–38. For a contrary view, see Paul Newell Campbell, "The Theatre Audience: An Abstraction," *Southern Speech Communication Journal* 46(1981):139–52.
3. For a more elaborate discussion of this point, see B. Beckerman, "Theatrical Perception," *Theatre Research International* 4(1979):157–71.

4. Edward Bullough commonly is credited with originating the concept. See Edward Bullough, " 'Psychical Distance' as a Factor in Art and an Aesthetic Principle," *British Journal of Psychology* 5 (June 1912):87–118.
5. Larry L. Barker, *Listening Behavior* (Englewood Cliffs, NJ: Prentice-Hall, 1971), 3–9.

Suggested Readings

Abdulla, Adnan K. *Catharsis in Literature.* Bloomington: Indiana University Press, 1985.

Barker, Larry L. *Listening Behavior.* Englewood Cliffs, NJ: Prentice-Hall, 1971.

Beckerman, B. "Theatrical Perception." *Theatre Research International* 4(1979):157–71.

Blau, Herbert. *The Audience.* Baltimore: Johns Hopkins University Press, 1990.

Bullough, Edward. " 'Psychical Distance' as a Factor in Art and an Aesthetic Principle." *British Journal of Psychology* 5(June 1912):87–118.

Burke, Kenneth. *The Philosophy of Literary Form,* rev. ed. New York: Vintage, 1957.

Campbell, Paul Newell. "The Performing Audience: An Abstraction." *Southern Speech Communication Journal* 46(1981):139–52.

Cole, Toby, and Helen Krich Chinoy, eds. *Actors on Acting.* New York: Crown, 1957.

Gillespie, Patti Peete. "The Performing Audience." *Southern Speech Communication Journal* 46(1981):124–38.

Graff, Gerald. *Literature Against Itself: Literary Ideas in a Modern Society.* Chicago: University of Chicago Press, 1979.

Hanna, Judith Lynne. *The Performer-Audience Connection: Emotion to Metaphor in Dance and Society.* Austin: University of Texas Press, 1983.

Holland, Norman N. *5 Readers Reading.* New Haven, CT: Yale University Press, 1975.

Kaplan, Stuart J., and G. P. Mohrmann. "Reader, Text, Audience: Oral Interpretation and Cognitive Tuning." *Quarterly Journal of Speech* 63(1977):59–65.

Langellier, Kristin M. "A Phenomenological Approach to Audience." *Literature in Performance* 3(April 1983):34–39.

Langer, Susanne K. *Philosophy in a New Key: A Study of the Symbolism of Reason, Rite and Art,* 3rd ed. Cambridge: Harvard University Press, 1957.

Lesser, Simon O. *Fiction and the Unconscious.* Boston: Beacon Press, 1957.

Loxley, Robert B. "Roles of the Audience: Aesthetic and Social Dimensions of the Performance Event." *Literature in Performance* 3(April 1983):40–44.

Mailloux, Steven. *Interpretive Conventions: The Reader in the Study of American Fiction.* Ithaca, NY: Cornell University Press, 1982.

Rosenblatt, Louise M. *Literature As Exploration,* rev. ed. New York: Noble & Noble, 1968.

Styan, J. L. *Drama, Stage and Audience.* Cambridge: Cambridge University Press, 1975.

Williams, David. "Audience Response and the Interpreter." In *Issues in Interpretation,* vol. II. Edited by Esther M. Doyle and Virginia Hastings Floyd, 199–206. Amsterdam: Editions Rodopi N.V., 1977.

Wolvin, Andrew, and C. G. Coakley, *Listening,* 2nd ed. Dubuque, IA: William C. Brown, 1985.

CHAPTER 10

The Evaluative Role
of the Audience

The preceding chapter noted that audience members typically form opinions of the aesthetic acts they encounter; as a matter of fact, most people spend considerably more time viewing and evaluating performances than doing them. This chapter examines that evaluative role and offers some guidelines for critical practice. The first section discusses the nature of the evaluative act, giving particular attention to the qualities of effective performance criticism. The second section focuses upon various critical models, demonstrating how the respective models establish distinct priorities for critical commentary. The third section looks at several evaluative issues that confront critics as they observe performers staging aesthetic texts. The final section raises some ethical questions that face performers and critics. By the end of the chapter, we should have a solid basis for making evaluative claims.

The Evaluative Act

Suppose someone said, "I really liked the performance. Every moment seemed real. When your hands were shaking as you picked up that letter, you were very believable." Embedded in this comment are three fundamental evaluative steps: description, judgment, and justification. Description specifies the particular auditory or visual details that the critic observed. Judgment is the value that the critic places upon what is heard or seen; it is a statement that falls somewhere on the continuum of good to bad. Justification offers a reason for the judgment; it implies or states a logic. We can break down the above comments as follows.

Description: "when your hands were shaking as you picked up that letter"

Judgment: "I really liked the performance"
Justification: [because] "every moment seemed real"
                       [because] "you were very believable"

Effective criticism involves accurately describing the performance, fairly judging its worth, and logically justifying the verdict. Each of these evaluative steps merits discussion.

To describe an aesthetic event accurately is a difficult task that calls upon critics to note the specific auditory and visual behaviors of the performer. Given the amount of stimuli that bombard spectators during aesthetic events, it is not surprising that they will miss some of the many details that performances offer. Often, critical discussions break down simply because the critics cannot agree upon what they saw and heard. Critics can easily miss each other's points if they do not establish a descriptive common ground. A particularly useful method for creating accurate descriptions of aesthetic events is dramatism. The dramatistic questions allow critics to focus upon aesthetic acts in a systematic and specific manner. Just as performers can use the dramatistic questions to explore aesthetic texts for performance, critics can apply the questions to texts in performance.

Think of a performance event that is vivid in your mind. Use the dramatistic questions identified in Chapter 4 to generate a descriptive account of the speaker(s) you saw in the performance event. Then explore the following:

PROBE 1

1. Compare the power of the dramatistic method for examining aesthetic texts for performance with its power to describe texts in aesthetic performances.
2. As you analyzed the performance event, to what extent were you able to remain descriptive? In other words, did your analysis ever become judgmental?
3. Argue for or against the usefulness of the dramatistic method for providing accurate descriptions of performance events.

Judgmental comments may be the only responses some people offer in critical discussions. Frequently, people simply say whether or not they liked a performance. They offer their verdict and, for them, the discussion ends. While the verdict may please or disappoint, stopping the discussion with only a statement of value is seldom helpful to the performer. Equally unsatisfying is the critic who withholds judgment. If critical remarks do not indicate whether the critic is positive or negative about the presentation, the discussion may seem empty and confusing. Articulation of judgments, however, carries some risks. Critics place themselves on the line by stating their views. Moreover, critics face the possibility of alienating those they critique. The burden of critical response is to negotiate interpersonal dynamics, as well as to develop a sound basis for any judgment. Before offering any specific guidelines for handling this burden, a discussion of the nature of justifying one's critical remarks is in order.

Justifying one's judgments demands careful argument. Critics take on the obligation to present a case for their views. To claim that what they saw (description) was good (judgment) begs the question of why they value what they do. Critics need to express the reasons for their opinions. They need to state the standards that inform their judgments. In doing so, their case relies upon a simple logic that unfolds as follows:

X was seen or heard.
X is good (or bad).
X is good (or bad) because of Y.

Notice that critics must obtain descriptive agreement before they can make their cases. If critics cannot establish that X was present, then the logic of their argument operates from a false premise. Likewise, if they cannot convince the audience of the reason for their positive or negative judgment, then their case will seem vacuous and irrelevant. Debate, then, might emerge over the reason for valuing a particular performance act.

How, then, might critics go about their business of offering useful responses? As suggested above, the first step is to reach descriptive consensus. In doing so, critics might rely upon the dramatistic method. The second step is to articulate one's judgment, and the final step is to make a case for the verdict. In following these steps, critics must handle interpersonal factors, as well as address substantive issues in a productive manner.

On the interpersonal level, good critics are *fair*, *sensitive*, and *honest*. Being fair demands that critics are responsive to the given performance. During the presentation, they are competent participants, open to an aesthetic transaction. They leave behind their own vested interests, preferring to address the given experience. They assume that performers have expended considerable energy and time in their attempts to stage others, and, hence, they take the performers' efforts seriously. In short, fairness requires critics to give of themselves. At the same time, good critics remain sensitive to the psychological needs of performers. Performers, by staging others, place themselves in a vulnerable position. Their efforts, offered publicly, are on display, exposed and subject to evaluation. Sensitive critics recognize the risks performers take and applaud them for it. Good critics remember that positive comments are just as instructive as negative ones. They carefully watch performers to see when their negative remarks are proving unproductive. If performers become defensive, the critical exchange is likely to suffer. Critics strive for an open and supportive forum in which genuine conversation can take place. This is most likely to occur when performers perceive critics as attempting to be helpful. Within this open and supportive context, good critics are honest. Offering false praise or omitting negative reactions from the discussion is not only deceptive, but also educationally unsound. Performers could easily take false praise and omissions as endorsements of problematic performance choices. Dishonest critics do not help performers; they hinder their growth.

While dealing with the interpersonal dynamics of the critical exchange, good critics present their views in a constructive manner. Their comments are *relevant*, *complete*, and *specific*. Relevant responses focus directly upon the given presentation and address matters of importance. Ideally, critics do not tell tangential stories or isolate an insignificant performance choice as the primary topic of discussion. Instead, good critics keep their focus upon the given performance and recognize what is important to acknowledge. They know what calls for only a passing remark and what demands considerable attention. They realize what is digressive and immaterial. Good critics are also complete. A complete critical response speaks to the entire performance. Complete critics examine all of the performance choices that merit comment. In the hands of complete critics, performers feel that they have received exhaustive, full responses to their efforts. Specific critics offer detailed remarks. They state their views with clarity and precision. They tell performers exactly what they are thinking. When offering negative remarks, they provide explicit alternatives for performers to consider. They avoid superficial and cliché responses. Critics who offer specific remarks demonstrate their close, in-depth attention to performers' work.

Good critics, then, proceed by negotiating the interpersonal forces at play and by structuring their evaluations in a useful manner. Their task is to be fair, sensitive, and honest in the critical exchange, as well as to be relevant, complete, and specific with their evaluations. At the same time, they are developing a critical case, based upon their observations and leading to a statement of value. Indeed, critics carry quite an obligation, one that is difficult to fulfill. Yet when performance criticism is functioning at its best, performers and audience members have much to learn. Critics are teachers, helping performers to develop their skills and to increase their insights into others. They also are guides, explicating the given performance in a rich and informative manner for the attending audience. They explore performances to see what may be problematic, but they leave performers intact and wiser than when they started.

Evaluative Models

The last section examined a critical remark in terms of description, judgment, and justification. We noted that the critic justifies positive judgments by claiming that the performance was "real" and "believable." Omitted from the discussion is why the critic thinks being "real" and "believable" are positive values for the given performance. Critical remarks carry implicit, over-riding norms that inform critics' justifications. All justifications, then, possess an embedded rationale. This point becomes clearer by returning to the basic logic of justifications and adding a final step.[1]

X was seen or heard	(Description)
X is good (or bad)	(Judgment)
X is good (or bad) because of Y	(Justification)
[Y is good (or bad) because of Z]	(Rationale)

To see how a critic's rationale may inform evaluations, we might briefly examine five distinct evaluative models.

Evaluative models offer critics theoretical frameworks that structure what they are likely to perceive. Each model sets a critical agenda, guiding perception and dictating values. Each indicates what demands attention and what requires priority. In short, models provide critics with schemes or systems for viewing performance events. We might best see the five models we shall explore as fundamental metaphors for understanding performance. We can state these metaphors as follows: performance as textual study, performance as artistic event, performance as communicative act, performance as cultural process, and performance as ethical practice.[2]

Critics, perceiving performance as textual study, primarily concern themselves with the power of performance to explicate aesthetic texts. Their fundamental interest is in texts. Performance, they believe, is a compelling method for examining their interest. It follows that their evaluations are textually based. They ask: To what degree did the performer present a faithful or equivalent rendering of the text? Given this central question, these critics would consider, to return to the earlier example, the notions of "real" and "believable" a legitimate justification only when the persona the performer was presenting was real and believable. In other words, these critics would value a given performance behavior to the extent that it reflected a dimension or aspect of the text.

Critics viewing performance as an artistic event assume that artistic events should possess certain qualities and should trigger certain responses. Considerable debate exists about what these qualities and responses should be. Nevertheless, most critics proceeding from this model would agree that performance is an art and that performers are artists. As artists, performers must not only demonstrate a mastery of craft and technique, but also offer an artistic experience. The ultimate evaluative question in this model is whether the performance was aesthetically sound. To return again to the previous example, these critics would see "real" and "believable" as aesthetic standards based in the historical tradition of theatrical realism. This tradition would allow many of these critics to accept "real" and "believable" as positive evaluative norms.

Critics seeing performance as a communicative act primarily focus upon the interchange between performers and listeners. Their concern is with how performers and listeners make performance events meaningful. Performances are utterances, open for interpretation by the participants. Performances, then, are transactions, dialogues between participants. The key critical question in this framework is whether genuine understanding emerged as a result of the exchange. These critics would value "real" and "believable" to the extent that real and believable actions facilitated understanding between the performer and the audience.

Critics conceptualizing performance as a cultural process see all performance events as an indication of cultural assumptions and beliefs. Performances, like other human achievements, tell people who they are and what they believe. However, one must look at performance practices closely for such insights to become evident. In the same way an anthropologist might use the unearthed pieces of a clay pot to infer things about a distant culture, critics may examine performances as cultural artifacts. In doing so, they discover the rules, conventions, and principles that guide and legitimize performance events. They acknowledge how such practices reflect a way of being in the world. They see the power of performance to change culture, to establish new ways of seeing. In this sense, performances are ongoing cultural practices, reaffirming cultural understandings as well as producing new cultural values and meanings. The basic evaluative concern is how performance and culture come together to teach people about who they are. Such critics would study how *real* and *believable* are understood within a given culture. They would explore the extent to which culture dictates how people see what is real and believable.

Critics conceiving of performance as ethical practice examine the implicit ethical issues involved in valuing some forms of speech over others. These critics occupy themselves with such subjects as the nature of the texts that performers present, the rights and obligations of people who have the opportunity to speak, and the political and moral ramifications of performance events. Such interests are guided by the belief that performance, in giving voice to one set of values, silences others. The fundamental evaluative question is whether the performance followed or adopted ethical principles. Thus, such critics might argue that to privilege "real" and "believable" actions over other forms of behavior may deny some individuals' right to expression. Moreover, they may see "real" and "believable" renderings of some voices (e.g., Hitler, white supremacists) as unethical acts.

Given these various evaluative models, it is not surprising that critics sometimes do not agree. In short, critics start with different assumptions about what to value. By using the example of the evaluative standards of "real" and "believable" across the various models, we understand why some critics would embrace these norms with greater comfort than others would. We should also see more clearly than before why performers may at times feel frustrated by the critical remarks they receive. If, indeed, the performer and critic are operating from different evaluative models, neither is likely to find the exchange satisfying.

What, then, might performers and critics do to increase the effectiveness of their communication? First, performers and critics must recognize the rationale for their evaluative remarks. This is no easy task, since critics may not restrict themselves to a given evaluative model. Their responses may range across all five frameworks identified above, as well as others. By questioning the basis of a given justification, however, performers and critics can often settle confusing points and establish a common ground for dialogue. Second, performers and critics must acknowledge that they can view performance in a number of ways. They should accept legitimate stances, such as the five models described above, with tolerance and understanding. There is no single correct perspective for evaluating performance; the various frameworks allow for an array of insights. The task for both performers and critics is the struggle to understand, to accept the others' comments with the same respect that they would have for their own.

PROBE 2

In the next discussion of a performance you hear, write down all of the evaluative remarks. Try to analyze the responses in terms of description, judgment, justification, and rationale.

1. How would you describe the evaluative commentary? Did the critics rely primarily upon description, judgment, justification, or rationale? How were these concepts intertwined in the discussion?
2. To what extent did the discussion favor one of the evaluative models described above? Were there some comments that do not seem to fit within any of the discussed models?
3. Isolate several critical statements and articulate the rationale informing them.

Issues in Evaluation

This section isolates several evaluative issues faced by critics when dealing with aesthetic performances. These issues confront critics from all theoretical perspectives, although different critics find certain issues more important than others. We can organize these issues around three fundamental concepts: texts, performers, and performances.

Text-centered Issues

One basic concern for critics is whether performers faithfully translate aesthetic texts into performance; or, to phrase the issue another way, to what degree the text selected for performance reflects the text in performance. Such a concern points to two key questions: (1) How much leeway does a performer have in interpreting the other's utterance? and (2) To what extent does placing an aesthetic text on stage shape or alter it?

Critics vary in the degree of interpretive leeway they are willing to grant to performers. Some critics permit performers considerable interpretive freedom; others insist upon rigid interpretive boundaries. In either case, when critics and performers disagree about the interpretation of a given text, they must deal with the incongruity. No two people are likely to understand a text in exactly the same way. But how much difference can be legitimately justified? Or, to put the question somewhat differently, is there such a thing as an incorrect interpretation? To the extent that they see performance as a method for understanding the communication of others, critics are likely to place some limits on performers' interpretive choices.

We might best define the range of interpretive choice in terms of three levels of textual meaning. On the first level, the language of texts provides *consensus understandings*, which are the agreed-upon meanings of a given text discovered by careful readers. Seldom open to debate, these understandings establish an interpretive common ground, a basis for further discussion about the meaning of a text. Further discussion leads to the level of *permissible understandings*—those that texts allow but that may not be agreed upon by all readers. Such understandings emerge from readers' thoughtful speculations about the meaning of a text. Following from consensus understandings, permissible understandings are reasoned claims, justifiable assertions. On the final level, there are *misunderstandings*—those interpretations that directly conflict with consensus understandings. Misunderstandings are incorrect readings, those that fail to take into account what all careful readers would grant. Critics, then, are likely to applaud those performances that reflect consensus understandings, to accept permissible understandings, and to reject misunderstandings.[3]

A simple example may help clarify these levels. Suppose someone said, "My name is Maryanne. I'm a twelve-year-old girl." Unless there were some reason to believe that the speaker was being deceitful, most people would quickly understand much of what is being said. Listeners would quickly grant the consensus understanding that the speaker is a female twelve-year-old named Maryanne. Less certain, however, are the questions of Maryanne's attitudes about her name and age and her motive for speaking. Maryanne's two sentences permit some interpretive leeway in how one might understand her utterance. If one said, however, that the speaker was not named Maryanne or that she was not a twelve-year-old female, then most people would say such claims are misunderstandings of the utterance. Critics, following this logic, would react positively to the performer who presented a female speaker that appeared to be twelve years old. Critics would also hold the performer accountable for those choices that were made concerning permissible interpretations. Here, the critics would not question whether the performer had the right or the wrong meaning. Instead, they would consider whether the performer featured an interesting or insightful aspect of the text. Critics would respond negatively to the performer who failed to create a twelve-year-old female.

PROBE 3   In preparation for one of your classmate's performances, read the text your classmate will present very carefully. Identify what you believe are consensus understandings, permissible understandings, and misunderstandings. Following the performance, compare your understandings with those of your classmate.

1. To what extent was your classmate's understanding of the text evident in the performance?
2. Discuss the value of this exercise for the performance critic. Does it help or hinder the critic to know a text before seeing it performed? Explain.

Another related issue is how the movement from one medium to another alters texts. Performers typically translate written language into oral utterances. They take texts that originally appeared in one context and place them within a theatrical frame. This movement from the page to the stage is highly important to critics who value faithful renderings of others' utterances. They know that any translation will lead to some differences between what appears on the page and what appears on stage. The differences may be a result of intentional performance choices, a product of practical constraints, or an unavoidable consequence of the act of translation.

Intentional performance choices resulting in page-stage differences are performers' purposeful decisions to break from texts. Critics who want performers to feature texts are unlikely to endorse such choices. Practical constraints may also lead to differences between the text on the page and the text in performance. Such constraints evolve around personal and interpersonal problems that performers encounter (e.g., sickness, available rehearsal time, budget, technical support). Text-centered critics commonly see differences emerging from such practical constraints as either simply unfortunate or a matter of poor planning. Translating communicative acts from one medium to another also may result in discrepancies between the page and the stage. Critics usually view such differences not as positive or negative, but as inevitable. Consider, for example, poems that offer little indication of the physical appearance of their personae. While poems may leave such a question open, performers cannot escape their own physical presence. Their bodies define personae in ways that texts may not specify and thus add a dimension to the texts that was not evident on the page. Indeterminate textual features become determinate as a consequence of translating utterances from one medium to another. Likewise, determinate textual features may become indeterminate in performance. This may emerge from the difficulty of doing on stage what can be done on the page. Describing a car chase scene on the page, for instance, is more easily accomplished than is executing that scene on the stage. Critics are likely to recognize and accept differences resulting from the act of translation. They realize that the translation process keeps an exact match or complete correspondence between the page and the stage from being possible.

PROBE 4

Read the letter from *Sandino's Daughters*, collected by Margaret Randall, in Appendix A. Perform the letter, asking the following questions.

1. Which textual dimensions became more determinate and which became less determinate as a result of your performance?
2. What might a critic mean by saying that your performance "featured the text"?

Performer-centered Issues

Critical comments about performers often revolve around two questions: (1) What constitutes a creative performance? and (2) What can critics legitimately say about performers' mental processes? Both of these questions are important considerations for the performance critic.

Creative performers are original and inventive in their work. This statement, however, begs the question of how critics determine what is original and inventive. On what basis does a critic claim that a given performer was creative? Is the creative performance one that is original and inventive for the performer? Is it one that appears new to the critic? Is it one that the critic knows is unique within theatrical tradition? The last question implies the best answer. Ideally, critics use the concept of creativity as an evaluative norm by reference to performance history. Performance history tells critics what people have done over time. Armed with a historical understanding, critics can contextualize the performances they encounter. They can recognize what is genuinely new within the performance tradition. What may be original and inventive for the performer may have a long record in performance practice. Thus, critics should know performance history in order to claim confidently that a given performance was creative.

The opposite of the creative performance is the plagiarized presentation. Critics should know when to argue that a given performer plagiarized the work of another. This problem typically arises when a performer presents an aesthetic text that another performer has staged before. Various recording devices make it possible for performers to take and pass off as their own others' performance choices. An example might prove instructive. Recently, a student-performer presented a speech Jack Nicholson gave in the film *The Witches of Eastwick*. The student had studied Nicholson's work very well, and he captured Nicholson's vocal and bodily behavior in exact detail. In short, the student gave a perfect imitation of Nicholson's performance. Critical response was divided. Those who had not seen the film reacted very positively; those who had seen the film expressed some disappointment. The latter were particularly disturbed that the student had not acknowledged that he was replicating what Nicholson had done. When asked if they would have responded positively if the performer had told them he was planning to impersonate Nicholson, most believed that they would have. They based their negative reaction on the belief that the student tried to deceive them, to present an aesthetic text as if he had made all the performance choices. They considered the student's work plagiarized because of how the performer framed it. Critics, then, call into play different evaluative norms when performers present their work as their own or as a copy of another's aesthetic act. When performers fail to give credit where credit is due, critics may rightly argue that their performances are plagiarized.

How critics might discuss the mental processes of performers is another important question. Critics may feel that performers should possess certain mental attitudes during performance. For example, they may believe that performers should concentrate on what they are doing, should be sincere in their attempts to stage others, and should empathize with the personae they are portraying. Concentration, sincerity, and empathy are all mental processes, internal states of mind. What critics see in performance may not be a valid indication of what is going on in the performer's head. In other words, mental states may not translate into specific behaviors. Thus, critics who assert that a performer was not concentrating, sincere, or empathizing may encounter the performer's simple retort, "Yes, I was." In such cases, critics are left in an indefensible position. This is not to say that critics cannot engage in productive dialogue about performers' internal processes. If a critic believes that a performer should possess certain mental attitudes during a presentation and wants to make the performer's internal state a part of the critical discussion, then the critic's only recourse is to ask the performer about the latter's mental processes. Ultimately, only performers have the authority to state what was going on in their minds.

PROBE 5

We have argued that critics cannot assume that performers' behaviors are an indication of their internal thoughts. Even so, we often feel quite sure that the external behaviors we see are a result of internal mental states. Consider whether or not the following critical comments are legitimate.

1. "Even if you are not sincere during the performance, you must show behaviors that convince your audience that you are."
2. "More often than not, audience members know if the performer is concentrating."
3. "When performers work with serious material, you can tell how well their presentations are going by how still their audiences become."
4. "Make sure the audience can see you empathizing."

Performance-centered Issues

Of the several evaluative issues that emerge when we think in general about performance events, we shall focus upon only two. The first centers upon the critic's and the audience's level of aesthetic engagement with performance events. The key question here is whether engagement can legitimately serve as an evaluative norm. A second issue involves the cultural values that guide the performance practices of a given community. The pivotal question here is the degree to which cultural values should dictate evaluative standards.

Various factors, as we saw in Chapter 9, contribute to whether or not critics become engaged in aesthetic events. The first question that critics confront, then, is whether their degree of engagement provides a legitimate basis for judgment. In one sense, critics have no other basis for evaluation. They can only respond in keeping with what they see and hear. Yet critics should remember that their own inclinations influence their perceptions. What may be quite engaging to one critic may be only mildly interesting to another. This is not to say criticism must be purely subjective, a matter of personal preference. Critics can consider whether their limited engagement was a problem in the aesthetic event or a matter of their own competencies and attitudes. In the first case, the critics' mandate is to identify the aspects of the performance that kept the critics from a fuller engagement with the work. In the second case, the critics' obligation is to acknowledge their own personal perspectives before commenting or to disqualify themselves as adequate judges of the event.

Critics who wish to rely upon their perceptions of audience response as a criterion for evaluation take on other responsibilities. It is difficult not to be influenced by strong reactions from an audience. Audiences send off signals, often providing clues about their responses to performances. Critics may note, for example, that the audience appeared to be completely enthralled or that the audience seemed to be quite restless. Two points are worth identifying about such claims. First, critics can only make inferences about audience reactions. Responses may translate into behaviors or they may not. Only audience members know what was going on in their heads. Audience members' responses, like performers' mental processes, are known to critics only by questioning. Second, even if critics determine how the audience members responded, it does not necessarily follow that the audience's evaluations are valid. Audiences may be sophisticated or naive judges. In using audience reactions as a basis for evaluation, the critics' task is to decide whether the audience members are trustworthy commentators.

A second general performance issue is the extent to which cultural values set evaluative standards. Critics face the question of whether their standards should hold for all performance events they encounter or whether their standards should change in keeping with the cultural values of a given performance community. Competitive performance events on the high school and college forensic circuit offer an interesting example. The forensic circuit has established a number of performance conventions and rules that the competitors must follow in order not to be disqualified: they must work within certain time limits, must have a manuscript present, must avoid costuming, and so on. The forensic performance community has generated a number of implicit and explicit critical values that they expect to inform performances and their evaluations. Critics unfamiliar with the forensic circuit have a difficult choice to make when judging in this context. They have three possible options: (1) they can learn the cultural values of the forensic circuit and evaluate accordingly; (2) they can disregard the operating cultural values and judge the performance events by their own standards; or (3) they can combine the first two options, responding in keeping with cultural norms and then articulating their alternative values. Only the first and third options seem fair to the performance community. Critics should not assume that all performance communities share their own standards.

Identify as many critical values as you can that have emerged within your class.

1. What does this performance community say is worthwhile? What constitutes a good performance for this community?
2. Do you agree with all of the values that this community seems to hold? If not, make a case for your viewpoint.

PROBE 6

Evaluation and Ethics

Human action has ethical consequences. Performance is no exception. All performance events carry ethical implications. Critics cannot escape the obligation to respond to the ethics of performance practice. On the most basic level, critics should consider whether a given performance event respected the rights of others.[4] Moreover, critics should understand how all performances are political acts, endorsing particular values.[5]

Critics, when examining if a performance respected the rights of others, scrutinize the performer's work with the speakers portrayed as well as the audience engaged. The following questions present a number of ethical issues about the rights of creators, personae, and audience members. These questions show the variety and complexity of ethical issues confronting critics. Critics might ask:

1. To what extent are performers obligated to utter the exact words of creators' texts? What, if any, changes can performers make in creators' texts?
2. What, if any, subjects or points of view would be unethical for performers to present? What responsibilities do performers have for the language and actions they present on stage? When should they forewarn audience members that their performances contain vulgar speech or nudity?
3. Is it ethically incumbent upon performers to strive for a dialogic engagement with those they stage? Would an intentionally superficial rendering be unethical? What constitutes the exploitation of another's utterance?
4. By what right do performers enter into the lives of others? How should performers be held accountable for their actions?
5. What implicit contract exists between performers and audience members in terms of what the audience will be asked to do when they attend performances? Should performers always honor that contract?

Such questions do not lend themselves to easy answers. Critics may argue that the performance context would determine their answers. They may claim that performers' ethical burdens depend upon the ethical practices of creators or audience members. They may insist that such questions neglect the rights of performers. Whatever the case, critics should consider the ethics of performers' actions. Performers, too, face the same ethical questions confronting critics. The imperative for both critics and performers is to recognize that performance choices have ethical consequences and to establish their own ethical guidelines.

Not only do critics need to reflect upon the ethics of performers' actions, but they should also recognize that performance events are political acts. This claim implies that performance is action in the world, a social process bound by historical circumstances. The performance community holds the power to privilege certain speakers and values. By performing particular texts, they favor particular voices. The performance community, for example, has often neglected texts by women and minorities. By maintaining certain performance conventions, they restrict the performance opportunities of others. They often cast Blacks, Mexicans, Asians, and Native Americans in disparaging and stereotypic roles. Even by charging money to performance events, they deny entry to certain members of the culture. For the most part, attending a performance is an opportunity enjoyed chiefly by the cultural elite. These few examples demonstrate the importance for critics to become attuned to the political nature of performance events. Critics have an ethical responsibility to consider how performance sanctions particular practices. Sensitive critics remain alert to whose voices are silenced and whose are given a forum.

Notes

1. For a parallel discussion, see Beverly Whitaker, "Critical Reasons and Literature in Performance," *Speech Teacher* 18(1969):191–93.
2. For a similar discussion, see Ronald J. Pelias, "Schools of Interpretation Thought and Performance Criticism," *Southern Speech Communication Journal* 50(1985):348–65.
3. See Beverly Whitaker Long, "Evaluating Performed Literature," in *Studies in Interpretation*, vol. II, ed. Esther M. Doyle and Virginia Hastings Floyd (Amsterdam: Editions Rodopi, N.V., 1977), 267–81; and Monroe C. Beardsley, "Right Readings and Good Readings," *Literature in Performance* 1(1980):10–22.
4. See Dwight Conquergood, "Performing as a Moral Act: Ethical Dimensions of the Ethnography of Performance," *Literature in Performance* 5(1985):1–13.
5. See Mary Susan Strine, ed., "Symposium: Post-Structuralism and Performance," *Literature in Performance* 4(1983):21–64.

Suggested Readings

Bharucha, Rustom. "Confessions of an Itinerant Critic." *Performing Arts Journal* 8(1984):9–27.

Conquergood, Dwight. "Performing as a Moral Act: Ethical Dimensions of the Ethnography of Performance." *Literature in Performance* 5(1985):1–13.

Dickie, George. *Evaluating Art*. Philadelphia: Temple University Press, 1988.

Emmet, Alfred. "A Short View of Dramatic Criticism." *Theatre Quarterly* 3(1973):3–5.

English, John W. *Criticizing the Critics*. New York: Hastings House, 1979.

Hernadi, Paul, ed. *What Is Criticism?* Bloomington: Indiana University Press, 1981.

HopKins, Mary Francis. "Sincerity and the Performing Artist: An Old Critical Concept Reestablished." In *Studies in Interpretation*, vol. II, edited by Esther M. Doyle and Virginia Hastings Floyd, 207–19, Amsterdam: Editions Rodopi, N.V., 1977.

Hornby, Richard. "Understanding Acting." *Journal of Aesthetic Education* 17(1983):19–37.

Long, Beverly Whitaker. "Evaluating Performed Literature." In *Studies in Interpretation*, vol. II, edited by Esther M. Doyle and Virginia Hastings Floyd, 267–81. Amsterdam: Editions Rodopi, N.V., 1977.

Long, Beverly Whitaker. "Performance as Doing: A Reconsideration of Evaluating Performed Literature." In *Festschrift for Isabel Crouch: Essays on the Theory, Practice, and Criticism of Performance*, edited by Wallace A. Bacon, 21–31. Las Cruces: New Mexico State University, 1987.

Meynell, Hugo A. *The Nature of Aesthetic Value*. Albany: State University of New York Press, 1986.

Mitchell, W. J. T., ed. *The Politics of Interpretation*. Chicago: University of Chicago Press, 1983.

Pelias, Ronald J. "Schools of Interpretation Thought and Performance Criticism." *Southern Speech Communication Journal* 50(1985):348–65.

Smith, Barbara Herrnstein. *Contingencies of Value: Alternative Perspectives for Critical Theory*. Cambridge: Harvard University Press, 1988.

Strelka, Joseph, ed. *Problems of Literary Evaluation*, vol. II. University Park: Pennsylvania State University Press, 1969.

Strine, Mary Susan, ed. "Symposium: Post-Structuralism and Performance." *Literature in Performance* 4(1983):21–64.

Strine, Mary S. "Art, Argument, and the Vitality of Interpretive Communities." In *Festschrift For Isabel Crouch: Essays on the Theory, Practice, and Criticism of Performance*, edited by Wallace A. Bacon, 58–70. Las Cruces: New Mexico State University, 1987.

Whitaker, Beverly. "Critical Reasons and Literature in Performance." *Speech Teacher* 18(1969):191–93.

Whitaker, Beverly. "Cognition and Audience in a Performance Class." *Speech Teacher* 23(1974):63–66.

Appendixes

APPENDIX A

Aesthetic Texts for Discussion

The Shield of Achilleus
Homer
translation by Richmond Lattimore

Hearing her the renowned smith of the strong arms answered her:
'Do not fear. Let not these things be a thought in your mind.
And I wish that I could hide him away from death and its sorrow
at that time when his hard fate comes upon him, as surely
as there shall be fine armour for him, such as another
man out of many men shall wonder at, when he looks on it.'
      So he spoke, and left her there, and went to his bellows.
He turned these toward the fire and gave them their orders for working.
And the bellows, all twenty of them, blew on the crucibles,
from all directions blasting forth wind to blow the flames high
now as he hurried to be at this place and now at another,
wherever Hephaistos might wish them to blow, and the work went forward.
He cast on the fire bronze which is weariless, and tin with it
and valuable gold, and silver, and thereafter set forth
upon its standard the great anvil, and gripped in one hand
the ponderous hammer, while in the other he grasped the pincers.
      First of all he forged a shield that was huge and heavy,
elaborating it about, and threw around it a shining
triple rim that glittered, and the shield strap was cast of silver.
There were five folds composing the shield itself, and upon it
he elaborated many things in his skill and craftsmanship.
      He made the earth upon it, and the sky, and the sea's water,
and the tireless sun, and the moon waxing into her fullness,
and on it all the constellations that festoon the heavens,
the Pleiades and the Hyades and the strength of Orion
and the Bear, whom men give also the name of the Wagon,

who turns about in a fixed place and looks at Orion
and she alone is never plunged in the wash of the Ocean.
On it he wrought in all their beauty two cities of mortal
men. And there were marriages in one, and festivals.
They were leading the brides along the city from their maiden chambers
under the flaring of torches, and the loud bride song was arising.
The young men followed the circles of the dance, and among them
the flutes and lyres kept up their clamour as in the meantime
the women standing each at the door of her court admired them.
The people were assembled in the market place, where a quarrel
had arisen, and two men were disputing over the blood price
for a man who had been killed. One man promised full restitution
in a public statement, but the other refused and would accept nothing.
Both then made for an arbitrator, to have a decision;
and people were speaking up on either side, to help both men.
But the heralds kept the people in hand, as meanwhile the elders
were in session on benches of polished stone in the sacred circle
and held in their hands the staves of the heralds who lift their voices.
The two men rushed before these, and took turns speaking their cases,
and between them lay on the ground two talents of gold, to be given
to that judge who in this case spoke the straightest opinion.
But around the other city were lying two forces of armed men
shining in their war gear. For one side counsel was divided
whether to storm and sack, or share between both sides the property
and all the possessions the lovely citadel held hard within it.
But the city's people were not giving way, and armed for an ambush.
Their beloved wives and their little children stood on the rampart
to hold it, and with them the men with age upon them, but meanwhile
the others went out. And Ares led them, and Pallas Athene.
These were gold, both, and golden raiment upon them, and they were
beautiful and huge in their armour, being divinities,
and conspicuous from afar, but the people around them were smaller.
These, when they were come to the place that was set for their ambush,
in a river, where there was a watering place for all animals,
there they sat down in place shrouding themselves in the bright bronze.
But apart from these were sitting two men to watch for the rest of them
and waiting until they could see the sheep and the shambling cattle,
who appeared presently, and two herdsmen went along with them
playing happily on pipes, and took no thought of the treachery.
Those others saw them, and made a rush, and quickly thereafter
cut off on both sides the herds of cattle and the beautiful
flocks of shining sheep, and killed the shepherds upon them.
But the other army, as soon as they heard the uproar arising
from the cattle, as they sat in their councils, suddenly mounted

behind their light-foot horses, and went after, and soon overtook them.
These stood their ground and fought a battle by the banks of the river,
and they were making casts at each other with their spears bronze-headed;
and Hate was there with Confusion among them, and Death the destructive;
she was holding a live man with a new wound, and another
one unhurt, and dragged a dead man by the feet through the carnage.
The clothing upon her shoulders showed strong red with the men's blood.
All closed together like living men and fought with each other
and dragged away from each other the corpses of those who had fallen.

    He made upon it a soft field, the pride of the tilled land,
wide and triple-ploughed, with many ploughmen upon it
who wheeled their teams at the turn and drove them in either direction.
And as these making their turn would reach the end-strip of the field,
a man would come up to them at this point and hand them a flagon
of honey-sweet wine, and they would turn again to the furrows
in their haste to come again to the end-strip of the deep field.
The earth darkened behind them and looked like earth that has been
    ploughed
though it was gold. Such was the wonder of the shield's forging.

    He made on it the precinct of a king, where the labourers
were reaping, with the sharp reaping hooks in their hands. Of the cut swathes
some fell along the lines of reaping, one after another,
while the sheaf-binders caught up others and tied them with bind-ropes.
There were three sheaf-binders who stood by, and behind them
were children picking up the cut swathes, and filled their arms with them
and carried and gave them always; and by them the king in silence
and holding his staff stood near the line of the reapers, happily.
And apart and under a tree the heralds made a feast ready
and trimmed a great ox they had slaughtered. Meanwhile the women
scattered, for the workmen to eat, abundant white barley.

    He made on it a great vineyard heavy with clusters,
lovely and in gold, but the grapes upon it were darkened
and the vines themselves stood out through poles of silver. About them
he made a field-ditch of dark metal, and drove all around this
a fence of tin; and there was only one path to the vineyard,
and along it ran the grape-bearers for the vineyard's stripping.
Young girls and young men, in all their light-hearted innocence,
carried the kind, sweet fruit away in their woven baskets,
and in their midst a youth with a singing lyre played charmingly
upon it for them, and sang the beautiful song for Linos
in a light voice, and they followed him, and with singing and whistling
and light dance-steps of their feet kept time to the music.

    He made upon it a herd of horn-straight oxen. The cattle
were wrought of gold and of tin, and thronged in speed and with lowing

out of the dung of the farmyard to a pasturing place by a sounding
river, and beside the moving field of a reed bed.
The herdsmen were of gold who went along with the cattle,
four of them, and nine dogs shifting their feet followed them.
But among the foremost of the cattle two formidable lions
had caught hold of a bellowing bull, and he with loud lowings
was dragged away, as the dogs and the young men went in pursuit of him.
But the two lions, breaking open the hide of the great ox,
gulped the black blood and the inward guts, as meanwhile the herdsmen
were in the act of setting and urging the quick dogs on them.
But they, before they could get their teeth in, turned back from the lions,
but would come and take their stand very close, and bayed, and kept clear.

And the renowned smith of the strong arms made on it a meadow
large and in a lovely valley for the glimmering sheepflocks,
with dwelling places upon it, and covered shelters, and sheepfolds.

And the renowned smith of the strong arms made elaborate on it
a dancing floor, like that which once in the wide spaces of Knosos
Daidalos built for Ariadne of the lovely tresses.
And there were young men on it and young girls, sought for their beauty
with gifts of oxen, dancing, and holding hands at the wrist. These
wore, the maidens long light robes, but the men wore tunics
of finespun work and shining softly, touched with olive oil.
And the girls wore fair garlands on their heads, while the young men
carried golden knives that hung from sword-belts of silver.
At whiles on their understanding feet they would run very lightly,
as when a potter crouching makes trial of his wheel, holding
it close in his hands, to see if it will run smooth. At another
time they would form rows, and run, rows crossing each other.
And around the lovely chorus of dancers stood a great multitude
happily watching, while among the dancers two acrobats
led the measures of song and dance revolving among them.

He made on it the great strength of the Ocean River
which ran around the uttermost rim of the shield's strong structure.

Then after he had wrought this shield, which was huge and heavy,
he wrought for him a corselet brighter than fire in its shining,
and wrought him a helmet, massive and fitting close to his temples,
lovely and intricate work, and laid a gold top-ridge along it,
and out of pliable tin wrought him leg-armour. Thereafter
when the renowned smith of the strong arms had finished the armour
he lifted it and laid it before the mother of Achilleus.
And she like a hawk came sweeping down from the snows of Olympos
and carried with her the shining armour, the gift of Hephaistos.

✧ ✧

Borges and I
Jorge Luis Borges
Translated by Anthony Kerrigan

Things happen to him, the other one, to Borges. I stroll about Buenos Aires and stop, almost mechanically now perhaps, to look at the arch of an entranceway and the ironwork gate; news of Borges reaches me in the mail and I see his name on an academic ballot or in a biographical dictionary. I like hourglasses, maps, eighteenth-century typography, etymologies, the taste of coffee, and Robert Louis Stevenson's prose; he shares these preferences, but with a vanity that turns them into the attributes of an actor. It would be an exaggeration to say that our relationship is a hostile one; I live, I go on living, so that Borges may contrive his literature; and that literature justifies me. I do not find it hard to admit that he has achieved some valid pages, but these pages can not save me, perhaps because what is good no longer belongs to anyone, not even to him, the other one, but to the language or to tradition. In any case, I am destined to perish, definitively, and only some instant of me may live on in him. Little by little, I yield him ground, the whole terrain, though I am quite aware of his perverse habit of magnifying and falsifying. Spinoza realized that all things strive to persist in their own nature: the stone eternally wishes to be stone and the tiger a tiger. I shall subsist in Borges, not in myself (assuming I am someone), and yet I recognize myself less in his books than in many another, or than in the intricate flourishes played on a guitar. Years ago I tried to free myself from him, and I went from the mythologies of the city suburbs to games with time and infinity, but now those games belong to Borges, and I will have to think up something else. Thus is my life a flight, and I lose everything, and everything belongs to oblivion, or to him.

I don't know which one of the two of us is writing this page.

✧ ✧

It Is a Beauteous Evening
William Wordsworth

It is a beauteous evening, calm and free,
The holy time is quiet as a nun
Breathless with adoration; the broad sun

Is sinking down in its tranquillity;
The gentleness of heaven broods o'er the sea:
Listen! the mighty being is awake,
And doth with his eternal motion make
A sound like thunder—everlastingly.
Dear Child! dear Girl! that walkest with me here,
If thou appear untouched by solemn thought,
Thy nature is not therefore less divine:
Thou liest in Abraham's bosom all the year;
And worship'st at the temple's inner shrine,
God being with thee when we know it not.

◇◇

From
Sandino's Daughters: Testimonies of Nicaraguan Women in Struggle
Margaret Randall

Note: *The following letter was written by Idania Fernandez. Her war name was Angela. She was twenty-four when she was killed by the National Guard in Leon on April 16, 1979. A month before her death she wrote these lines to her daughter Claudia. They remain a legacy from all revolutionary mothers to all children. Margaret Randall*

March 8, 1979

My dear daughter:

This is a very important time for people everywhere; today in Nicaragua, and later in other countries in Latin America and throughout the world. The Revolution demands all each of us has to give, and our own consciousness demands that as individuals we act in an exemplary way, to be as useful as possible to this process.

I hope that someday, not too far off, you may be able to live in a free society where you can grow and develop as human beings should, where people are brothers and sisters, not enemies. I'd like to be able to walk with you, holding hands, walk through the streets and see everyone smiling, the laughter of children, the parks and rivers. And we, ourselves, smile with joy as we see our people grow like a happy child and watch them become new human beings, conscious of their responsibility toward people everywhere.

You must learn the value of the paradise of peace and freedom you are going to be able to enjoy. I say this because the best of our brave people have given their precious blood and they've given it willingly, with great love for their people, for freedom and for peace, for the generations to come and for children like you. They've given their lives so children won't have to live under this repression, humiliation and misery so many men, women and children have suffered in our beautiful Nicaragua.

I'm telling you all this in case I'm not able to tell you personally or no one else tells you these things. A mother isn't just someone who gives birth and cares for her child; a mother feels the pain of all children, the pain of all peoples as if they had been born from her womb. My greatest desire is that one day you will become a true woman with a great love of humanity. And that you'll know how to defend justice, always defend it against whatever and whomever would trample it.

To become this kind of person, read and assimilate the works of the great leaders of our revolution and of the revolutions of other countries, take the best of each as example and put these into practice so that you will continue to grow always. I know you'll do this and that you can do it. And that gives me great peace.

I don't want to leave you words, promises or empty morals. I want to leave you an attitude to life, my own (although I know it isn't yet the best) and that of all my Sandinist brothers and sisters. I know you will learn how to use it.

Well, my plump one, if I have the privilege of being able to see you again—which is also a possibility—we'll have long talks about life and the Revolution. We'll work hard carrying out the tasks we're given. We'll play the guitar and sing and play together. And through all this, we'll come to know each other better and learn from one another.

> *Come, show me your pretty face*
> *Lovely like flowers and freedom*
> *And give me energy to struggle*
> *Uniting your laughter and our reality*
> *Daily I think of you*
> *Imagining always how you are*
> *Always love our people, and humanity*
>
> *With all the love of your mother, Idania.*
>   *Until our victory, forever.*
>   *Free Homeland, or Death.*

✧ ✧

A Sorrowful Woman
Gail Godwin

Once upon a time there was a wife and mother one too many times.

One winter evening she looked at them: the husband durable, receptive, gentle: the child a tender golden three. The sight of them made her so sad and sick she did not want to see them ever again.

She told the husband these thoughts. He was attuned to her; he understood such things. He said he understood. What would she like him to do? "If you could put the boy to bed and read him the story about the monkey who ate too many bananas, I would be grateful." "Of course," he said. "Why, that's a pleasure." And he sent her off to bed.

The next night it happened again. Putting the warm dishes away in the cupboard, she turned and saw the child's grey eyes approving her movements. In the next room was the man, his chin sunk in the open collar of his favorite wool shirt. He was dozing after her good supper. The shirt was the grey of the child's trusting gaze. She began yelping without tears, retching in between. The man woke in alarm and carried her in his arms to bed. The boy followed them up the stairs, saying, "It's all right, Mommy," but this made her scream. "Mommy is sick," the father said, "go and wait for me in your room."

The husband undressed her, abandoning her only long enough to root beneath the eiderdown for her flannel gown. She stood naked except for her bra, which hung by one strap down the side of her body; she had not the impetus to shrug it off. She looked down at the right nipple, shriveled with chill, and thought, How absurd, a vertical bra. "If only there were instant sleep," she said, hicupping, and the husband bundled her into the gown and went out and came back with a sleeping draft guaranteed swift. She was to drink a little glass of cognac followed by a big glass of dark liquid and afterwards there was just time to say Thank you and could you get him a clean pair of pajamas out of the laundry, it came back today.

The next day was Sunday and the husband brought her breakfast in bed and let her sleep until it grew dark again. He took the child for a walk, and when they returned, red-cheeked and boisterous, the father made supper. She heard them laughing in the kitchen. He brought her up a tray of buttered toast, celery sticks, and black bean soup. "I am the luckiest woman," she said, crying real tears. "Nonsense," he said. "You need a rest from us," and went to prepare the sleeping draft, find the child's pajamas, select the story for the night.

She got up on Monday and moved about the house till noon. The boy, delighted to have her back, pretended he was a vicious tiger and followed her from room to room, growling and scratching. Whenever she came close, he would growl and scratch at her. One of his sharp little claws ripped her flesh, just above the wrist, and together they paused to watch a thin red line materialize on the inside of her pale arm and spill over in little beads. "Go away," she said. She got herself upstairs and locked the door. She called the husband's office and said, "I've locked myself away from him. I'm afraid." The husband told her in his richest voice to lie down, take it easy, and he was already on the phone to call one of the baby-sitters they often employed. Shortly after, she heard the girl let herself in, heard the girl coaxing the frightened child to come and play.

After supper several nights later, she hit the child. She had known she was going to do it when the father would see. "I'm sorry," she said, collapsing on the floor. The weeping child had run to hide. "What has happened to me, I'm not myself anymore." The man picked her tenderly from the floor and looked at her with much concern. "Would it help if we got, you know, a girl in? We could fix the room downstairs. I want you to feel freer," he said, understanding these things. "We have the money for a girl. I want you to think about it."

And now the sleeping draft was a nightly thing, she did not have to ask. He went down to the kitchen to mix it, he set it nightly beside her bed. The little glass and the big one, amber and deep rich brown, the flannel gown and the eiderdown.

The man put out the word and found the perfect girl. She was young, dynamic, and not pretty. "Don't bother with the room, I'll fix it up myself." Laughing, she employed her thousand energies. She painted the room white, fed the child lunch, read edifying books, raced the boy to the mailbox, hung her own watercolors on the fresh-painted walls, made spinach soufflé, cleaned a spot from the mother's coat, made them all laugh, danced in stocking feet to music in the white room after reading the child to sleep. She knitted dresses for herself and played chess with the husband. She washed and set the mother's soft ash-blonde hair and gave her neck rubs, offered to.

The woman now spent her winter afternoons in the big bedroom. She made a fire in the hearth and put on slacks and an old sweater she had loved at school, and sat in the big chair and stared out the window at snow-ridden branches, or went away into novels about other people moving through other winters.

The girl brought the child in twice a day, once in the later afternoon when he would tell of his day, all of it tumbling out quickly because there was not much time, and before he went to bed. Often now, the man took his wife to dinner. He made a courtship ceremony of it, inviting her beforehand so she could get used to the idea. They dressed and were beautiful together again and went out into the frosty night. Over candlelight he would say, "I think you are better, you know." "Perhaps I am," she would murmur. "You look . . . like a cloistered queen," he said once, his voice breaking curiously.

One afternoon the girl brought the child into the bedroom. "We've been out playing in the park. He found something he wants to give you, a surprise." The little boy approached her, smiling mysteriously. He placed his cupped hands in hers and left a live dry thing that spat brown juice in her palm and leapt away. She screamed and wrung her hands to be rid of the brown juice. "Oh, it was only a grasshopper," said the girl. Nimbly she crept to the edge of a curtain, did a quick knee bend and reclaimed the creature, led the boy competently from the room.

"The girl upsets me," said the woman to her husband. He sat frowning on the side of the bed he had not entered for so long. "I'm sorry, but there it is." The husband stroked his creased brow and said he was sorry too. He really did not know what they would do without that treasure of a girl. "Why don't you stay here with me in bed," the woman said.

Next morning she fired the girl who cried and said, "I loved the little boy, what will become of him now?" But the mother turned away her face and the girl took down the watercolors from the walls, sheathed the records she had danced to, and went away.

"I don't know what we'll do. It's all my fault, I know. I'm such a burden, I know that."

"Let me think. I'll think of something." (Still understanding these things.)

"I know you will. You always do," she said.

With great care he rearranged his life. He got up hours early, did the shopping, cooked the breakfast, took the boy to nursery school. "We will manage," he said, "until you're better, however long that is." He did his work, collected the boy from the school, came home and made the supper, washed the dishes, got the child to bed. He managed everything. One evening, just as she was on the verge of swallowing her draft, there was a timid knock on her door. The little boy came in wearing his pajamas. "Daddy has fallen asleep on my bed and I can't get in. There's no room."

Very sedately she left her bed and went to the child's room. Things were much changed. Books were rearranged, toys. He'd done some new drawings. She came as a visitor to her son's room, wakened the father, and helped him to bed. "Ah, he shouldn't have bothered you," said the man, leaning on his wife. "I've told him not to." He dropped into his own bed and fell asleep with a moan. Meticulously she undressed him. She folded and hung his clothes. She covered his body with the bedclothes. She flicked off the light that shone in his face.

The next day she moved her things into the girl's white room. She put her hairbrush on the dresser; she put a note pad and pen beside the bed. She stocked the little room with cigarettes, books, bread, and cheese. She didn't need much.

At first the husband was dismayed. But he was receptive to her needs. He understood these things. ''Perhaps the best thing is for you to follow it through,'' he said. ''I want to be big enough to contain whatever you must do.''

All day long she stayed in the white room. She was a young queen, a virgin in a tower; she was the previous inhabitant, the girl with all the energies. She tried these personalities on like costumes, then discarded them. The room had a new view of streets she'd never seen that way before. The sun hit the room in late afternoon and she took to brushing her hair in the sun. One day she decided to write a poem. ''Perhaps a sonnet.'' She took up her pen and pad and began working from words that had lately lain in her mind. She had choices for the sonnet, ABAB or ABBA for a start. She pondered these possibilities until she tottered into a larger choice: she did not have to write a sonnet. Her poem, could be six, eight, ten, thirteen lines, it could be any number of lines, and it did not even have to rhyme.

She put down the pen on top of the pad.

In the evenings, very briefly, she saw the two of them. They knocked on her door, a big knock and a little, and she would call Come in, and the husband would smile though he looked a bit tired, yet somehow this tiredness suited him. He would put her sleeping draft on the bedside table and say, ''The boy and I have done all right today,'' and the child would kiss her. One night she tasted for the first time the power of his baby spit.

''I don't think I can see him anymore,'' she whispered sadly to the man. And the husband turned away, but recovered admirably and said, ''Of course, I see.''

So the husband came alone. ''I have explained to the boy,'' he said. ''And we are doing fine. We are managing.'' He squeezed his wife's pale arm and put the two glasses on her table. After he had gone, she sat looking at the arm.

''I'm afraid it's come to that,'' she said. ''Just push the notes under the door; I'll read them. And don't forget to leave the draft outside.''

The man sat for a long time with his head in his hands. Then he rose and went away from her. She heard him in the kitchen where he mixed the draft in batches now to last a week at a time, storing it in a corner of the cupboard. She heard him come back, leave the big glass and the little one outside on the floor.

Outside her window the snow was melting from the branches, there were more people on the streets. She brushed her hair a lot and seldom read anymore. She sat in her window and brushed her hair for hours, and saw a boy fall off his new bicycle again and again, a dog chasing a squirrel, an old woman peek slyly over her shoulder and then extract a parcel from a garbage can.

In the evening she read the notes they slipped under her door. The child could not write, so he drew and sometimes painted his. The notes were painstaking at first: the man and boy offering the final strength of their day to her. But sometimes, when they seemed to have had a bad day, there were only hurried scrawls.

One night, when the husband's note had been extremely short, loving but short, and there had been nothing from the boy, she stole out of her room as she often did to get more supplies, but crept upstairs instead and stood outside their doors, listening to the regular breathing of the man and boy asleep. She hurried back to her room and drank the draft.

She woke earlier now. It was spring, there were birds. She listened for sounds of the man and the boy eating breakfast; she listened for the roar of the motor when they drove away. One beautiful noon, she went out to look at her kitchen in the daylight. Things were changed. He had bought some new dish towels. Had the old ones worn out? The canisters seemed closer to the sink. She inspected the cupboard and saw new things among the old. She got out flour, baking powder, salt, milk (he bought a different brand of butter), and baked a loaf of bread and left it cooling on the table.

The force of the two joyful notes slipped under her door that evening pressed her into the corner of the little room; she hardly had space to breathe. As soon as possible, she drank the draft.

Now the days were too short. She was always busy. She woke with the first bird. Worked till the sun set. No time for hair brushing. Her fingers raced the hours.

Finally, in the nick of time, it was finished one late afternoon. Her veins pumped and her forehead sparkled. She went to the cupboard, took what was hers, closed herself into the little white room, and brushed her hair for a while.

The man and boy came home and found: five loaves of warm bread, a roast stuffed turkey, a glazed ham, three pies of different fillings, eight molds of the boy's favorite custard, two weeks' supply of fresh-laundered sheets and shirts and towels, and hand-knitted sweaters (both of the same grey color), a sheath of marvelous water-color beasts accompanied by mad and fanciful stories nobody could ever make up again, and a tablet full of love sonnets addressed to the man. The house smelled redolently of renewal and spring. The man ran to the little room, could not contain himself to knock, flung back the door.

"Look, Mommy is sleeping," said the boy. "She's tired from doing all our things again." He dawdled in a stream of the last sun for that day and watched his father roll tenderly back her eyelids, lay his ear softly to her breast, test the delicate bones of her wrist. The father put down his face into her fresh-washed hair.

"Can we eat the turkey for supper?" the boy asked.

❖ ❖

"In Westminster Abbey"
John Betjeman

Let me take this other glove off
    As the *vox humana* swells,
And the beauteous fields of Eden
    Bask beneath the Abbey bells.
Here, where England's statesmen lie,
Listen to a lady's cry.

Gracious Lord, oh bomb the Germans.
    Spare their women for Thy Sake,
And if that is not too easy
    We still pardon Thy Mistake.
But, gracious Lord, whate'er shall be,
Don't let anyone bomb me.

Keep our Empire undismembered
    Guide our Forces by Thy Hand,
Gallant Blacks from far Jamaica,
    Honduras, and Togoland;
Protect them Lord in all their fights,
And, even more, protect the whites.

Think of what our Nation stands for,
    Books from Boots' and country lanes,
Free speech, free passes, class distinction,
    Democracy, and proper drains.
Lord, put beneath Thy special care
One-eighty-nine Cadogan Square.

Although dear Lord I am a sinner,
    I have done no major crime;
Now I'll come to Evening Service
    Whensoever I have time.
So, Lord, reserve for me a crown,
And do not let my shares go down.

I will labor for Thy Kingdom,
    Help our lads to win the war,

Send white feathers to the cowards
  Join the Women's Army Corps,
Then wash the Steps around Thy Throne
In the Eternal Safety Zone.

Now I feel a little better,
  What a treat to hear Thy Word,
Where the bones of leading statesmen,
  Have so often been interred.
And now, dear Lord, I cannot wait
Because I have a luncheon date.

✧ ✧

From
Hard Times
Studs Terkel

Michael, 19

What does the Depression mean to me? I don't know. I'm not depressed. I can pot out any time I want. A Depression is to me when I can't sit down on my chaise lounge and have a beer and this boob tube right in my face.

Tad, 20

It's something that has been filtered through by my parents. I didn't know much about it, and they don't mind my not knowing much about it. They control the source of information — sort of like the high priest: you can't approach the altar too closely, or you'll be struck dead. This purple heart in their background has become a justification for their present affluence. If we got the idea they didn't have it so bad, they'd have less psychological control over us. That's why they don't approve of the hippies. These people are saying: our parents told us it was this way. Now we're doin' it, and it's not so bad. Our parents don't like that. They want to keep it a secret. They try to control the information that filters down to us. They're screwed up and they don't want people to find out about it.

They say, "You have it soft now." The point is, *they* have it soft now. They sort of feel guilty about it. If they make other people feel guilty about it, it won't be so noticeable in their own instance.

Robert Gard

Professor of Drama, University of Wisconsin

I set out for the University of Kansas on a September morning with $30 that I'd borrowed from my local bank. I had one suit and one necktie and one pair of shoes. My mother had spent several days putting together a couple of wooden cases of canned fruits and vegetables. My father, a country lawyer, had taken as a legal fee a 1915 Buick touring car. It was not in particularly good condition, but it was good enough to get me there. It fell to pieces and it never got back home anymore.

I had no idea how long the $30 would last, but it sure would have to go a long way because I had nothing else. The semester fee was $22, so that left me $8 to go. Fortunately, I got a job driving a car for the dean of the law school. That's how I got through the first year.

What a pleasure it was to get a pound of hamburger, which you could buy for about five cents, take it up to the Union Pacific Railroad tracks and have a cookout. And some excellent conversation. And maybe swim in the Kaw River.

One friend of mine came to college equipped. He had an old Model T Ford Sedan, about a 1919 model. He had this thing fitted up as a house. He lived in it all year long. He cooked and slept and studied inside that Model T Ford Sedan. How he managed I will never know. I once went there for dinner. He cooked a pretty good one on a little stove he had in this thing. He was a brilliant student. I don't know where he is now, but I shouldn't be surprised if he's the head of some big corporation. (Laughs.) Survival. . . .

The weak ones, I don't suppose, really survived. There were many breakdowns. From malnutrition very likely. I know there were students actually starving.

Some of them engaged in strange occupations. There was a biological company that would pay a penny apiece for cockroaches. They needed these in research, I guess. Some students went cockroach hunting every night. They'd box 'em and sell them to this firm.

I remember the feverish intellectual discussion we had. There were many new movements. On the literary scene, there was something called the Proletarian Novel. There was the Federal Theater and the Living Newspaper. For the first time, we began to get socially conscious. We began to wonder about ourselves and our society.

We were mostly farm boys and, to some extent, these ideas were alien to us. We had never really thought about them before. But it was a period of necessity. It brought us face to face with these economic problems and the rest. . . . All in all, a painful time, but a glorious time.

✧ ✧

The Hospital Window
James Dickey

I have just come down from my father.
Higher and higher he lies
Above me in a blue light
Shed by a tinted window.
I drop through six white floors
And then step out onto pavement.

Still feeling my father ascend,
I start to cross the firm street,
My shoulder blades shining with all
The glass the huge building can raise.
Now I must turn round and face it,
And know his one pane from the others.

Each window possesses the sun
As though it burned there on a wick.
I wave, like a man catching fire.
All the deep-dyed windowpanes flash,
And, behind them, all the white rooms
They turn to the color of Heaven.

Ceremoniously, gravely, and weakly,
Dozens of pale hands are waving
Back, from inside their flames.
Yet one pure pane among these
Is the bright, erased blankness of nothing.
I know that my father is there,

In the shape of his death still living.
The traffic increases around me
Like a madness called down on my head.
The horns blast at me like shotguns,
And drivers lean out, driven crazy—
But now my propped-up father

Lifts his arm out of stillness at last.
The light from the window strikes me

And I turn as blue as a soul,
As the moment when I was born.
I am not afraid for my father —
Look! He is grinning; he is not

Afraid for my life, either,
As the wild engines stand at my knees
Shredding their gears and roaring,
And I hold each car in its place
For miles, inciting its horn
To blow down the walls of the world

That the dying may float without fear
In the bold blue gaze of my father.
Slowly I move to the sidewalk
With my pin-tingling hand half dead
At the end of my bloodless arm.
I carry it off in amazement,

High, still higher, still waving,
My recognized face fully mortal,
Yet not; not at all, in the pale,
Drained, otherworldly, stricken,
Created hue of stained glass.
I have just come down from my father.

✧ ✧

Big Boy
Theresa M. Carilli

Joe

You really wanna know about my fightin days. I'll tell you then. I was born in
Hartford, this big street kid, back during the depression. My parents were a
couple of Sicilian immigrants — arranged marriage here in America. I took
up boxing to help make a couple of bucks for the family. I had eight brothers
and sisters. I was good at boxing and my friends gave me a nickname, "Big
Boy" cause I was big and had a boyish face. I hated that god damned name,
always did. My real name is Umberto. My mother named me after the king of
Italy at the time. My brother changed my name to "Joe" because back then, in

the 40's, who ever heard of a boxer named Umberto. That was a sissy name. Joe Big Boy.

Daughter

See this crack on the wall? This was one of the Christmas cracks. This one here was an Easter crack. When I was a kid, mom used to hang my art work over the cracks that dad used to make — either with his fist or head. After awhile there were so many cracks, mom stopped putting up my art work. It looked more natural that way. He'd get mad and he'd ram his head into the wall. Sometimes but seldom, his fist. And if he was really mad, he'd get down on his hands and knees and smash his head into the metal radiators until it would bleed.

Joe

So here I am at 17 years old, boxing for money. My son of a bitchen father was beating my mother up and he still wasn't working. I had a good strong right arm and in two years, I'm a professional boxer at Madison Square Garden. Smash some guy in the face until he bleeds and make some money. It was a means to an end. That's not what I wanted for my life. I wanted to be educated, to study literature and theater, especially since my parents were illiterate. But, people think that big guys like me don't have brains. Big people scare most people. I used to cry every time I fought so I always kept two books in my locker to calm me down. One was Robert Browning and the other, Spinoza. I really wanted to be a lawyer.

Daughter

I remember the day dad came home after gambling the house away. It was some business deal he said. But we all knew. He turned white, broke all the windows in the house, took some downers that the doctor prescribed for his nerves and then he split to "jump off a bridge." It was Christmas eve. The police found him on the bridge and brought him home. Mom would have left him if he didn't have a nervous breakdown. Mom would have left him if she weren't afraid he would kill her.

Joe

I met Joe Louis at the garden. He took a liking to me and I became his sparring partner for 25 bucks a day. Back in 1942, that was good money. Blacks and Italians. We're known to be good at two things, and the other one's fightin. One day Louis and I were sparring at Riverside Stadium in Washington D.C. In front of 15,000 people I threw a punch directly at Louis. The only thing he couldn't handle was a punch thrown directly at him. I was more surprised than he was. They took him to the hospital because they thought I broke his jaw. I became a big celebrity.

Daughter

He punched mom on my ninth birthday in front of my cousin. I was so embarrassed. Mom had to go to the hospital.

Joe

But, I never was successful as a fighter. I never been successful at anything because I don't have no god damned guts and no luck either. When my first chance for glory came up, I got drafted, sent to Italy and Africa. When my second chance came up, the troops got moved.

Daughter

Mom said that dad was screwing around on her their first year of marriage. She understood though. He was in Europe during the war, and she knew his past history as a fighter. She'd say, "How can you put the boy back on the farm, after he's seen Paris."

Joe

I hated fighting. Broke my nose five times. Lost up to eight pounds in a fight. Once I got knocked in the head so hard I didn't know where I was for three days. A friend led me around. I did learn a few things from boxing — you can do anything you want in this world because most everybody's so god damned stupid. That's why I tell my daughters to do anything they want.

Daughter

What did I get from dad? A sense of humor. A great sense of humor. Once you see someone break a wall down just once, you realize that you have a lot to be happy about.

Joe

Affected me? Sure. Yeah. It's affected me.

Daughter

My sister had shock therapy, 12 times. She was diagnosed as a paranoid schizophrenic. I spent two years in a suicidal depression. I had a therapist who spent two years explaining to me that normal wasn't violence or abuse.

Joe

Affected me. Sure. Yeah. It's affected me.

Daughter

There are some things he's told us and a lot I'm sure he hasn't. He's punch drunk. He doesn't talk in complete sentences. He fashions himself a philosopher but there's no logic that runs through anything he says. Its like a bad Monty Python movie. I wonder what he would have been like if he hadn't been a fighter.

Joe

I get angry sometimes. Sometimes I get so mad, I'm afraid I'm gonna kill someone. If there was a next time, I'd want it all, not be just some big dumb street kid. I guess I'm just one unlucky bastard.

The Fox and the Woodcutter
from Aesop's Fables
Translated by Babrius Hull

A fox was fleeing. As she fled
A hunter fast behind her sped.
But being wearied, when she spied
An old man cutting wood, she cried,
"By all the gods that keep you well,
Hide me among these trees you fell,
And don't reveal the place, I pray."
He swore that he would not betray
The wily vixen; so she hid,
And then the hunter came to bid
The old man tell him if she'd fled,
Or if she'd hidden there. He said,

"I did not see her," but he showed
The place the cunning beast was stowed
By pointing at it with his finger.
But still the hunter did not linger.
He put no faith in leering eye,
But trusting in the words, went by.
Escaped from danger for a while
The fox peeked out with coaxing smile.
The old man said to her, "You owe
Me thanks for saving you, you know."
"Most certainly; for I was there
As witness of your expert care.
But now farewell. And don't forget,
The god of oaths will catch you yet
For saving with your voice and lips
While slaying with your finger tips."

✧ ✧

The Gasoline Wars
Jean Thompson

We are looking at plantations, Henry and I. The plantations have names like Asphodel and Hermitage and St. Francis. They are all large and white and pillared. They remind me of a set of white china birds in the parlor of an elderly lady. It costs money to go inside, money we don't have, so we skulk through parking lots, peer through wire fences, seeing what we can.

Wait a minute, I say. I want to take a picture of this one.

Save your film, says Henry. It isn't a good shot.

And he is right because when the picture is developed it will show a large white pillared mansion, trees dripping Spanish moss, and our yellow Volkswagen parked in the driveway. But I have announced that I am taking this picture so I steady the camera and shoot.

Why don't you just buy postcards, he says.

Because we can't afford them.

And I am right because we can't spare a dime for a pay toilet. Looking at plantations was Henry's idea. It has taken us far out of our way. I tell myself it is not his fault that the plantations aren't much fun or that we can't see the river because the grass-covered levee is so high. But these things don't help.

Why don't you relax, he tells me.

We don't have enough money to buy gas, I say. We'll run out.

We'll think of something, Henry says.

We are both right.

Actually Henry still believes we have enough money, enough gas. He believes it because he wants to. It is one of his mental habits I find exasperating. I could count the money and figure mileage and prove mathematically that we'll run out of gas. This is one of my habits that exasperates him. I will save it for later, when I will also remind him that it was he who put premium in the car by mistake.

Henry is looking at the map. If we double back to that last highway, he says, there's another plantation eight miles farther.

He is watching me craftily. I close my face to him. And then, he says, there's another one four, make that five miles down the road.

He is trying to goad me. Later, Henry, I think.

We have been in New Orleans for the last week, staying in the Carmen Rae Motel, coral stucco, six dollars a night. In the mornings we felt the warm damp air clinging to us like a sheet, and it was good to wake up slowly. We drank liquor and ate seafood until our stomachs felt like aquariums. We had only one serious argument, and that was about the advisability of a left turn onto Bienville Street.

We visit two more plantations. They are large and white and chipped, like ancient bathtubs. Well, says Henry. I've never seen so many historic buildings. Very impressive.

I make no reply.

Guess we better get moving. Better look for a place to cross the river.

It is 3:00 P.M. We have been in the car for five hours. We are a little bit south of Baton Rouge. We have a place to sleep in Nashville. Yes, I say, time for a final burst of speed.

He gives me a look that says Later, Marie. The gas gauge is the fuse on a bomb. We watch it burning down.

We find a ferry but have to wait for it. Although it is only March it is hot sitting on the pebbly dirt beside the river. The scrubby cottonwoods have brown water up to their knees. Henry turns on the radio and static cuts a line between my ears like a can opener.

Henry and I fight like people thirty years older than ourselves, like cartoons in an old *Saturday Evening Post*. I wish it were funnier. I criticize his driving, his sloppiness, his lack of foresight. He can't stand my nagging, my nervousness, my scheduling. At times I see him shrinking, balding, see myself growing a heavy jaw and a preposterous flowered hat.

I look at Henry. His eyes are closed and he is slouched behind the wheel. Henry, I tell him, in all sincerity I admire your flexibility.

He doubts my sincerity and would like to ask me what brought that on. But now the ferry is coming, hooting, churning the coffee-colored water. It flies the pelican flag of Louisiana. A large man in a torn plaid shirt, his hair like fuzz on a tennis ball, directs the cars. His mouth is loose, collapsed-looking, shapeless. Henry drives too close to the rail, makes a coil of rope wobble on its post. Back, the man shouts, back, waving his arms. Henry mutters and puts the car in reverse.

I have always liked ferries. They calm me. Maybe it is the act of crossing water. We are standing at the rail watching the boat peel back the river. It is cooler here. Henry's hand cups the back of my neck. I nibble his shirt collar. Let's try to relax, he says. Whatever happens. I agree.

At times we are a handsome couple.

Behind us footsteps ring on the metal deck. The man in the plaid shirt is walking toward us. He walks the same way a boulder rolls down a hill.

Now I have lived in the South before, though you couldn't tell it from my accent. I do not have the Northerner's usual fears of being dismembered by the Klan in a swamp. I like the South, like being called Ma'am, like the little rituals and politenesses that mark dealings between strangers. Henry has a moustache but his light hair is clipped. Henry can talk his way out of nearly anything. But I must admit to a momentary nervousness when this large man bears down on us in the middle of the brown river.

He taps Henry on the shoulder and his shapeless mouth forms shapeless words: Woo yew lak to come up? Pointing to the glassed-in cabin on the deck above our heads.

Sure, says Henry. Thanks, we would. We follow the man, who I think is smiling, up twisting white metal stairs, emerging timidly into the cabin. It is larger than you might think, it is white and tidy and the controls take up two walls. A man sits on a stool in front of the wheel. He overflows the stool, the flesh of his arms sags from his sleeves, his face rallies briefly around his black cigar. How you all today, he asks us.

Fine, thank you, we reply. And yourself?

Tol'able, he says, gumming the cigar. He asks us if we are on vacation.

Yes, says Henry. All the way from Illinois.

Henry asks if a ferry is difficult to steer. The pilot lets him take the wheel. The man in the plaid shirt stands behind us. He is definitely smiling.

The pilot beckons to me, his old broad hand blue with knotty veins. See that lever, he says, Pull it. I do so. There is a long mooing whistle. I giggle. Now you told em we're coming, he says.

We thank them and pick our way downstairs, watch the riverbank rise before us, wave as we drive away. Henry and I nod with mutual pleasure at having shared a glimpse into a colorful and perhaps vanishing bit of America.

You see there are the good times.

We must have chosen the wrong way to get into Baton Rouge. There are endless detours, hand-painted signs tacked to highway markers, arrows pointing both ways. It is a long slow route. We pass construction sites, rusty barges floating in the rusty river, steel towers and pipes and sulfurous chemical works. Henry takes it personally when I ask if he's sure we're on the right road.

Of course I'm sure, he says, and if we're not I'll get back on it.

I'm hungry, I say. Are you getting hungry? Yes, he is. In the car we have doughnuts and shrimp, both bought this morning in New Orleans, before our fiscal crisis became apparent. The shrimp are whole, unpeeled, already boiled in the fish market. We crack the shells and dunk them in a bottle of cocktail sauce. It is good food but a little peculiar. Eating it reminds us we are on rations.

As neutrally as possible I say I guess we better get gas while we're here.

Henry is developing a little crease in the bridge of his nose. His eyes are sinking toward it. I know that Marie, he says. Why don't you get off my back?

I wasn't trying to criticize, I tell him. Why do you always assume the worst about me?

I don't.

You just did.

It is the kind of argument that could go on, but we are too tired to introduce new variations. The highway leads us through what looks like a black area of town, frame houses collapsing at their centers like underdone cakes, soap-streaked windows, tottering groceries, Dairy Queens. Henry peers at the gas stations. This is absurd, he says. They're out of gas.

Why is it absurd. It's been going on lots of places.

Because this town is one big oil refinery, he says. The unfairness of it gives us a common gripe. Standard Oil wears army boots, he says. Shell blows dead bears, I say.

We find a gas station that will sell five dollars of gas to each car and we take our place in line. A girl in a fringed red cowgirl outfit emerges from the office with a sign saying Last Car for Gas. She ambles down the line, slows at the car before us. Henry grits his teeth and mutters Over here, Tex, or I'll blast your tits off. She complies.

It is after four when we leave Baton Rouge. I am driving. Henry has the map out. I think we should go to Vicksburg, he says. It's not out of our way.

I have heard this kind of thing before. Henry, I say, much as I admire your childlike capacity for living for the moment, it is indeed out of our way. We can pick up the Interstate right here to Memphis.

You know I hate Interstates, says Henry.

They are not meant to inspire ardor, I say. We only have enough money for one more tank of gas. It is getting late. Why the hell do you want to go to Vicksburg?

Henry says I've never seen a Civil War battlefield. I've always wanted to see one.

I have seen a number of Civil War battlefields. I agree they are interesting. But not today. The inside of the Volkswagen begins to smell briny from the shrimp. It is as if an ocean has washed over us, left behind a residue of Coke cans, cellophane, sticky towels and paper sacks.

We are on our way to Vicksburg. I drive with every muscle locked. We do not speak. In our arguments we become everything we accuse each other of being. He is irresponsible. I am shrill, vindictive. If I were not the person Henry accuses me of being, I might enjoy the view. As we approach Vicksburg the land gets hillier, the trees lacier, the sun lower. Ribbons of red light cross the road.

Henry has been napping. He wakes, yawns, peers over me to look at the gas gauge. Well, he says, looks like we'll have to try to cash a check after all.

With our wildly out-of-state accounts. I say nothing. I follow the signs to the battlefield site, brake the car viciously. The sun is setting as we get out. We walk six feet apart. There is no one else around.

If I were not being the person Henry accuses me of being, I might be absorbed by Vicksburg. Soft deep shadows lie between the hills. Dying men tried to crawl as far as these trees. The states have placed memorials to mark the positions of their troops. The battle lines are only a few yards apart in some places. Henry is trudging on the ridge, along the Confederate markers. He is artificially, tensely jaunty, his hands in his pockets. I am below him on the Union lines. The ruddy light makes him an easy target. The 47th Pennsylvania Infantry is on my right, seasoned troops, I can depend on them to cover me.

Henry turns in my direction. He shouts I suppose you're really pleased that you were right about the gas.

Why should I be pleased about running out of gas at night in Mississippi?

Why don't you have any credit cards?

Why don't you have a credit rating?

Why did you buy that whole bottle of awful brandy?

Why don't you stop screaming?

I could charge him now. Uphill. Geography is on his side, but history is on mine. The Father of Waters will again go unvexed to the sea. Instead I turn and march back to the car, the short grass snapping under my feet.

We make the rounds of gas stations. Henry does the talking. I know it's against your policy, he says, but I'd really appreciate it if you could cash my fiancée's check.

When we deal with the public like this I become his fiancée.

Politely the gas station men turn us down. They stand in the halo of their blue humming lights and let their chins sink as they shake their heads. Sorry. Sorry. You might try over at the Sunoco. The Phillips.

It is quite dark. Henry gets back in the car. Let's drive to Canton to pick up the Interstate, he says. We'll try there.

It won't work, I say. Nothing will work.

Will you calm down?

I can't. I told you this would happen. You never listen to me.

You should listen to yourself sometime. Like one of those tropical birds whose feathers rise when they screech.

The Volkswagen grinds through ten miles of lumpy road. Henry is rustling a paper bag. Want a shrimp, he says.

No thank you.

Why do we get in such fixes?

We are speaking calmly.

Because you let everything turn into a crisis, I say, and then we have to do something unnerving to get out of it.

You're always worrying, Henry says. Why can't you trust me?

I can't answer his question. Behind it is my larger fear, that if we don't get out of this car soon we will remain the people we accuse each other of being.

Another ten miles goes by and I say I wonder if we could sell the gas can.

I think it is a reasonable suggestion. The gas can is a brand-new five-gallon job. It's never even had gas in it. But Henry purchased it three days ago over my objections.

Sure, he says bitterly. You'd like that.

I assure him I am not liking any of it.

At Canton we spot a large, flood-lit Marathon station. Its brightness gives us hope. We pull up discreetly at its side. Henry looks at me critically. Comb your hair, he says.

We prepare to be a charming young couple.

There is just one man running these five shining sets of gas pumps, these red white and blue cylinders that now look to me as elegant and stirring as a fleet of newly painted sailboats. He is a young man with a nubbly crew cut, a round plump face, and a very clean white T-shirt. Henry strolls up as if we were the most casual of evening walkers. Hi there, he says.

The man nods, his face pleasant but noncommittal.

I wonder if you could do us a big favor, says Henry. We're stuck, really stuck. You wouldn't take a check for gas, would you?

Well no. We can't take no checks.

That's what I figured. I don't blame you. It's asking for trouble these days. But. There is a way you could help us that wouldn't be any risk to you. Come on, I'll show you.

Henry leads the three of us to the car. I try to look as distantly sexy as the broads that pose across the hoods of new Cadillacs, but I am stumbling with fatigue. Henry opens our trunk and brings out the gas can. The price sticker is still on it, $5.68. A trade, says Henry.

The man scratches his head. Laughs a little. Sure is new, he says.

We wouldn't try to fool you, says Henry.

Oh please, I say, blinking moistly. We'd really appreciate it. I don't know what we'll do otherwise.

Henry drapes an arm around me. You see my fiancée is a diabetic and if we don't get back to her medicine we'll have to go to a hospital.

I try to look both sexy and sickly. At least he didn't say I had leukemia. Or, My woman, she's near her time.

The man looks uncomfortable. Possibly moved. We will come back at Christmas and ask for donations for orphans. Henry says Look, we'll give you a deal on the can, four dollars worth of regular for it. We wouldn't expect what we paid for it.

Please, I say.

The man sighs. If it was up to me . . . he says. I'll have to call my boss. He turns and walks back to the station.

The boss. Henry and I despair. This man is nice enough but I'm not sure I trust him to convey our special qualities of wholesomeness and pathos over the telephone. What we need, I say, is a swaddled infant.

So we sleep in the car tonight, says Henry. And try again tomorrow. It won't be the end of the world.

Yes it will, I say.

The man returns. Boss says it's OK. Four dollars worth.

We are fulsome in our thanks. We'll splurge and get Cokes, says Henry. Want anything?

Only if it's sugar-free, dear.

We drive off. We have enough money now for gas to Nashville. Thank God we get good mileage, Henry says. Diabetes, I say.

He grins over the steering wheel. It worked, didn't it?

I think I've been prostituted.

For an amateur you're pretty good at it.

Henry, I say, you were right. We pulled it off. I should have more faith in you. Really and truly. But why can't I ever contradict you without a fight?

If you would not raise your dulcet voice, my dear.

But we are not fighting now. There is something reassuring to me about being on the Interstate, a smooth dark humming track that will take us easily where we want to go. Life with Henry makes me yearn for Interstates. We will chat pleasantly. We will remember the good times. We eat the last of the doughnuts with a shrimp chaser. Henry picks a radio station that plays rich fruity songs sung by aging vocalists. I make no protests.

Henry, I say, I will admit that life with you has a certain undeniable zest to it.

Marie, he says, you can be a steadying influence on me.

When I open my eyes the same radio station is on, but blobs of static adhere to it. How far are we from Memphis, I ask.

Only thirty miles.

How's the gas?

We'll get some in Memphis.

I yawn. The road passes over a truck stop, revolving Standard sign, busy lights. I sit up straight. Henry, I say, what time is it?

Twelve-thirty.

I think we should get gas back there. I think we should turn back.

We have enough to get to Memphis.

Yes, but—I have lived in Memphis. I explain certain things to Henry about the predominance of Southern Baptists, the paucity of night life, the absence of what might be called cosmopolitan niceties. We may not be able to find a station open, I say.

Don't be absurd. It's a major city. Of course there'll be a station open.

I'm sure you're right, Henry. Somewhere in Memphis there is an open gas station. However. We may not find it easily. By actual count Memphis has more churches than gas stations. Please turn back.

Here you go again, Henry says. The same old fretting.

Henry, I say, you don't have to believe me. Just as a personal favor. Let's get gas now. Please.

I am not going to cater to your paranoia. That's final.

The Interstate loops around Memphis, a thick gray tongue lit with hideous yellow lights. We drive slowly. There is hardly any traffic. I don't see anything from here, says Henry. Guess we'll have to get off and look.

I say nothing as we glide through the empty streets. We circle gas stations, dimly lit or dark, a forlorn moth looking for a flame. I am practicing speeches to use over the telephone to old neighbors. Mrs. Kaiser? Sorry to disturb you, this is Marie Reynolds, my sister Alice used to play with LaVerne. You remember? We had the collie? I know it's terribly late but I'm stuck in town and my fiancé has liver trouble . . .

My tongue is a red-hot bolt that will sizzle anything it touches. We idle at a stop sign.

How the hell do we get back to the Interstate, Henry says. Is it this road?

You're lost aren't you? Admit it.

You bitch, says Henry. I should walk away and let you handle this yourself.

If you'd done that this morning, I say, I'd be asleep in Nashville right now.

The poisonous yellow light contains violence, smoke, hot metal. It floats between us for a moment, then Henry wrenches the car forward and we roar toward the highway.

We're not far from the airport, I say. Try there.

The Memphis Airport Terminal has been compared to a flying tray of martini glasses. It is starkly lit concrete in a vast shadowy plain. There is one man nodding to himself in a parking toll booth. Henry stops the car, gets out to talk to him. I make sure the windows are shut.

I scream You are a fucking asshole idiot prick whoremonger.

Henry returns. No luck, he says.

Back on the Interstate. We are beginning to feel like the Donner Party. Soon we will start eating each other. Henry's face resembles a slab of aged beef. I stare out the window. I am uncertain of my eyes. I clutch Henry's elbow. I do not trust my voice. I point. Henry dives towards the exit, spitting gravel from the wheels.

The man at the gas station is cheerful, used to being up all night. Oh yes, he says, most everybody coming through here late has to stop at my place. Where you all driving from?

Quito, Ecuador, I say. Henry uncreases our limp dollar bills. He asks How long will it take to get to Nashville?

Maybe three hours, says the man. Don't speed. They pick em up. Bring you right back. Be careful now.

You want me to drive, I ask Henry.

He shakes his head. I can manage for awhile.

It is 2:00 A.M. We do not apologize or touch, but we are oddly peaceful, anesthetized. I peel Henry some shrimp. This is good shrimp, he says. I'm glad we have it.

I nod. I'm dreaming but I'm not sure I'm asleep. In my dream Henry is at the wheel of a ship. Tall masts vanish in the fog above our heads. Henry is saying We can't get off until you admit you were wrong. About what, I say. What? I open my eyes. The car is stopped in the bay of a rest area. Henry comes around to my side. I don't think I can drive anymore, he says.

I slide behind the wheel. How far are we, I ask. He says I'm not sure, lies down with his head in my lap. I bend down and kiss him on the lips. His mouth is soft, shivering. In a moment he is asleep.

I feel rested but I know it won't last. The only thing in really bad shape are my eyes. We pass a road sign; I can't read it. I think it has numbers, three digits. The radio plays only ghosts of voices, nothing that will keep me awake. I switch if off and sing to myself. I sing all the songs I know, beginning with the Beatles' albums, each side, each album as near as I can remember. Henry's head rocks in my lap like a grapefruit on the edge of the tide. I sing folk songs I would not be caught dead listening to. How many seas must a white bu-urd sail . . .

This highway is very dark. Far ahead of me is a red taillight. I lock my eyes on it. I have trouble seeing the edges of the road. I sing old rock 'n' roll. I remember all the good old songs. Fatigue is a black velvet hood muffling my head. Henry moans in his sleep. Henry is really a very attractive man. I remember the good old times. The Christmas he bought me the nightgown from Frederick's of Hollywood. The time we got drunk on tequila and asked the bartender to page Sylvia Plath. Maybe we will not become the people we accuse each other of being. I will not get diabetes. He will not have liver trouble. We will continue to get good mileage.

Ahead of me the red light winks out. I think the car is going up and down hills, though the headlights are level. I sing hymns I have not heard for years, Rock of Ages and The Old Rugged Cross, humming when I forget a line. I sing musicals. Once Henry and I saw a musical where the leading man started to sing, announced he was too nervous, and spoke the lyrics instead. Henry and I were the only people in the theater who laughed. What show was that, Brigadoon? My Fair Lady? I can't remember. Then I have a terrible thought. The wheel jumps under my hands. Did we see that musical or just hear about it? Am I making it all up? Henry, I say. I jab him with my elbow. Wake up. Tell me I'm wrong. His sleep is unbroken. I won't try to wake him again. I think we will make it to Nashville, but I have run out of songs.

✧ ✧

The Merry Chase
Gordon Lish

Don't tell me. Do me a favor and let me guess. Be honest with me, tell the truth, don't make me laugh. Tell me, don't make me have to tell you, do I have to tell you that when you're hot you're hot, that when you're dead you're dead? Because you know what I know? I know you like I know myself, I know you like the back of my hand, I know you like a book, I know you inside out. You know what? I know you like you'll never know.

You think I don't know whereof I speak?

I know, I know. I know the day will come, the day will dawn.

Didn't I tell you you never know? Because I guarantee it, no one will dance a jig, no one will do a dance, no one will cater to you so fast or wait on you hand and foot. You think they could care less?

But I could never get enough of it. I could never get enough. Look at me, I could take a bite out of it, I could eat it up alive, but you want to make a monkey out of me, don't you? You want me to talk myself blue in the face for you, beat my head against a brick wall for you, come running when you have the least little wish. What am I, your slave? You couldn't be happy except over my dead body? You think I don't know whereof I speak? I promise you, one day you will sing a different tune.

But in the interim, first things first. Because it won't kill you to do without, tomorrow is another day, let me look at it, let me see it, there is no time like the present, let me kiss it and make it well.

Let me tell you something, everyone in the whole wide world should only have it half as good as you.

You know what this is? You want to know what this is? Because this is some deal, this is some set-up, this is some joke. You could vomit from what a joke this is.

I want you to hear something, I want you to hear the unvarnished truth.

You know what you are?

That's what you are!

You sit, I'll go — I already had enough to choke a horse.

Go ahead and talk my arm off. Talk me deaf, dumb, and blind. Nobody is asking, nobody is talking, nobody wants to know. In all decency, in all honesty, in all candor, in all modesty, you have some gall, some nerve, and I mean that in all sincerity. The crust on you, my God!

I am telling you, I am pleading with you, I am down to you on bended knee — just don't get cute with me, just don't make any excuses to me — because in broad daylight, in the dead of night, at the crack of dawn.

You think the whole world is going to do a dance around you? No one is going to do a dance around you. No one even knows you are alive.

But if it is not one thing, then it is another.

Just who do you think you are, coming in here like a lord and lording it all over all of us? Do you think you are a law unto yourself? I am going to give you some advice. Don't flatter yourself — you are not the queen of the May, not by a long shot. Act your age — share and share alike.

Ages ago, years ago, so long ago I couldn't begin to remember, past history, ancient history — you don't want to know, another age, another life, another theory altogether.

Don't ask. Don't even begin to ask. Don't make me any promises. Don't tell me one thing and do another. Don't look at me cross-eyed. Don't look at me like that. Don't hand me that crap. Look around you, for pity's sake. Don't you know that one hand washes the other?

Talk sense.

Take stock.

Give me some credit for intelligence. Show me I'm not wasting my breath. Don't make me sick. You are making me sick. Why are you doing this to me? Do you get pleasure from doing this to me? Don't think I don't know what you are trying to do to me.

Don't make me do your thinking for you.

Shame on you, be ashamed of yourself, have you absolutely no shame?

Why must I always have to tell you?

Why must I always drop everything and come running?

Does nothing ever occur to you?

Can't you see with your own two eyes?

You are your own worst enemy.

What's the sense of talking to you? I might as well talk to myself. Say something. Try to look like you've got a brain in your head.

You think this is a picnic? This is no picnic. Don't stand on ceremony with me. The whole world is not going to step to your tune. I warn you — wake up before it's too late.

You know what? A little birdie just told me. You know what? You have got a lot to learn — *that's* what.

I can't hear myself talk. I can't hear myself think. I cannot remember from one minute to the next.

Why do I always have to tell you again and again?

Give me a minute to think. Just let me catch my breath.

Don't you ever stop to ask?

I'm going to tell you something. I'm going to give you the benefit of my advice. Do you want some good advice?

You think the sun rises and sets on you, don't you? You should get down on your hands and knees and thank God. You should count your blessings. Why don't you look around yourself and really see for once in your life? You just don't know when you're well off. You have no idea how the rest of the world lives. You are as innocent as the day you were born. You should thank your lucky stars. You should try to make amends. You should do your best to put it all out of your mind. Worry never got anybody anywhere.

But by the same token.

Whatever you do, promise me this—just promise me that you will do your best to keep an open mind.

What do I say to you, where do I start with you, how do I make myself heard with you? I don't know where to begin with you, I don't know where to start with you, I don't know how to impress on you the importance of every single solitary word. Thank God I am alive to tell you, thank God I am here to tell you, thank God you've got someone to tell you, I only wish I could begin to tell you, if there were only some way someone could tell you, if only there were someone here to tell you, but you don't want to listen, you don't want to learn, you don't want to know, you don't want to help yourself, you just want to have it all your own sweet way and go on as if nothing has changed. Who can talk to you? Can anyone talk to you? You don't want anyone to talk to you. So far as you are concerned, the whole world could drop dead.

You think death is a picnic? Death is no picnic. Face facts, don't kid yourself, people are trying to talk some sense into you, it's not all just fun and fancy free, it's not all just high, wide, and handsome, it's not just a bed of roses and peaches and cream.

You take the cake, you take my breath away—you are really one for the books.

Be smart and play it down. Be smart and stay in the wings. Be smart and let somebody else carry the ball for a change.

You know what I've got to do? I've got to talk to you like a baby. I've got to talk to you like a Dutch uncle. I've got to handle you with kid gloves.

Let me tell you something no one else would have the heart to tell you. Look far and wide—because they are few and far between!

Go ahead, go to the ends of the earth, go to the highest mountain, go to any lengths, because they won't lift a finger for you—or didn't you know that some things are not for man to know, that some things are better left unsaid, that some things you shouldn't wish on a dog, not on a bet, not on your life, not in a month of Sundays?

What do you want? You want the whole world to revolve around you, you want the whole world at your beck and call? That's what you want, isn't it? Be honest with me.

Answer me this one question—how can you look me in the face?

Don't you dare act as if you didn't hear me.

You want to know what's wrong with you? This is what is wrong with you. You are going to the dogs, you are lying down with dogs, you are waking sleeping dogs—don't you know enough to go home before the last dog is dead?

When are you going to learn to leave well enough alone?

You know what you are? Let me tell you what you are. You are betwixt and between.

I'm on to you, I've got your number, I can see right through you — I warn you, don't you dare try to put anything over on me or get on my good side or lead me a merry chase.

So who's going to do your dirty work for you now? *You?* Do me a favor and don't make me laugh!

Oh, sure, you think you can rise above it, you think you can live all your life with your head in the clouds, in a cave, without rhyme or reason, without a hitch, without batting an eyelash, without blemish, without a leg to stand on, without fail, without cause, without a little bit of butter on your bread, but let me tell you something—you're all wet!

You know what? You're trying to get away with false pretenses, that's what! You think you're modesty itself, that's what! You think you look good in clothes, that's what! But you know what is wrong with you? Because I am here to tell you what is wrong with you. There is no happy medium with you, there is no live and let live with you, because talking to you is like talking to a brick wall until a person can break a blood vessel and turn blue in the face.

Pardon my French, but you know what I say?

I say put up or shut up!

Pay attention to me!

You think I am talking just to hear myself talk?

✧ ✧

My Breath
Orpingalik
(Netsilik Eskimo man)

This is what I call my song, because it is as important for me to sing it, as it is to draw breath.

This is my song: a powerful song.
Unaija-unaija.
Since autumn I have lain here,
helpless and ill,
as if I were my own child.

Sorrowfully, I wish my woman
to another hut,
another man for refuge,
firm and safe as the winter-ice.
Unaija-unaija.

And I wish my woman
a more fortunate protector,
now I lack the strength
to raise myself from bed.
Unaija-unaija.

Do you know yourself?
How little of yourself you understand!
Stretched out feebly on my bench,
my only strength is in my memories.
Unaija-unaija.

Game! Big game,
chasing ahead of me!
Allow me to re-live that!
Let me forget my frailty,
by calling up the past!
Unaija-unaija.

I bring to mind that great white one,
the polar bear,
approaching with raised hind-quarters,

his nose in the snow —
convinced, as he rushed at me,
that of the two of us,
he was the only male!
Unaija-unaija.
Again and again he threw me down:
but spent at last,
he settled by a hump of ice,
and rested there,
ignorant that I was going to finish him.
He thought he was the only male around!
But I too was a man!
Unaija-unaija.

Nor will I forget that great blubbery one,
the fjord-seal, that I slaughtered
from an ice-floe before dawn,
while friends at home
were laid out like the dead,
feeble with hunger,
famished with bad luck.
I hurried home,
laden with meat and blubber,
as though I were just running across the ice
to view a breathing-hole.
Yet this had been an old and cunning bull,
who'd scented me at once —
but before he had drawn breath,
my spear was sinking
through his neck.

This is how it was.
Now I lie on my bench,
too sick to even fetch
a little seal oil for my woman's lamp.
Time, time scarcely seems to pass,
though dawn follows dawn,
and spring approaches the village.
Unaija-unaija.

How much longer must I lie here?
How long? How long must she go begging
oil for the lamp,
reindeer-skins for her clothes,

and meat for her meal?
I, a feeble wretch:
she, a defenceless woman.
Unaija-unaija.

Do you know yourself?
How little of yourself you understand!
Dawn follows dawn,
and spring is approaching the village.
Unaija-unaija.

✧ ✧

From
Battered Women, Shattered Lives
Kathleen H. *Hofeller*

Corrie

When I interviewed Corrie, I was struck by the fact that she looked much older than her twenty-two years would have suggested. Her face was pale, and she appeared tired and drawn. Dressed in a simple, slightly wrinkled white blouse and a faded red skirt, the person who peered out at me from vacant, brown eyes looked as though she had nearly been defeated by life.

Corrie had been born and raised in Texas. The eldest of eight children, her father was a sharecropper. Although she had been living in California for several years, she had not entirely lost her accent.

"I guess some people'd say that I had it hard. We never had much, but my daddy and momma are good, church goin' people, and there was lots of love in our family. Seein' as I was the oldest, I was always helpin' Momma look after my brothers and sisters. Now, I know some girls like me, who had to care for little ones, grew up sayin' they didn't want no kids at all, 'cause they was sick of 'em. But not me. I loved my family—all of 'em—and one thing I did look forward to was havin' babies of my own. My kids are the best thing I ever had.

I met Joe when I was fourteen. Joe was eighteen, and he was the first boy who ever cared about me. I must say it was real flatterin'. He was a smooth talker, that one. He used to say all sorts of nice things, and crazy me, I believed him. Once we started goin' out, he told everyone that if any other boy ever laid a hand on me, he'd murder him. I believed him, and everybody else

did, too, 'cause Joe had a reputation for bein' tough. He was always pickin'
fights with someone.

Well, it couldn't have been more than six, eight months before Joe
wanted us to go to bed. Now, I'd been taught that that sort of thing was a sin.
But Joe had a way of bein' awful convincin'. He said when two people was
really in love like us, that God understood and that what we wanted to do was
alright. Well, he finally talked me into it. I felt real bad afterwards and I
thought for sure he'd dump me off and be with some other girl the next day.
But he didn't. He stayed with me. I was glad of that, but you know, things have
a way of goin' wrong. About a month later, I found out I was pregnant. At first I
thought Joe'd be angry. But when I told him, he said he was glad and wanted
to get married. I *was* kinda young to settle down, but there weren't no way I
could ask my family to take me. I mean, things was hard enough already. Besides, I *had* been to bed with him, and all. So, I said yes, and we set the
date. Now, my momma was real sad. She was sorry to see me a married
woman at the age of fifteen. But I told her it would be one less mouth to feed,
and that she was a bride at sixteen and things had worked out okay for her.

Well, everythin' seemed fine until a couple of days before the weddin'.
Joe and I was sittin' and talkin' one evenin'. I don't remember why, but somehow we started into an argument. And right in the middle of all this, without
no warnin' at all, Joe takes his hand and slaps me across the face. Now, I'd
had a switch taken to me when I was young, but never anythin' like that. It
made me think twice about spendin' the rest of my life with him. I mean, it's
one thing to go beatin' up on other men, but hittin' a woman — well, that's
somethin' else again. I was not at all sure I wanted to be Mrs. ———— , but I just
couldn't see no way out.

Well, Joe showed up the next mornin' all sorry and tellin' me how he
couldn't live without me, and how he'd never hit a woman before, and he
would never do it again, and how he wanted our baby. And 'cept for that one
time, he'd been mostly good to me. And he always took care of his family.
See, his daddy deserted 'em when he was little, so soon as he was old
enough, Joe went to work. Him and his older brother, Earl, supported his
mother and the two younger ones for years. But for all he done for his
momma, she didn't appreciate him none. She and Joe didn't get along 'cause
she was always sayin' how much he reminded her of his no-good daddy, and
how Joe was goin' to turn out bad just like him. Anyway, he seemed so sincere, I just couldn't say 'no.' So, we got married.

After the weddin' Joe dropped out of school to get a fulltime job on a
farm. We moved into a little two room house. It wasn't very much, but we
were happy — at least at the beginnin'. The whole time I was pregnant, Joe
just treated me like a queen. He didn't want me to overdo and he seemed
proud of the way I looked. He used to show me off. Well, trouble started soon
as that baby came. I had a real hard labor, so I was pretty well exhausted by
the time little Johnny came into this world. And it was real tough when he'd

cry at night and Joe had to sleep. It made Joe angry—and I could understand—he worked hard all day and he needed a good night's rest. So, I'd walk the floor with the baby and do my best to keep him quiet. See, Johnny was kind of sickly—not real bad, but not quite right, neither. We had these doctor bills start piling up, and pretty soon we was in debt. Well, Joe had to take a second job as a parttime janitor in town, three nights a week. We did okay, but it was awful hard on Joe, and he started drinkin' on weekends to relax.

The worst of it was how he always changed when he was drunk. He's like two different people. When he's sober he can be real nice. He's good to me, tellin' me how much he likes my cookin' and things like that. But when he's been drinkin', he's a real monster. You ever see that television show, "The Incredible Hulk"? That's Joe. When he gets drunk, he can likely pull a door off its hinges. 'Fact, once he tore off our screen door. It jammed when he was tryin' to get out, so he just takes it and he rips it right off. I mean, that's scary, that's scary.

And when Joe was drunk, the kids were afraid of him, too. They'd run and hide. I don't blame 'em. One time, when Johnny was about two, Joe took his belt and spanked him so hard that he had black and blue marks all over his legs and bottom, and I told Joe that if he ever tried that again, I'd take a gun and blow his brains out. 'Cause, it's one thing to beat up on a grown person, but there's no excusin' hittin' on a defenseless little child. Well, after that, Joe never hit any of 'em, but he'd still yell at 'em, call 'em names, and tell 'em how stupid they was. It's no wonder the kids don't like their daddy.

The first time Joe beat me after we was married was when Johnny was about two months old. Joe came in one night real late, and expected me to hop up and fix his supper. I told him 'no,' that Johnny'd just gone to sleep after his two o'clock feedin', that I was tired, and I'd wrapped his dinner and left it in the icebox for him. Well, he didn't take too kindly to that. In fact, what he took was his fist, and he punched me smack in the face. I started cryin' and he grabbed me by the shoulders and he shook me until I thought I'd fall apart. He said, 'You get in there, you little bitch, and you fix your husband some supper like you should.' I wasn't about to argue, but by the time I had it ready, he'd fallen asleep on the couch. He never did eat it. Next mornin', when he saw my cheek all bruised, he said he couldn't believe he'd done that to me. He swore it was just 'cause he'd been drinkin' and he promised he'd cut down. I really couldn't hold it against him. After all, he had an awful lot on him. Here he is, only eighteen and all of a sudden he's got a wife and baby to provide for. And he was still givin' some money to his momma each week.

Well, things went okay for about a year. Then his boss caught him drinkin' on the job and he fired him. I started takin' in some mendin' and laundry to help out. But, you know, seems no matter what I did, about every couple of months he'd be drunk and he'd just pop off and hit me one. It wasn't too bad, really, just some bruises. I'd stay in the house and not see any-body for a few days. I 'specially wanted to keep it from my parents 'cause they'd worry.

Then I found out I was pregnant again. I wasn't surprised—Joe was always after me. I don't know, maybe some men are like that, but so help me every time I'd turn around he wanted me in bed with him. Frankly, I don't see what all the fuss is about. He says it's my wifely duty to satisfy him when and where he wants it, and I suppose he's right. But much as I like babies, I was the one had to carry 'em, and after the first one, Joe wasn't so nice to me. I guess he saw I'd done it once and there weren't nothin' much to it, so I should be able to do it any number of times without too much trouble. Lucky for me our second one, our little girl, wasn't so bad.

Well, after she was born, things got real bad for us. Joe's truck broke down and we had to borrow money to get it fixed. Just seemed we was gettin' deeper and deeper in debt. What's worse, Joe started drinkin' more. I'd get real angry over that. I mean, wastin' good money on beer. He said he needed it to relax, but I told him my daddy never took a drop and he always done just fine.

Joe and I used to have arguments over that. I remember one night he come home drunk and he'd spent nearly all his paycheck on beer. Well, we needed that money, so I really got after him, you know? So he says, 'Woman, you better shut up,' and he hits me right in the mouth. It started bleedin' real bad, so I ran to the bathroom and locked the door. I guess Joe figured he'd got what he wanted, 'cause he went off to bed. Next mornin' my lip was still oozin' blood and looked ugly, so I went to the doctor. After the doctor fixed me up, he said, 'How'd you do this, Corrie?' And I lied. I'm not goin' to tell him I've got a man that beats up on me. So, I said that I tripped and fell on somethin'. He looked at me real suspicious, but he just said, 'You take care.' Well, I didn't speak to Joe for near two days. I couldn't hardly even look at him. I was really beginnin' to think I couldn't live with this man no longer. Then, Joe decided to come out here to California and do construction work like Earl. Joe said he'd stay with Earl and his wife and would make real good pay. Well, we certainly did need the money, 'specially since I was pregnant again. And believe me, I was all for havin' him gone. So, he left for a whole six months. He sent money back pretty regular, and I had my kids and relations to keep me company.

Right after Joe came back, Joe Jr. was born. He was a good, strong, healthy baby, so I was real happy. Then one night Joe walks in and says that we was all movin' to California. He'd already found a place for us out here, near where Earl lived. That was terrible news to me. I'd lived my whole life in Texas, close to my family and all. Movin' this far away just scared me to death. But I was his lawful wife, and it was my duty to go with him. So I packed up everything we owned, said 'good-bye,' and off we went.

Well, turns out comin' here was mostly a bad thing. Joe seemed to be drinkin' an awful lot. He'd stop off after work with Earl and his other buddies, so he come in drunk or close to it almost every evenin'. I think it was 'cause of those construction men. I really do. They was hard drinkers, and they treated their wives like dirt. Joe'd tell me how they all kept women on the side and how they'd fool their wives about it. And Joe started wantin' me to do all these crazy things. He wanted sex a different way every night. No decent woman would ever do some of the things he asked. It just wasn't the way I was raised. He never forced me, except once when he was mighty drunk, but I could tell he was disgusted with me 'cause I couldn't keep up with him and his new set of friends.

'Bout the only good thing out here was meetin' Earl's wife, Nancy. She was a California girl and real nice to me. She worked part-time as a secretary, and she was the independent type—not like me. More 'n once she'd said if Earl didn't lay off her soon, she'd leave him. She was my only real friend out here. She saw the bruises on me from time to time, and finally I just couldn't lie no more. She said the next time it happened I should send Johnny to get the neighbors to call the police.

Well, Nancy seemed pretty smart, you know, so next time he started in on me, I done what she said. I can't say as it did a whole lota good, though. When the police got there, I told 'em, 'Take him away, I never want to see him again.' But since nothin' on me was bleedin', (he hadn't cut me or broken any bones) this policeman says, 'Now calm down. I didn't see it so I can't make an arrest.' I said, 'I don't care. You take him away—you take him away. I want him in jail.' But they just wouldn't take me serious. Well, they did talk him into leaving, and they asked me if I needed to see a doctor or go to the hospital. I said no, I figured nothin' was broken, and that I'd mend. So off they went. When Joe come back, he didn't hit me or nothin', but he said that if I ever so much as *thought* about calling the police again, he'd just as soon kill me as not. And, you know what he said about killin'? Well, it actually come true, just like them prophecies in the Bible.

You see, it wasn't too long before Joe comes in one night drunk and real nasty. Seems Nancy had just told Earl she was goin' to leave him, so him and Joe had gone out drinkin' and talkin', and the more they talked, the angrier they got. So, by the time Joe got home he was in a foul mood. Soon as he come in he started in a-yellin' at me about how horrible Nancy was and how horrible all women was and he used all sorts of words I wouldn't ever repeat. Then he asks me where his dinner is. I mean, it must have been close to eleven o'clock, so I told him it was in the refrigerator. Then he yells at me 'cause the house is kinda messy. Now, he knowed I was pregnant again and that I'd been feelin' real poorly. I'd done the best I could. Well, that just seemed to make him angrier, and he slapped me so hard across the face that I fell to the ground. And then he started kickin' me. I was afraid he'd get me in the face, so I put my arms over my head, but he kicked me in the stomach! I couldn't hardly believe he'd do such a thing, and I screamed at him to stop, that he'd hurt the baby, but he wouldn't stop. He just kept kickin' me. All of a sudden I felt this horrible pain — cramps so awful I just doubled over. Then I started bleedin'. Well, Joe could see he done somethin' real bad, but instead of helpin' me he just says, 'Serves you right,' and walks out the door. For awhile I just laid there, cryin'. Of course the kids was up with the noise and all, too scared to come out 'til their daddy left. Well, when they all come in and they saw me layin' there like that, they started cryin', too. I knew I'd have to get to a doctor, so I told Johnny to go call Aunt Nancy. I thank the Lord for Nancy. Anyway, she come right over and took me to the hospital.

The doctor there was real nice. But then he asked me what had happened, and I said I'd fell. He didn't believe me, though, 'cause he asked me again how it had happened. So I said I guessed that God just didn't want this baby to get born. Well, that doctor looked me straight in the eye and he said that God didn't have nothin' to do with it and that the person who done that to me had murdered my baby. Well, that was more than I could take. I just broke down and cried, and I told him everything. And so he tells me after I get out of the hospital that I should leave my husband. I was really pretty lucky 'cause no lastin' harm was done. They gave me somethin' called a 'D and C', and after a few days I was ready to go home.

Well, I'd had lots of time to think, layin' there in that hospital. What that doctor said kept comin' back to me. I decided I couldn't live with no murderer. Besides, even before that horrible night I'd been thinkin' these terrible thoughts, about how nice it'd be if Joe was dead. Fact, a couple of times I even thought of killin' him myself. Now, I'd never had such sinful thoughts before, and it scared me. I prayed about it a long time. I figured I could take livin' with Joe, but I was worried about my kids. It's real hard on them to see their momma get beat up. And I don't want any of them to grow up thinkin' that's the way things is supposed to be. So I done what I had to. When I got out of the hospital, instead of goin' back to Joe, we went and stayed with Nancy. She'd just moved out on Earl, and she said it was fine if we lived there 'til things got settled. That was mighty kind of her, 'cause her place wasn't very big. She helped me go down and apply for welfare. I sure hated doin' that. My daddy ain't never taken a handout, even when times was real bad. But, I just didn't have no choice. You know, life don't always work out the way you want it, and you just got to do the best you can. Anyhow, after about two weeks, I decided I couldn't stay out here no more. Even Joe thinks I belong back home. He says I'm too backward and stupid to make it out here. So, I'm goin'. My daddy said he'd sell one of the hogs and send me the bus fare. I guess it'll come in a week or so. I can't say as I know what's goin' to happen, but my momma and daddy said we'd find some way to manage.''

◇ ◇

The Do-All Ax
Harold Courlander

No, don't know as I can tell you anything with magic in it. How you expect I can tell you about magic when they ain't no such thing? Of course, there's two-three exceptions, like those flyin' slaves in the old days. Folks say there was a couple of field hands down around Johnson's Landing who didn't like the way they was bein' treated as slaves, and they just flapped their arms and took off. When last seen they was over the water headed east like a ball of fire.

Then there was that do-all ax. It sure got magic in it, what I mean.

The way it was, in the old days there was a man who had this do-all ax. When it was time to clear the trees off the ground to do some plantin', this man'd take his ax and his rockin' chair and go out and sit down in the shade. Then he's sing a kind of song:

Bo kee meeny, dah ko dee,
Field need plantin', get off my knee.

That ax would just jump off his knee and start choppin' wood without no one holdin' onto the handle or anything. All by itself it went around cuttin' down the timber till the field was cleared. Then it chopped up the trees into stovewood lengths and threw 'em in a pile in the barnyard.

And next thing you know, this ax turn itself into a plow and went to plowin' up the field to make ready for plantin'. And when that's done, the plow turn into a corn planter and plant the corn.

All the time this man who owned it was rockin' back and forth in the shade, fannin' himself with a leaf. Well, that corn was sure-enough magic corn, grew up almost as fast as it went in the ground; little sprouts start to pop out 'fore the sun went down.

'Bout this time the man sing another song:

Kah bo denny, brukko bay
Time for dinner, quit this play.

Then the corn planter turned itself back into an ax and stopped workin'.

Well, three-four days later that corn was tall and ready for hoein'. Man went out with his ax, and it turned into a hoe. It went up and down the rows by itself, hoein' corn till the whole field was done. Next week the man came back and the hoe turn itself into a corn knife to cut all them stalks down. You see, the whole job was done just by this here magic ax.

Other folks used to come around and watch all these goin's-on. Everybody figure if they only had an ax like that, life would be a powerful lot better for them.

There was one man named Kwako who wanted that ax more'n anyone else. Said he reckoned he'd about die if he didn't get that ax. And when there wasn't nobody home one time, this Kwako went in and took it. Figured he'd get his own work done and then bring the ax back and wouldn't nobody know the difference.

He ran home and got his own rockin' chair and went out in the field. Laid the ax across his lap and sang like the other man did:

Bo kee meeny, dah ko dee,
Field need plantin', get off my knee.

Man, that ax went to work. Chopped down all the trees, cut the wood up in stovewood lengths, and stacked it by the house. Then it turned itself to a plow and plowed the ground. Then it turned to a corn planter and planted corn. 'Bout the time it was done plantin', the corn sprouts was already pokin' through the ground.

Kwako he was mighty pleased when he see all that. He sat rockin' back and forth in the shade enjoyin' himself real good. So when the corn was all planted he hollered, "That's enough for now, come on home." But corn planter didn't pay no attention, just kept jumpin' all around. Kwako hollered, "Didn't you hear what I said? Quit all this foolishness and come on home." Trouble was, he didn't know the song to stop it. He should have said:

Kah bo denny, brukko bay,
Time for dinner, quit this play.

But he didn't know the words, and he just kept hollerin', and the corn planter just kept jumpin' around, plantin' corn every-which-way till the seed was all gone. Then it turned into a hoe and started hoein' up the field. Now, that corn wasn't tall enough to be hoed, and it got all chopped to little pieces. Man, that field was a mess. Kwako he ran back and forth tryin' to catch the hoe, but he couldn't make it, hoe moved around too fast. Next thing you know, the hoe turned into a corn knife and started cuttin' in the air. But wasn't no corn to cut. So it went over in the cotton field and started cuttin' down the cotton. Just laid that cotton field low. And then it moved west, cuttin' down everything in the way. And when last seen it was followin' the settin' sun. After that it was gone for good.

Since that time there hasn't ever been a magic do-all ax in this part of the world, and folks has to do their farmin' the hard way.

But get it out of your head that there's magic things roundabout. What I told you is true, but it's an *exception*.

◇ ◇

Excerpt from a Conversational Improvisation Rehearsal
Bryan K. Crow

The following excerpt is transcribed from an audiotape of a rehearsal for an original production called Conversation Pieces. *The production was scripted from tapes of real-life conversations recorded by intimate couples in their homes. The four performers who portrayed the two couples studied the original tapes extensively and attempted to reproduce them as accurately as possible. The first and third acts of the production showed each couple conversing in their separate homes, but in the middle act the two couples were brought together for an evening of getting acquainted. Since this meeting had never taken place in real life, the performers generated new conversations as a foursome, trying to remain consistent to the characters they were portraying while also weaving in anecdotes from their own lives. The best "bits" from these spontaneously generated conversations were polished during workshop improvisations and were eventually presented on stage as "rehearsed improvisations." The following excerpt from one of the workshop improvisations was selected for inclusion here because it demonstrates not only the potential performance value of conversational material, but also the inherently aesthetic quality of unscripted, collaboratively emergent personal narrative. The couples are Dee and Bea, Jay and Kay. As we join them, they have been discussing their youthful experiences of the "first kiss."*

Key to transcription symbols

=	Preceding and following words are latched together with no gap and no overlap.
:	Preceding sound is stretched.
?	Rising intonation.
heh	Single laugh token.
(( ))	Description of behavioral event.
word	Word or syllable receiving greater stress.
[	Indicates point of overlap between speakers.
word-	Indicates abrupt cutoff of word.
/	Rising intonation of less prominence than "?".
(.)	Untimed brief pause.
(2.0)	Timed pause, in seconds.

Pause at syntactically relevant place, with falling intonation.

End of scene.

WORD   More extreme stress on word.

( )   Uncertain transcription or unhearable utterance.

" "   Utterance marked as a performance of a quotation.

001   B: What about *you* Dee?
002   (2.8)

003   D: ((laughs))
                    [
004   B: heheheh! *uh*oh! heheheh!

005   D: I remember uh the *first* girl I ever kissed was when I
006   was five years old

007   B: (.) Fhhh*ive* ((laughs))
                        [
008   K: Five! ((laughs))

009   J: Y'started *young* then (heh)
            [
010   D: Yes and uh:::
011   Her name was Erin Baumann
012   (3.0)

013   D: And uh sh- Erin was- Erin was uh (.)
014   Erin's parents and my parents were best friends, right?

015   B: Uh huh?

016   D: So uh (.)

017   K: ((laughs))

018   D: Erin used ta always come over 'n we'd play together

019   B: Uh huh/
            [
020   D: And uh- my (.) my parents would always put us (.)
                    [
021   J: Uh hu:h!   uh huh (heh)
                                            [
022   D: our
023   parents would always put us to *bed* y'know about
024   nine o'clock 'n they'd continue to play cards 'n stuff?

```
025   B:    Uh::huh! (heh)
                         [
026   D:                    Erin was loud I always tended to
027         be more quiet during those years,
                                             [
028   B:                          Uh huh?
029   D:    .hh And uh ((softer)) she came into my bedroom,
030         right?=
031   B:    =No way!
                   [
032   K:    =Mm hm
033   J:    In silky lingerie
                   [
034   D:    Well because- I- the reason why was cause I called-
                                                   [
035   B:                                  ((giant laugh))
                                                      [
036   K:                                         ((laugh))
037   B:    She's fi::ve!     .hhh     heheheheheheh
                       [
038   D:        Heheh!     She was only fi:ve
                       [
039   K:            Hahahahahaha
040   D:    Yeah! she did! and I- I uh
                           [
041   B:                .hhh ((blows nose))
                                          [
042   D:                                I- I called her in
043         right/, and I s- I told her
                                      [
044   J:                    You called her (to come in)
045   D:    I said- I said to her,
                     [
046   K:            "Pssst! Hey!" ((laugh))
                                         [
047   D:                          "Do you wanna- do you wanna
```

048   make out."
049   K: heheheh
050   B: D- ((guffaw)) Where did you *hear* that at five!!
                        [
051   D: (She- no she just- jus-) ((stuttering))
052   Well w- I'd been out with older kids,
                 [
053   J: (Tell about it   )
054   D: 'n you'd always hear that stuff on the bus
055   (kids make out)
                 [
056   B: ((laugh))
                    [
057   J: Y'know? *actually*,
57A   K: I believe it
                    [
058   D: So anyways I said y- I said to her
059   "Y- do you wanna make out" 'n she said to me
060   "What's that." (.) "What's that," and I said to
061   her, uh, that's where (.) you uh ya *kiss* each other
062   a buncha times,"
063   B: ((laughs))
                 [
064   K: ((laughs))
                     [
065   D: And then she said "That's all you just kiss each
066   other?"
067   And I said "Well there's *two* things."
068   (.) I said "Ya can't tell anybody (.) and ya have to
069   like it."
070   B: ((wildly)) Hahahahaha!
                 [
071   K: ((wildly)) Hahahahaha! ((continuing to laugh))
                                    [
072   B: *Love* those
073   qualifications!
074   .hhh That's wild!
                 [

```
075  D:   I said, ((laughing)) "Ya can't tell anybody and ya have
076       to like it" so she goes (.)
                   [
077  B:              Dee! ((laugh))
078  D:   She goes "OK", she goes "OK" right?
079       .hhh So uh (.)
080  B:   ((laughing quietly))
                   [
081  D:              So (.)      we kissed each other right?
082       'n as soon as we kissed each other she goes,
083       .hhh "MO:::MMY,"
084  B:   ((loud laughter))
              [
085  K:   ((loud laughter))
                        [
086  D:                   "Dee kissed me!"
087       ((stuttering)) 'n I- I- I felt like (.)
                   [
088  B:          Oh:::::::: No::::::::::::! ((laugh))
089  D:   crawlin' under those blankets 'n just goin' to sleep
                                  [
090  B:                             Nothin' like kissin'
091       'n tellin' ((laughs))
                     [
092  K:              Yeah::! ((laughs)) ((indecipherable
093       utterance))
               [
094  D:   "MO::MMY, Dee kissed me!"
095  K:   ((laughing)) Oh God!
                       [
096  B:                   Oh::::::::::::, heh
097  D:   Erin Baumann
098       Yep, she was (.)
099  J:   Heh
100  B:   Heh:::::
101  D:   She just got married a couple years ago
102  K:   Wow hehheheheh
```

103 D: She got married to one of my buddies in high school,
104   Kevin Jaeger
105 J: He probably kissed better
          [
106 D: Two Germans, y'know?
107 K: Yeah ((iaughs))
            [
108 B: ((laughs))
                [
109 D: Two Germans
110 K: Heheheh (God)
              [
111 B: Oh that's funny!
112 K: The first time I ever ki-
                    [
113 B: *Five*??
114 D: Yeah!
          [
115 K: Heheheh
          [
116 B: My:: Go::d! eheh
117 K: God
      # # # #

◇ ◇

Twirler
Jane Martin

A young woman stands center stage. She is dressed in a spangled, one-piece swimsuit, the kind for baton twirlers. She holds a shining silver baton in her hand.

I started when I was six. Momma sawed off a broom handle, and Uncle Carbo slapped some sort of silver paint, well, gray, really, on it and I went down in the basement and twirled. Later on Momma hit the daily double on horses named Spin Dry and Silver Revolver and she said that was a sign so she gave me lessons at the Dainty Deb Dance Studio, where the lady, Miss Aurelia, taught some twirling on the side.

I won the Ohio Juniors title when I was six and the Midwest Young Adult Division three years later, and then in high school I finished fourth in the nationals. Momma and I wore look-alike Statue of Liberty costumes that she had to send clear to Nebraska to get, and Daddy was there in a T-shirt with my name, April — my first name is April and my last name is March. There were four thousand people there, and when they yelled my name golden balloons fell out of the ceiling. Nobody, not even Charlene Ann Morrison, ever finished fourth at my age.

Oh, I've flown high and known tragedy, both. My daddy says it's put spirit in my soul and steel in my heart. My left hand was crushed in a riding accident by a horse named Big Blood Red, and though I came back to twirl, I couldn't do it at the highest level. That was denied me by Big Blood Red, who clipped my wings. You mustn't pity me, though. Oh, by no means! Being denied showed me the way, showed me the glory that sits inside life where you can't see it.

People think you're a twit if you twirl. It's a prejudice of the unknowing. Twirlers are the niggers of a white university. Yes, they are. One time I was doing fire batons at a night game, and all of a sudden I see this guy walk out of the stands. I was doing triples and he walks right out past the half-time marshals, comes up to me — he had this blue bead headband, I can still see it. Walks right up, and when I come front after a back reverse he spits in my face. That's the only, single time I ever dropped a baton. Dropped 'em both in front of sixty thousand people, and he smiles, see, and he says this thing I won't repeat. He called me a bodily part in front of half of Ohio. It was like being raped. It shows that beauty inspires hate and that hating beauty is Satan.

You haven't twirled, have you? I can see that by your hands. Would you like to hold my silver baton? Here, hold it.

You can't imagine what it feels like to have that baton up in the air. I used to twirl with that baton up in the air. I used to twirl with this girl who called it blue-collar Zen. The 'tons catch the sun when they're up, and when they go up, you go up, too. You can't twirl if you're not *inside* the 'ton. When you've got 'em up over twenty feet, it's like flying or gliding. Your hands are still down, but your insides spin and rise and leave the ground. Only a twirler knows that, so we're not niggers.

The secret for a twirler is the light. You live or die with the light. It's your fate. The best is a February sky clouded right over in the late afternoon. It's all background then, and what happens is that the 'tons leave tracks, traces, they etch the air, and if you're hot, if your hands have it, you can draw on the sky.

God, Charlene Ann Morrison. God, Charlene Ann! She was inspired by something beyond man. She won the nationals nine years in a row. Unparalleled and unrepeatable. The last two years she had leukemia and at the end you could see through her hands when she twirled. Charlene Ann died with a 'ton thirty feet up, her momma swears on that. I roomed with Charlene at a regional in Fargo, and she may have been fibbin', but she said there was a day when her 'tons erased while they turned. Like the sky was a sheet of rain and the 'tons were car wipers and when she had erased this certain part of the sky you could see the face of the Lord God Jesus, and his hair was all rhinestones and he was doing this incredible singing like the sound of a piccolo. The people who said that Charlene was crazy probably never twirled a day in their life.

Twirling is the physical parallel of revelation. You can't know that. Twirling is the throwing of yourself up to God. It's a pure gift, hidden from Satan because it is wrapped and disguised in the midst of football. It is God-throwing, spirit fire, and very few come to it. You have to grow eyes in your heart to understand its message, and when it opens to you it becomes your path to suffer ridicule, to be crucified by misunderstanding, and to be spit upon. I need my baton now.

There is one twirling no one sees. At the winter solstice we go to a meadow God showed us just outside of Green Bay. The God throwers come there on December twenty-first. There's snow, sometimes deep snow, and our clothes fall away, and we stand unprotected while acolytes bring the 'tons. They are ebony 'tons with razors set all along the shaft. They are three feet long. One by one the twirlers throw, two 'tons each, thirty feet up, and as they fall back they cut your hands. The razors arch into the air and find God and then fly down to take your blood in a crucifixion, and the red drops draw God on the ground, and if you are up with the batons you can look down and see Him revealed. Red on white. Red on white. You can't imagine. You can't imagine how wonderful that is.

I started twirling when I was six, but I never really twirled until my hand was crushed by the horse named Big Blood Red. I have seen God's face from thirty feet up in the air, and I know Him.

Listen. I will leave my silver baton here for you. Lying here as if I forgot it. And when the people file out you can wait back and pick it up, it can be yours, it can be your burden. It is the eye of the needle. I leave it for you.

[*The lights fade.*]

✧ ✧

Women's Laughter
Marge Piercy

1.
When did I first become aware —
hearing myself on the radio?
listening to tapes of women in groups? —
of that diffident laugh that punctuates,
that giggle that apologizes,
that bows fixing parentheses before, after.
That little laugh sticking
in the throat like a chicken bone.

That perfunctory dry laugh
carries no mirth, no joy
but makes a low curtsy, a kowtow
imploring with praying hands;
forgive me, for I do not
take myself seriously.
Do not squash me.

2.
Phyllis, on the deck we sit
telling horror stories

from the *Marvel Comics* of our lives.
We exchange agonies, battles and after each
we laugh madly and embrace.

That raucous female laughter
is drummed from the belly.
It rackets about kitchens,
flapping crows
up from a carcass.
Hot in the mouth as horseradish,
it clears the sinuses
and the brain.

3.
Phyllis, I had a friend
who used to laugh with me
braying defiance, as we roar
with bared teeth.
After the locked ward
where they dimmed her with drugs
and exploded her synapses,
she has now that cough
fluttering in her throat
like a sick pigeon
as she says, but of course
I was sick, you know,
and laughs blood.

✧ ✧

Address to the National Institute of Arts and Letters, 1971
Kurt Vonnegut, Jr.

I was here for the first time last year. My impression then was, "My gosh—how thick the walls are!" (My father was an architect. My grandfather, too.)

When I was invited to give this address, it was explained to me that I need not be serious. I was offended. I hadn't asked permission to be foolish—yet that was what was given to me.

I can be as serious as anyone here, with a few obvious exceptions. And I will prove it. I will speak of happiness, it's true — but I will speak of anthropology and biochemistry and unhappiness as well.

I wish in particular to call your attention to the work of Dr. M. Sydney Margoles, a Los Angeles endocrinologist, who is able to distinguish between male homosexuals and heterosexuals by means of urinalysis. He doesn't even have to meet them. What other sweet mysteries of life are chemicals? All of them, I believe. Biochemistry is everything. The speculations of artists about the human condition are trash.

Happiness is chemical. Before I knew that, I used to investigate happiness by means of questions and answers. (If I had my life to live over, I would learn how to perform a urinalysis.) And I asked my father when he was an old man, "Father — what has been the happiest day in your life so far?"

"It was a Sunday," he said.

Soon after he was married, he said, he bought a new Oldsmobile. This was before the First World War. (The Oldsmobile was not then the tin-knocker's wet dream it has since become.) This was in Indianapolis, Indiana. My father was an architect, as I've said — and a painter, too. And my father, the young architect and painter, took his new wife in his new Oldsmobile to the Indianapolis 500-mile Speedway on a Sunday afternoon. He burglarized a gate. He drove the Oldsmobile onto the track, which was made of bricks. And he and my mother drove around and around and around.

That was a happy day. My father was the widower of a suicide when he told me about that happiest day.

My father told me, too, what he supposed the happiest day in the life of *his* father had been. My paternal grandfather was probably happiest as a boy in Indiana, sitting with a friend on the cowcatcher of a moving locomotive. The locomotive was puffing from Indianapolis to Louisville. There was some wilderness still, and the bridges were made of wood.

When night fell, the sky was filled with fireworks from the stack of the locomotive. What could be nicer than that? Nothing.

My father and grandfather were good artists. I'm sorry they can't be here today. They deserved your warm company in this cool tomb.

(They deserved your cool company in this warm tomb.)

My own son asked me a month ago what the happiest day of my life had been so far. He called down into my grave, so to speak. This speech is *full* of tombs. My son considered me practically dead, since I smoked so many Pall Malls every day. (He's right, too.)

I looked up from the pit, and I told him this: "The happiest day of my life, so far, was in October of 1945. I had just been discharged from the United States Army, which was still an honorable organization in those Walt Disney times. I had just been admitted to the Department of Anthropology of the University of Chicago.

"At last! I was going to study man!"

I began with physical anthropology. I was taught how to measure the size of the brain of a human being who had been dead a long time, who was all dried out. I bored a hole in his skull, and I filled it with grains of polished rice. Then I emptied the rice into a graduated cylinder. I found this tedious.

I switched to archaeology, and I learned something I already knew: that man had been a maker and smasher of crockery since the dawn of time. And I went to my faculty adviser, and I confessed that science did not charm me, that I longed for poetry instead. I was depressed. I knew my wife and my father would want to kill me, if I went into poetry.

My adviser smiled. "How would you like to study poetry which *pretends* to be scientific?" he asked me.

"Is such a thing possible?" I said.

He shook my hand. "Welcome to the field of social or cultural anthropology," he said. He told me that Ruth Benedict and Margaret Mead were already in it—and some sensitive gentlemen as well.

One of those gentlemen was Dr. Robert Redfield, the head of the Department of Anthropology at Chicago. He became the most satisfying teacher in my life. He scarcely noticed me. He sometimes looked at me as though I were a small, furry animal trapped in an office wastebasket. (I stole that image from George Plimpton, by the way. God love him.)

Dr. Redfield is dead now. Perhaps some physical anthropologist of the future will fill his skull with grains of polished rice, and empty it out again—into a graduated cylinder. While he lived, he had in his head a lovely dream which he called "The Folk Society." He published this dream in *The American Journal of Sociology*, Volume 52, 1947, pages 293 through 308.

He acknowledged that primitive societies were bewilderingly various. He begged us to admit, though, that all of them had certain characteristics in common. For instance: They were all so small that everybody knew everybody well, and associations lasted for life. The members communicated intimately with one another, and very little with anybody else.

The members communicated only by word of mouth. There was no access to the experience and thought of the past, except through memory. The old were treasured for their memories. There was little change. What one man knew and believed was the same as what all men knew and believed. There wasn't much of a division of labor. What one person did was pretty much what another person did.

And so on. And Dr. Redfield invited us to call any such society "a Folk Society," a thing I often do. I will now give you a sample of Dr. Redfield's prose, and an opportunity to taste his nostalgia for a sort of society once inhabited by all races of men.

In a folk society, says Dr. Redfield, and I quote him now:

. . . behavior is personal, not impersonal. A "person" may be defined as that social object which I feel to respond to situations as I do, with all the sentiments and interests which I feel to be my own; a person is myself in another form, his qualities and values are inherent within him, and his significance for me is not merely one of utility. A "thing," on the other hand, is a social object which has no claim upon my sympathies, which responds to me, as I conceive it, mechanically; its value for me exists in so far as it serves my end. In the folk society, all human beings admitted to the society are treated as persons; one does not deal impersonally ("thing fashion") with any other participant in the little world of that society.

Moreover [Dr. Redfield goes on], in the folk society much besides human beings is treated personally. The pattern of behavior which is first suggested by the inner experience of the individual — his wishes, fears, sensitivities, and interests of all sorts — is projected into all objects with which he comes in contact. Thus nature, too, is treated personally; the elements, the features of the landscape, the animals, and especially anything in the environment which by its appearance or behavior suggests the attributes of mankind — to all these are attributed qualities of the human person. [I stop quoting now.]

And I say to you that we are full of chemicals which require us to belong to folk societies, or failing that, to feel lousy all the time. We are chemically engineered to live in folk societies, just as fish are chemically engineered to live in clean water — and there aren't any folk societies for us anymore.

How lucky you are to be here today, for I can explain *everything*. Sigmund Freud admitted that he did not know what women wanted. I know what they want. *Cosmopolitan* magazine says they want orgasms, which can only be a partial answer at best. Here is what women really want: They want lives in folk societies, wherein everyone is a friendly relative, and no act or object is without holiness. Chemicals make them want that. Chemicals make us all want that.

Chemicals make us furious when we are treated as things rather than persons. When anything happens to us which would not happen to us in a folk society, our chemicals make us feel like fish out of water. Our chemicals demand that we get back into water again. If we become increasingly wild and preposterous in modern times — well, so do fish on river banks, for a little while.

If we become increasingly apathetic in modern times — well, so do fish on river banks, after a little while. Our children often come to resemble apathetic fish — except that fish can't play guitars. And what do many of our children attempt to do? They attempt to form folk societies, which they call "communes." They fail. The generation gap is an argument between those who believe folk societies are still possible and those who know they aren't.

Older persons form clubs and corporations and the like. Those who form them pretend to be interested in this or that narrow aspect of life. Members of the Lions Club pretend to be interested in the cure and prevention of diseases of the eye. They are in fact lonesome Neanderthalers, obeying the First Law of Life, which is this: "Human beings become increasingly contented as they approach the simpleminded, brotherly conditions of a folk society."

The American Academy of Arts and Letters and the National Institute of Arts and Letters don't really give a damn for arts and letters, in my opinion. They, too, are chemically-induced efforts to form a superstitious, affectionate clan or village or tribe. To them I say this, "Lots of luck, boys and girls."

There are other good clubs. The Loyal Order of the Moose is open to any male who is Christian and white. I myself admire The War Dads of America. In order to become a War Dad, one must have had a friend or a relative who served in the armed forces of the United States sometime during the past 195 years. The friend or relative need not have received an honorable discharge, though that helps, I'm told.

It also helps to be stupid. My father and grandfather were not stupid, so they did not join the Moose or anything. They chose solitude instead. Solitude can be nearly as comforting as drugs or fraternities, since there are no other people to remind a solitary person how little like a folk society his society has become. My father had only his young wife with him on his happiest day. My parents were one flesh that day. My grandfather had only a friend with him on his happiest day. There was very little talking — because the locomotive made so much noise.

As for my own happiest day: I was happy because I believed that the Department of Anthropology at the University of Chicago was a small, like-minded family which I was being allowed to join. This was not true.

As I have said before, I can explain *everything* in terms of this biochemical-anthropological theory of mine. Only two men are less mystified by the human condition than I am today: Billy Graham and Maharishi. If my theory is mistaken, it scarcely matters, since I was told that this need not be a serious speech anyway.

Also, whether I am mistaken or not, we are surely doomed, and so are our artifacts. I have the word of an astronomer on this. Our sun is going to exhaust its fuel eventually. When the heat stops rushing out from its core, our sun will collapse on itself. It will continue to collapse until it is a ball perhaps forty miles in diameter. We could put it between here and Bridgeport.

It will wish to collapse even more, but the atomic nuclei will prevent this. An irresistible force will meet an immovable object, so to speak. There will be a tremendous explosion. Our sun will become a supernova, a flash such as the Star of Bethlehem is thought to have been. Earth Day cannot prevent this.

Somewhere in that flash will be the remains of a 1912 Oldsmobile, a cowcatcher from a locomotive, the University of Chicago, and the paperclip from this year's Blashfield Address.

I thank you.

Sample Dramatistic Analysis

The Focus of Attention in Edmund Spenser's "One Day I Wrote Her Name"
Joey Barton

ONE DAY I WROTE HER NAME

One day I wrote her name upon the strand,
But came the waves and washed it away;
Again I wrote it with a second hand,
But came the tide, and made my pains his prey.
"Vain man," said she, "that dost in vain essay
A mortal thing so to immortalize,
For I myself shall like to this decay,
And eke my name be wiped out likewise."
"Not so (quoth I) let baser things devise
To die in dust, but you shall live by fame;
My verse your virtues rare shall eternize,
And in the heavens write your glorious name,
Where whenas death shall all the world subdue,
Our love shall live, and later life renew."

A common theme in Renaissance poetry is the transitory nature of love and life. Edmund Spenser's "One Day I Wrote Her Name" is representative. While the poem is about love and life, it is even more so a poem about its speaker. Particularly interesting is how Spenser guides the readers' attention

*Joey Barton is an undergraduate student at Southern Illinois University, Carbondale.

to the speaker in the poem. Spenser has readers direct their interests primarily to the speaker within the poem. While the readers are aware of both the identified woman and the idea of capturing immortality through verse, readers see these considerations as secondary to the interest in and attention to the speaker. Several aspects of the poem create the impression that the speaker is the central focus.

Much, if not all, of the poem calls attention to the speaker's actions. Initially, the title indicates that the subject of the poem is, at least in part, the action of the speaker writing or having written someone's name. Moving through the poem, readers find the persona speaking of a past event which automatically places an emphasis on the action of "telling." Readers never lose sight of the fact that the speaker is describing a past event. The past tense verbs used in the first four lines clearly establish this. The speaker interrupts both quotes with the identification tags of "said she" and "quoth I" for the purpose of clarifying to his present audience who said what to whom. Readers, then, are highly conscious of the speaker telling about this past event.

The speaker also draws considerable attention to himself by describing the action within the past event. The speaker wrote someone's name twice "upon the strand" and observed that the waves washed away his efforts. He listened to what was said to him and he responded. Within his response, he claims he will do other actions—immortalize the woman by his verse and write her name "in the heavens."

Another way that the speaker guides the readers' attention to himself is through his relationship to his audience. Readers know the persona is not presently speaking to the woman by the use of the "her" and "she" pronouns. It is also unlikely that the speaker would quote the details of the event to someone who was present during the event. Hence, the audience is external to the past event but is presently hearing the speaker's story. The fact that the speaker carefully indicates who said what to whom supports the idea of a listening audience. This sense of someone being spoken to places the speaker in a conversational scene. But since the persona is the only one who talks within this scene, the readers direct their attention toward him.

Placing the speaker in this conversational scene, readers soon question what motivates him to relate this story. Since the persona is not speaking to the woman in the poem, readers feel that he must be more interested in his audience's reaction than the woman's reaction. This would negate the idea that the persona is speaking for the purpose of courting the woman and would suggest that he feels he will gain some satisfaction from telling this story to his listeners. From this perspective, readers might see the persona as a braggart who is expounding on his own cunning and wit. After all, he had a clever and final answer to the woman's claim that his efforts were vain. Or, readers might view him as asking if his argument appears credible since he carefully spells out the argument within his story. Another possible interpretation might be that the speaker thinks this story is humorous and, hence, worth telling. The humor arises from the assumption that the woman accepts his argument—an argument that the speaker himself questions as valid. All these and other possible interpretations are just speculations, but with each of them, readers find once again that the speaker pulls attention to himself.

The speaker's argument also makes readers focus on him. Readers can view the argument from several perspectives. From one viewpoint, both the woman and the speaker appear to follow a strange logic. After the speaker indicates that he wrote the woman's name twice and that both times the waves washed it away, the woman assumes that the speaker is trying to immortalize her by this action and that this action is vain. The speaker claims his efforts are not vain since he will immortalize her through his poem. Here, the speaker implies that the woman believes that he is trying to immortalize her just by writing her name or that he is writing the poem in the sand! When the speaker responds that she will live through his verse, the argument continues following her line of thought. Instead of accepting her thinking, he could have denied that he had any intention of trying to immortalize her in the sand. When readers view the argument this way, they keep their focus on the speaker since he is in control of the final direction of the argument and performed an act which motivated the woman to speak.

There is another way readers might see the argument. In this view, the speaker's poem is present, not written in the sand, but possibly being read by the woman while he is writing her name. In this instance, the woman and the speaker could be referring to a poem that he had already written. No line in the poem specifies whether or not the speaker has written the poem that he thinks will give their love eternal life. When readers accept that the speaker has already written the poem, they are focusing on another of the speaker's actions.

Finally, and most probable, the argument comes together when readers view it metaphorically. In this case, both the speaker and the woman know that simply writing a name on a shore is not a serious attempt to immortalize someone and, hence, in and of itself, not vain. What is vain, suggests the woman, are writings which try to immortalize her since, "I myself shall," like the waves which wash my name away, "decay." Here, the readers notice the speaker because he emerges as the defendant in a carefully constructed case. It is left to him to convince the jury that he is not vain.

It appears, then, that the speaker is constantly drawing attention to himself. While the poem is about the woman that the speaker loves, it is much more so about himself. He seems to ask the audience to recognize how clever he is. Perhaps, this is not his intent, but readers cannot help seeing him as the center of the poem. Even more, readers cannot escape the fact that he did what he said he would: he immortalized their love in his poem.

BIBLIOGRAPHY OF AESTHETIC TEXTS

Literary Forms

Abcarian, Richard, and Marvin Klotz, eds. *Literature: The Human Experience*, 4th ed. New York: St. Martin's Press, 1988.

Allen, Donald, and George F. Butterick, eds. *The Postmoderns: The New American Poetry Revised.* New York: Grove Press, 1982.

Allison, Alexander W., Arthur J. Carr, and Arthur M. Eastman, eds. *Masterpieces of Drama*, 5th ed. New York: Macmillan, 1986.

Aly, Bower, ed. *Speeches in English.* New York: Random House, 1968.

Arbuthnot, Mary Hill, and Dorothy M. Broder, eds. *The Arbuthnot Anthology of Children's Literature.* Glenview, IL: Scott, Foresman, 1976.

Arkin, Marian, and Barbara Scholler, eds. *Longman Anthology of Literature by Women.* New York: Longman, 1989.

Bain, Carl E., Jerome Beaty, and J. Paul Hunter, eds. *The Norton Introduction to Literature*, 4th ed. New York: W. W. Norton, 1986.

Barber, William, ed. *Within Doors: Poems Written by Residents of a Nursing Home.* Veneta, CA: Printed Word, 1977.

Beaty, Jerome, and J. Paul Hunter, eds. *New Worlds of Literature.* New York: W. W. Norton, 1989.

Benedikt, Michael, ed. *The Prose Poem: An International Anthology.* New York: Dell, 1976.

Berg, Stephen, and Robert Mezey, eds. *The New Naked Poetry: Recent American Poetry in Open Forms.* Indianapolis: Bobbs-Merrill, 1976.

Bergman, David, ed. *The Story.* New York: Macmillan, 1988.

Boesak, Allen. *The Finger of God: Sermons on Faith and Socio-Political Responsibility.* Los Angeles: Orbis Books, 1982.

Brooks, Cleanth, and Robert Penn Warren, eds. *Understanding Poetry*, 4th ed. New York: Holt, Rinehart & Winston, 1976.

Brooks, Cleanth, and Robert Penn Warren, eds. *Understanding Fiction*, 3rd ed. Englewood Cliffs, NJ: Prentice-Hall, 1979.

Canan, Janine, ed. *She Rises like the Sun: Invocations of the Goddess by Contemporary American Poets.* Freedom, CA: The Crossing Press, 1989.

Cassill, R. V., ed. *The Norton Anthology of Short Fiction*, 3rd ed. New York: W. W. Norton, 1986.

Crossley-Holland, Kevin, ed. *The Oxford Book of Travel Verse*. New York: Oxford University Press, 1987.

Dacey, Philip, and David Jauss, eds. *Strong Measures: Contemporary American Poetry in Traditional Forms*. New York: Harper & Row, 1986.

DeMont, Benjamin, ed. *Close Imagining: An Introduction to Literature*. New York: St. Martin's Press, 1988.

Dobrin, Arthur, ed. *Lace: Poetry from the Poor, the Homeless, the Aged, the Physically and Emotionally Disabled*. Springfield, MA: Cross Culture, 1979.

Ehrhart, W. D., ed. *Unaccustomed Mercy: Soldier Poets from the Vietnam War*. Lubbock, TX: Texas Tech University Press, 1989.

Ellmann, Richard, ed. *The New Oxford Book of American Verse*. New York: Oxford University Press, 1976.

Ellmann, Richard, and Robert O'Clair, eds. *The Norton Anthology of Modern Poetry*. New York: W. W. Norton, 1988.

Elsen, Johnathan, and Stuart Troy, eds. *The Novel Reader: Short Fiction, Poetry and Prose in Literature*. New York: Crown, 1987.

Florsheim, Stewart J., ed. *Ghosts of the Holocaust: An Anthology of Poetry from the Second Generation*. Detroit: Wayne State University Press, 1989.

Goodman, Roger B., ed. *75 Short Masterpieces: Stories from the World's Literature*. New York: Bantam Books, 1961.

Gray, Gayle A., ed. *Womanscript: Writing about Women by Women*. Springfield, MA: One Horse Press, 1987.

Greenfield, Stanley B., and A. Kingsley Weatherhead, eds. *The Poem: An Anthology*, 2nd ed. New York: Appleton-Century-Crofts, 1972.

Hall, Donald, and David Lehman, eds. *The Best American Poetry, 1989*. New York: Collier, 1989.

Halpern, Daniel, ed. *The Art of the Tale: An International Anthology*. New York: Viking Penguin, 1986.

Henderson, Stephen, ed. *Understanding the New Black Poetry*. New York: William Morrow, 1973.

Hogan, Michael, ed. *Do Not Go Gentle: Poetry and Prose from Behind the Walls*. Lewiston, ID: Blue Moon Press, 1977.

Holson, Geary, ed. *The Hemewlet Earth: An Anthology of Native American Literature*. Albuquerque: University of New Mexico Press, 1981.

Howard, Maureen, ed. *Contemporary American Essays*. New York: Penguin, 1984.

Howe, Florence, and Ellen Bass, eds. *No More Masks! An Anthology of Poems by Women*. New York: Doubleday Anchor Books, 1973.

Hunt, Douglas, ed. *The Riverside Anthology of Literature*. Boston: Houghton Mifflin, 1988.

Hurt, Charles, and Andrew Bauer, eds. *A Treasury of Great American Speeches*. New York: Hawthorn, 1970.

Ferguson, Mary Anne, ed. *Images of Women in Literature*, 3rd ed. Boston: Houghton Mifflin, 1981.

Kennedy, X. J. *An Introduction to Poetry*, 5th ed. Boston: Little, Brown, 1982.

Knickerbocker, K. L., and H. Willard Reninger, eds. *Interpreting Literature*. New York: Holt, Rinehart & Winston, 1979.

Konek, Carol, and Dorothy Walters, eds. *I Hear My Sisters Saying: Poems by Twentieth-Century Women*. New York: Thomas Y. Crowell, 1976.

Lelie, Naton, and Villiani Lelie, eds. *Third World*. Youngstown, OH: Pig Iron Press, 1988.

Mach, Maynard, et al., eds. *The Norton Anthology of World Masterpieces*. New York: W. W. Norton, 1980.

Meyer, Michael, ed. *The Bedford Introduction to Literature*, 2nd ed. New York: St. Martin's Press, 1990.

Moraga, Cherrie, and Gloria Anzaldua, eds. *This Bridge Called My Back: Writings by Radical Women of Color*. New York: Kitchen Table/Woman of Color Press, 1981.

Paulin, Tom, ed. *The Faber Book of Political Verse*. Winchester, MA: Faber & Faber, 1986.

Payne, Karen, ed. *Between Ourselves: Letters Between Mothers and Daughters*. Boston: Houghton Mifflin, 1983.

Paz, Octavio, ed. *Mexican Poetry: An Anthology*. New York: Grove, 1985.

Perlman, James, et al., eds. *Brother Songs: A Male Anthology of Poetry*. Duluth, MN: Holy Cow, 1979.

Peterson, Owen, ed. *Representative American Speeches*. New York: Wilson, 1987.

Pickering, James H., ed. *Fiction 100: An Anthology of Short Stories*, 4th ed. New York: Macmillan, 1985.

Richter, David H., ed. *The Borzoi Book of Short Fiction*. New York: Alfred A. Knopf, 1983.

Sadler, William Alan, ed. *Master Sermons Through the Ages*. New York: Harper & Row, 1963.

Seller, Maxine Schartz, ed. *Immigrant Women*. Philadelphia: Temple University Press, 1981.

Shapard, Robert, and James Thomas, eds. *Sudden Fiction*. Layton, UT: Peregrine Smith, 1986.

Sherman, Joan R., ed. *Collected Black Women's Poetry*. New York: Oxford University Press, 1988.

Shimer, Dorothy Blair, ed. *Rice Brown Women: Writings by and about the Women of China and Japan*. New York: New American Library, 1982.

Simonson, Harold P., ed. *Quartet: A Book of Stories, Plays, Poems, and Critical Essays*, 2nd ed. New York: Harper & Row, 1973.

Smedley, Agnes, ed. *Daughter of the Earth*. New York: Feminist Press, 1976.

Smith, Dave, and David Bottoms, eds. *The Morrow Anthology of Younger American Poets*. New York: Quill, 1985.

Solt, Mary Ellen, ed. *Concrete Poetry: A World View*. Bloomington: Indiana University Press, 1970.

Stenger, Wallace, and Mary Stenger, eds. *Great American Short Stories*. New York: Dell, 1985.

Stevick, Philip, ed. *Anti-Story: An Anthology of Experimental Fiction*. New York: The Free Press, 1971.

Stoneman, Richard, ed. *Daphene into Laurel: Translations of Classical Poetry from Chaucer to the Present*. Wolfeboro, NH: Longwood, 1982.

Stratford, Will, ed. *Many Voices—Many Lands*. Orinda, CA: Poetry Center Press, 1988.

Thompson, Denys, ed. *Distant Voices: Poetry of the Preliterates*. Lanham, MD: Rowman, 1978.

Walsh, T., ed. *Hispanic Anthology*. New York: Gordon, 1985.

Warren, Robert Penn, and Albert Erskine, eds. *Short Story Masterpieces*. New York: Dell, 1954.

Webber, Jeannette L., and Joan Grumman, eds. *Women as Writer*. Boston: Houghton Mifflin, 1978.

White, Steven, ed. *Poets of Nicaragua*. Greensboro: Unicorn Press, 1982.

Wiersbe, William W., ed. *Treasury of the World's Great Sermons*. Grand Rapids, MI: Kregel, 1977.

Wildman, Eugene, ed. *Experiments in Prose*. Chicago: Swallow Press, 1969.

Williams, Emmett, ed. *An Anthology of Concrete Poetry*. New York: Something Else Press, 1967.

Wright, Charles, ed. *Country Music: Selected Early Poems*. Middletown, CT: Wesleyan University Press, 1982.

Conversational Forms

Alexander, A. E., ed. *Russian Folklore*. Belmont, MA.: Norland, 1975.

Alexander, Maxine, ed. *Speaking for Ourselves: Women of the South*. New York: Pantheon Books, 1984.

Bennett, Charles Henry. *Bennett's Fables from Aesop and Others Translated into Human Nature*. New York: Viking, 1978.

Blair, Walter, ed. *Tall Tale America*. New York: Coward-McCann, 1944.

Botkin, B. A., ed. *Treasury of Western Folklore*. New York: Crown, 1975.

Brown, Dee, ed. *Bury My Heart at Wounded Knee*. New York: Holt, Rinehart, & Winston, 1971.

Brunvand, Jan Harold, ed. *The Choking Doberman and Other "New" Urban Legends*. New York: W. W. Norton, 1984.

Buss, Fran Leeper, ed. *Dignity: Lower Income Women Tell of Their Lives and Struggles*. Ann Arbor: University of Michigan Press, 1985.

Clarkson, Atelia, and Gilbert B. Cross, eds. *World Folktales*. New York: Charles Scribner's Sons, 1980.

Cole, Anna, ed. *Best Loved Folktales of the World*. Garden City, NY: Doubleday, 1982.

Coles, Robert, and Jane Hollowell Coles, eds. *Women of Crisis: Lives of Struggle and Hope*. New York: Delacorte Press, 1978.

Goss, Linda, and Marian E. Barnes. *Talk That Talk: An Anthology of African American Storytelling*. San Diego: Harcourt Brace Jovanovich, 1988.

Graves, Robert. *The Greek Myths*. New York: Penguin, 1955.

Halligan, Terry, ed. *Funny Skits and Sketches*. New York: Sterling, 1987.

Hanson, Carol, and Karin Liden, eds. *Moscow Women: Thirteen Interviews*. New York: Pantheon, 1977.

Hofeller, Kathleen, ed. *Battered Women, Shattered Lives.* Palo Alto, CA: R and E Associates, 1983.

Howe, Louise Kapp, ed. *Pink Collar Workers: Inside the World of Women's Work.* New York: Avon Books, 1977.

Kormoff, Manuel, ed. *The Great Fables of All Nations.* New York: Tudor, 1928.

McCrindle, Jean, and Shiled Rowbotham, eds. *Dutiful Daughters: Women Talk About Their Lives.* Austin: University of Texas Press, 1977.

Messer, Ellen, and Kathryn E. May, eds. *Back Rooms: An Oral History of the Illegal Abortion Era.* New York: Simon & Schuster, 1988.

Mieder, Wolfgang, ed. *The Prentice-Hall Encyclopedia of World Proverbs.* Englewood Cliffs, NJ: Prentice-Hall, 1986.

Neithammer, Carolyn, ed. *Daughters of the Earth: The Lives and Legends of Native American Women.* New York: Macmillan, 1977.

Parker, Chris, ed. *B Flat, Bebop, Scat: Jazz Short Stories and Poems.* Scranton, PA: Salem House, 1987.

Power, Effie, ed. *Bag O' Tales.* New York: E.P. Dutton, 1934.

Randall, Margaret, ed. *Cuban Women Now: Interviews with Cuban Women.* Toronto: The Women's Press, 1974.

Seifer, Nancy Barbara, ed. *Nobody Speaks for Me! Self Portraits of American Working Class Women.* New York: Simon & Schuster, 1976.

Terkel, Studs. *Working: People Talk About What They Do All Day and How They Feel About What They Do.* New York: Pantheon, 1972.

Wertheimer, Barbara, ed. *We Were There: The Story of Working Women in America.* New York: Pantheon, 1977.

Yershov, Igor, and Krenia Yerhova, eds. *The Fire Bird: Russian Fairy Tales.* New York: Imported Publishers, 1976.

Ceremonial Forms

Asante, Moleti K., et al., eds. *Changing Seasons: Afrocentric Rites of Passage.* Chicago: Third World, 1988.

Bierherst, J. *The Sacred Path: Spells and Power Songs of American Indians.* New York: Quill Press, 1984.

David, Andrew, ed. *Famous Political Trials.* Minneapolis: Lerner, 1980.

Fitch, Ed, ed. *Magical Rites from the Crystal Well.* Saint Paul: Llewellyn, 1984.

Gonzalez-Wipper, Migene. *The Complete Book of Spells, Ceremonies and Magic.* New York: Crown, 1988.

Leland, C. G., ed. *Gypsy, Sorcery and Fortune Telling.* New York: University Books, 1963.

Mortimer, John, ed. *Famous Trials.* New York: Hippocrene Books, 1986.

Mumm, Susan M., ed. *Rituals for a New Age: Alternative Weddings, Funerals, Holidays, Etc.* Ann Arbor, MI: Quantum, 1987.

Ross, John, ed. *Trial in Collections.* Metuchen, NJ: Scarecrow Press, 1983.

Teish, Luisah, ed. *Jambalaya: The Natural Women's Book of Personal Charms and Practical Rituals.* New York: Harper & Row, 1985.

GLOSSARY

accentual verse   Poetry that uses the same number of stresses in each line.

adjustive identification   An act of convergence in which an individual accommodates to the other, allowing the other to dominate the nature of the empathic encounter.

adoption   The third of three steps in the empathic process, in which individuals firmly establish the others' feelings as their own. A person might adopt another's feelings based upon stereotypic, dispositional, or individualistic understandings.

aesthetics   The study of the arts and of people's responses to them.

aesthetic communication   Both the text or utterance that the performer presents and the actual presentation given by the performer; a culturally defined act in which a speaker structures language in an expressive and unified manner, triggering audience response.

aesthetic distance   The psychological and physical position a spectator assumes in relationship to an artistic event.

aesthetic text   Written or spoken artistic words or utterances.

aesthetic transaction   An artistic communicative exchange in which the participants have sufficient competencies, recognize their respective roles, and are engaged in the event.

alliteration   Repetition of identical consonant sounds, usually at the beginning of words in close proximity: e.g., *w*ild and *w*oolly.

allusion   A figure of speech that makes an implied or direct reference to a presumably familiar person, place, or thing outside the text. Often refers to a historical, biblical, or literary person or event.

apostrophe   A figure of speech in which a speaker addresses an absent person or a personified abstraction as if physically present.

art   The combination of technical skill and creativity that produces an aesthetic act.

articulation   Intelligibility of speech.

assonance   Repetition of identical vowel sounds in words in close proximity.

audience   Listeners or spectators who participate within and contribute to aesthetic events.

central speaker   One who has a significant role in the forefront of the utterance.

ceremonial forms   Types of aesthetic texts including initiation rites, pledges/oaths, religious rituals, chants, and commemorations.

character   One of several labels given to the speaker in the text; broadly, any person who exists within a speaker's aesthetic text.

characterized speaker   One who is fully developed, multidimensional; one whose utterances provide considerable self-characterization.

character speech   The utterances of speakers within aesthetic texts. May be presented as direct or indirect discourse.

choosing   The third of five steps for exploring personae through voice and body, in which the performer selects from the valid options uncovered through the playing and testing steps the ones the performer wants to present on stage.

clarity   The degree to which words are clearly articulated and correctly pronounced.

closed scene   Private utterance wherein the performer gives the impression of not seeing the audience, since the audience is not part of the scene the performer is trying to stage.

communication apprehension   Fear associated with the act of communicating, marked by signs of physiological and emotional stress. Also referred to as stage fright and presentational energy.

conflict   Forces pulling in opposite directions. Often unfolds in terms of complication and resolution as in traditional literary plays (exposition, challenge, rising action, crisis, climax, and resolution) or as in social dramas (breach, crisis, redressive measures, and reconciliation or permanent breach).

connotation   The associative and suggestive meanings of a word.

consensus understandings   Generally or widely accepted interpretation of textual meaning, grounded in solid textual evidence.

consonance   Repetition of consonant sounds, especially at the end of stressed syllables without the similar correspondence of vowels: e.g., stro*ke* and luc*k*.

convergence   The second of three steps in the empathic process, in which the participants form a bond, joining together through an understanding and sharing of feelings.

conversational forms   Types of aesthetic texts including storytelling, verbal dueling, joke telling, toasts, fables, proverbs, tall tales, legends, myths, and fairy tales.

creators   The originators of aesthetic texts. In literary circles, often referred to as writers or authors; in theatrical circles, as actors or performers.

credible speaker   One who is believable.

denotation   The literal, dictionary definition of a word.

dialogic engagement   Process in which an exchange of understanding occurs between the performer and performed or the performer and the audience.

diction   A speaker's word choices and their arrangements.

direct discourse   The presentation of the exact speech of a character, usually identified by quotation marks. See *character speech*.

drama   A communicative act characterized by conflict. Also synonymous with literary plays, a literary form intended for performance by actors on stage.

dramatic mode   The relationship between a speaker and audience in which the speaker is closed off from direct interaction with the audience and addresses another speaker within the fictive world.

dramatism   A method of inquiry in which a theatrical vocabulary is used to investigate the processes of human action. The dramatistic dimensions can be summarized by reference to the pentad of act, agent, agency, scene, and purpose.

elocutionists   Performers who emphasized delivery practices based upon the natural order during the neo-classical and romantic periods.

empathy   The capacity for understanding and sharing in the feelings of another.

epic mode   A combination of the lyric and dramatic modes in which a story-teller speaks directly to an audience and through other speakers who appear to speak for themselves.

evaluation   A statement of aesthetic worth based upon description, judgment, justification, and rationale.

expressive language   Speech that is figurative, sensuous, rhythmic, and reflexive.

figurative language   Speech that expresses one thing in terms normally denoting another; often works by comparison or association.

focus   Where a performer chooses to look during performance; a performance technique for distinguishing characters by visually specifying a physical location for each given character.

framing   Marks how a speaker wants the audience to see a given communicative act. Calls upon listeners to acknowledge the speaker's intent.

free verse   Poetry that does not rely upon an established metrical pattern, but instead calls upon other means for organizing the poem, such as natural speech rhythms and breath units.

genre   A way of classifying texts.

gleeman   A wandering minstrel of Anglo-Saxon England.

Homeridai   Rhapsodes responsible for the recording of Homer's epic poems, *The Iliad* and *The Odyssey*.

hyperbole   A figure of speech in which the speaker uses a deliberate exaggeration for emphasis.

implied author   The impressions we form of a creator from an encounter with the creator's work.

indirect discourse   Speech in which a teller presents a character's perspective and perhaps diction while continuing to remind the audience that the teller is speaking. See *character speech*.

jongleur   A minstrel or wandering entertainer of medieval France.

kinesics   The study of the relationship between body motions (gestures, movements, postures, and facial expressions) and communication.

kinesthesia   Sensory experience of physical actions.

lyric mode   A personal utterance, often characterized by the presence of an *I*, in which a speaker addresses an audience alone.

metaphor A figure of speech in which an implied rather than directly stated comparison is made.

meter The rhythm of an utterance established by the regular recurrence of accents. Metrical patterns emerge through the arrangement of stressed and unstressed syllables. Four basic forms occur in English verse: iambic (unstressed-stressed), trochaic (stressed-unstressed), anapestic (unstressed-unstressed-stressed), and dactylic (stressed-unstressed-unstressed). Less common are the spondee (stressed-stressed) and the pyrrhic (unstressed-unstressed). Each repetition of a pattern constitutes a foot.

monometer	one foot
dimeter	two feet
trimeter	three feet
tetrameter	four feet
pentameter	five feet
hexameter	six feet
heptameter	seven feet
octameter	eight feet

A metric line, then, is identified by its rhythmic pattern as well as by the number of times the pattern is repeated in a line.

metonymy A figure of speech in which a speaker uses one word to represent another.

misunderstandings Interpretations of a text that are not grounded in textual evidence or that disregard existent textual evidence.

mode A way of classifying aesthetic texts according to the speaker's relationship to the audience. In the lyric mode, a single speaker communicates alone to an audience; in the dramatic mode, two or more speakers communicate with each other within a fictive world; in the epic mode, one speaker communicates alone to an audience and others communicate to each other within a fictive world.

neutral listening Attending to a communicative act without imposing one's preconceptions and prejudices.

object language The manipulation of physical objects in the presentation of self; includes such things as manner of dress, choice of hairstyle, body ornamentation, etc.

objective speaker One who appears to report only the facts.

onomatopoeia Words whose sounds suggest their sense.

open scene One in which a speaker directly addresses a general audience; no one in particular is identified as the specific audience.

oral cultures Those that have little or no experience with writing.

oral interpretation The field of study that examines literary texts from communicative, artistic, therapeutic, and critical perspectives. The historical foundation for the discipline of performance studies.

oxymoron A figure of speech in which a speaker joins together two apparently contradictory terms.

participation   An active engagement in an aesthetic exchange.

pentad   See *dramatism*.

performers   Speakers who present aesthetic texts within a theatrical frame.

performance studies   The field that analyzes aesthetic communication through the act of performance.

permissible understandings   Understandings that texts allow but that may not be agreed upon by all readers.

personae   Speakers within aesthetic texts, composed by their creators to express what they want to say. Also see *character*.

personification   A figure of speech in which human qualities are attributed to nonhuman organisms, abstract ideas, or inanimate objects.

pitch   Frequency of vibration of vocal fold corresponding to a point on a musical scale from high to low.

playing   The first of five steps for exploring personae through voice and body, in which the performer considers what is possible for presentation.

plot   The arrangement of action into meaningful relationships.

point of view   Perspective from which a speaker's utterance unfolds; how a speaker shapes and controls the utterance.

presenting   The fifth of five steps for exploring personae through voice and body, in which the performer publicly stages an aesthetic text for spectators and considers their responses.

print cultures   Those that have the technology to produce writing in print form.

privileged speakers   Those who have the ability to see into the minds of those they discuss.

projective identification   An act of convergence in which individuals assimilate the others, using themselves to dominate the nature of the empathic encounter.

pronunciation   Correctness of speech.

proxemics   Study of relational and environmental space and its impact upon communication.

recognition   The first of three steps in the empathic process, in which an individual comes to understand another's point of view.

reflexive language   Speech that allows people to reflect upon themselves, to talk about their own actions.

reliable speaker   Degree to which the beliefs and attitudes of the creator and persona appear similar.

repeating   The fourth of five steps for exploring personae through voice and body, in which the performer sets and refines vocal and physical choices based upon extensive repetitions.

rhapsode   A performer who appeared in ancient Greece around the 6th century B.C. and who recited memorized texts and used a staff to mark time.

rhyme   Repetition of similar or identical accented vowel sounds and any following sounds.

rhythmic language   Speech that repeats a given sound pattern.

role speech   A type of conversational aesthetic text wherein individuals adopt a particular social character, complete with carefully wrought scripts, and, at times, elaborate costumes, props, set and light designs: e.g., auctioneers, carnival hawkers.

scansion   Analysis of a poem's metrical pattern.

scop   An Anglo-Saxon minstrel who entertained the courts with tales of heroic deeds.

script cultures   Those that have the ability to write but not the capacity to produce writing in print form.

selective listening   Calls upon audience members to perceive the essential dimensions of aesthetic acts.

sensuous language   Speech that appeals to the senses.

sequencing   Arranging an aesthetic text according to perceptual, temporal/spatial, argumentative, or ritualistic patterns.

sign language   Nonverbal behaviors that serve as word substitutions.

simile   A figure of speech in which a speaker makes an explicit comparison, usually using *like* or *as*.

singer   Performer of ancient Greece who simultaneously composed and sang his tales by relying upon set formulas and themes.

speaker   A person, real or fictive, who communicates.

speech play   A type of conversational aesthetic text in which speakers indicate, usually through tone, that their utterances should be understood as fun or playful: e.g., teasing, mock threats, mimicking.

syllabic verse   Poetry that uses the same number of syllables in each line.

synecdoche   Figure of speech that uses a part to represent the whole.

tactile communication   How people touch themselves, others, and physical objects, and the resultant impact on communication.

tempo   Rate of speed at which sounds are produced.

testing   The second of five steps for exploring personae through voice and body, in which the performer probes initial understandings of texts in order to see which appear valid.

traditional literary forms   Type of aesthetic text including poetry, prose fiction, drama, letters, diaries, autobiographies, speeches, and essays.

transactional communication   Process by which participants exchange information, messages, or meanings through their interpretive and behavioral skills.

troubador   Lyric poets and performers of southern France in the twelfth and thirteenth centuries.

understatement   A figure of speech in which a speaker, in saying something, downplays its significance.

unified language   Speech that functions together to form its entirety; a complete, coherent whole.

utterance   A communicative act or aesthetic text.

vocal inflection   The upward or downward movement of the pitch of the voice.

vocal quality   The degree to which the sound of a speaker's voice is pleasing.

vocal variety   The degree to which a speaker's pitch, volume, and tempo vary.

volume   Force or intensity used when speaking; the degree of loudness.

245

INDEX

Note: Page numbers in *italic* indicate authors of text selections in Appendix A.

Accent(s), 66, 67
Act (in pentad), 49
Action, 123
Active listening, 148
Adoption, in empathic process, 94–95, 96
Aeneid (Virgil), 32
Aesop's Fables, 190–91
Aesthetic, defined, 18
Aesthetic communication, 12, 18–19, 23–24,
    51–60
  classification of, 56–60
  language of, 109–16
  modes of, 56–58, 60, 103–4
  participants in, 107–8
  speakers of, 51–56
  of speakers, 56–60
  See also Aesthetic text(s)
Aesthetic conversational text forms, 104–5
Aesthetic distance, 147, 148
Aesthetics, 12
Aesthetic text(s), 12–13, 15, 17, 24, 56
  bibliography of, 233–37
  classification of, 103–6
  and dramatism, 48, 51–60
  and evaluation, 159–63
  forms of, 104–6
  framing, 114–15, 116
  language of, 109–16
  participants in, 107–8
  speakers of, 19, 51–56 (*see also* Speakers)
  structure of, 115, 119–37
  types of, 103–6, 119
  See also Aesthetic communication; Aesthetic
    transactions

Aesthetic transaction(s), 19, 147–50
  language of aesthetic texts in, 109–16
  models of, 116, 137
  participants in, 107–8, 147–50
  structure of aesthetic texts in, 115, 119–37
  See also Aesthetic texts; Aesthetic
    communication
Affect displays, 74
Agency (in pentad), 50
Agent (in pentad), 48–49
Age of Reason, 35
Alliteration, 133
Allusions, 112
Analytic process, 64–85
  body and, 64–68, 73–76
  steps in, 65–68
  voice and, 64–73
Apostrophe, 112
Arnold, Matthew, 134–35
Artistic event, performance as, 156–57
Artistic performance, 8–12, 156–57
Articulation, 69, 72
Art of Acting and Public Reading, The (Tallcott),
  38
Assessment, by performer, 142–43
Assonance, 133
Audience, 17, 19, 22–24, 58, 59, 129–30
  active role of, 24, 107–8, 141, 147
  in dramatic mode, 57
  evaluative role of, 146, 152–66
  expectations of, 145
  as participant, 107–8
  performative role of, 141–50
  as performer, 144–46

Audience (*Continued*)
  performer as, 141–43
  relationship to speaker, 58–60, 103, 107–8,
      120, 129–30
  response(s) of, 51, 67–68, 107–8, 131, 132, 164
  "sense-making" role of, 23, 145–46
  as speakers, 54–55
  and theatrical conventions, 22, 23
Authorization, empathy and, 88–89

Bauman, Richard, 9–10
Beowulf, 33
Betjeman, John, 53, *183–84*
Bible, 33
Boccaccio, 34
Body
  as analytic tool, 64–68
  coordinating bodily and vocal behavior, 82–83
  dimensions of, 73–76
  working with, 78–85
Borges, Jorge Luis, *175*
Brockett, Oscar G., 10, 12
Browning, Elizabeth Barrett, 59
Browning, Robert, 65
Bulwer, John, 35
Burke, Kenneth, 47–48

Canterbury Tales (Chaucer), 33–34
Carilli, Theresa, M., *187–90*
Ceremonial text forms, 12, 106
Chamber Theatre, 39
Character, 130. *See also* Persona(e)
Characterization, 59, 64–68, 92, 130. *See also*
      Body; Empathy; Voice
Character speech, 131–32
Chaucer, Geoffrey, 33–34
Chautauqua, 37–38
Choosing, in analytic process, 66–67, 82–83
Cicero, 32
Clark, S. H., 38
Clichés, 110–11
Coleridge, Samuel Taylor, 37
Comedy, 9–10, 22, 70
Communication, 5–6
  aesthetic (*see* Aesthetic communication)
  breakdown in, 16
  and culture, 5–6, 10, 11, 18
  and interpretation, 6

linguistic factors in, 5–6
  and motivation, 5
  nonverbal, 73–74
  as performance, 3–6, 8, 11, 23
  performance as, 157
  as process, 6
  tactile, 76, 77
  as transactional, 16, 18, 23
Communication apprehension, 79–80
Competence, of participants, 107, 116, 147–50
Composition, 30, 35, 52
Confessions (St. Augustine), 32
Conflict, 7, 121–24
  complication/resolution pattern of, 121–23
  stages of, 123
Connotation, 133
Consonance, 133
Context, situational and cultural, 145
Convergence, empathic, 93–94, 95, 96
Conversation, 35, 59, 104–5. *See also* Dialogue
Conversational forms, aesthetic, 12, 104–5
Costumes, 75
Courlander, Harold, *212–13*
Craft, 18, 107
Creativity, 18, 67, 107, 116, 162
Creator(s), 130
  as speakers, 51–52, 53, 55
Credibility, 91
Criticism, 153
  constructive, 155
  evaluative models for, 156–58
  See also Evaluation
Critics, 153–58. *See also* Audience
Crow, Bryan K., *214–19*
Cultural factors
  in communication, 5–6, 18
  in performance, 10, 11, 157, 164
Culture, 5–6
Curry, S. S., 37

Dante, 34
Decameron (Boccaccio), 34
Delivery, 35
Delsarte, François, 36–37, 38
Denotation, 133
Description, 126
  in evaluation, 152, 153
Developmental factors, in empathy, 88

Dialogic engagement, 16–18, 23, 149
Dialogue, 16–17, 64, 125
Dickey, James, *186–87*
Diction, 133
Discourse, direct and indirect, 131
Divine Comedy (Dante), 34
Drama, 7–8
    social, 123
    stages of conflict in, 123
Dramatic mode, 57, 60
Dramatism, 7–8, 39, 47–62, 153
    fundamental assumptions of, 47–48
    and the pentad, 48–51
    speakers and, 51–60
Dramatistic analysis, 64, 66, 87
    sample, 229–31
Dramatistic features, in performance, 7–8
Dryden, John, 35

Eliot, T. S., 16, 111
Elocutionists, 35–36, 37, 38
Emerson, Charles Wesley, 37
Empathic claim, 88
Empathic process, 90–98
    adoption in, 94–95, 96
    convergence in, 93–94, 96
    questions to guide, 97–98
    recognition in, 90–92, 96
Empathy, 87–98, 149
    defined, 87–90
    and empathic process, 90–98
    and performance, 95–98
    as qualitative process, 88
Enactment, 21
Engagement, of participants, 107, 147–50, 164
Environment, behavior and, 75
Epic mode, 57–58, 60
Eskimo song duels, 8–9, 11
Ethical issues, in evaluation, 157, 165–66
Evaluation, 152–66
    audience, 146, 152–66
    issues in, 159–65
    models for, 156–58
    performance-centered, 163–65
    performer-centered, 162–63
    text-centered, 159–61
Evaluative act, 152–55
Execution, by performer, 142

Expectations, audience, 145
Experience, performance and, 20–21
Expression, 37, 38
    schools of, 37–38
Eye contact, 58, 74

Fairness, critical, 154
Feedback, 67, 68
Figures of speech, 110–13
Fine, Elizabeth C., 40
First-person texts, 90–91
Focus, 59, 130
Forensic performance, 164–65
Framing, 114–15, 116
Free verse, 136

Genre, 103
Gesture(s), 34–35, 36–37, 74. *See also* Kinesics
Gleemen (minstrels), 33
Godwin, Gail, 92, 131, *178–82*
Greece, ancient, performance practice in, 29, 31–32
Gregory, Dick, 9–10
Group performance, 13, 38–39
Gutenberg, Johannes, 26
Gutenbery Galaxy, The (McLuhan), 28

Hemingway, Ernest, 91
History of performance, 29–39, 162
    in ancient Greece and Rome, 31–32
    in middle ages, 32–34
    in Renaissance, 34–35
    in neo-classical period, 35–36
    in romantic era, 36–38
    in twentieth century, 38–39
History of the Theatre (Brockett), 10
Hofeller, Kathleen H., *206–11*
Homer, 29, 31–32, *171–74*
Homeridai (rhapsodes), 31
Homo histrio, 6
Honesty, critical, 155
Horace, 32
Human behavior, dramatism and, 47–48
Human communication. *See* Communication
Humor, 9–10, 70
Hyperbole, 112

Identification, projective and adjustive, 94, 96
Iliad (Homer), 29
Implied author, 52
Inflection, 70
Inhibitions, 78
Interpretation, 60–61
    communication and, 6, 39
    and textual meaning, 159–60
Interpretation of the Printed Page (Clark), 38
Irony, 53

Jokes, 70, 78, 115. *See also* Humor
Jongleurs, 33
Judgment, in evaluation, 152, 153–54
Justification, in evaluation, 152–53, 154

Keats, John, 133
Key, vocal, 70
Kinesics, 74, 76
Kinesthesia, 81, 97
King, Martin Luther, 19

Language, 5–6, 11, 26–27, 28, 35, 109–16
    expressive, 109–13, 116, 120
    figurative, 110–13
    and figures of speech, 110–13
    literal, 110
    reflexive, 113
    repetition and rhythm in, 113
    repressive, 120
    sensuous, 109
    shared, 144, 145
    unified, 109, 113–15, 116
Latin, 34
Learning, by performer, 143
Lessing, Doris, 131–32
Lewis, Richard, 8–9
Lincoln, Abraham, 120
Linguistic factors, in communication, 5–6. *See also* Language
Lish, Gordon, *200–203*
Listening behavior, 148–149
Listening skills, 148–49
Literacy, 26–30, 32
Literary criticism, 39
Literary forms, traditional, 12, 104
Literate (or script) cultures, 27, 57
Literature, 11, 31, 56, 104. *See also* Aesthetic text(s)

Lord, Albert B., 29
Lyceum, 37–38
Lyric mode, 57, 60

MacKaye, Steele, 36
McLuhan, Marshall, 28
"Magic if," 94
Marshall, Archibald, 91
Martin, Jane, *220–22*
Marvell, Andrew, 59
Meaning, 16
Medieval period, performance practice in, 32–34
Medium, translation of (page-to-stage), 160–61
Memorization, 28, 30, 83–84
Metaphor, 111
Meter, 29–30, 133–36
    types of, 133–34
Metonymy, 112
Metrical patterns, 133–35
Milton, John, 111, 112
Minstrels, 33
Modes, 56–58, 60, 103–4
    dramatic, 57, 60, 103
    epic, 57–58, 60, 103
    lyric, 57, 60, 103
Monotone, 70
Motivation, 5, 47, 83
Movable-type press, 26, 34

National Association of Academic Teachers of Public Speaking, 38
Neo-classical period, performance practice in, 35–36
Neutrality, as listening skill, 149
Nonverbal behavior, 73–74, 81–82

Objectivity, 91
Object language, 75–76, 77
Observation, 80–81
Odyssey (Homer), 29
O'Hara, Frank, 124
Omniscience, 92
Ong, Walter, 26–27
Onomatopoeia, 132
Oral cultures, 27, 28, 29–30
    performance practice in, 29–30
Oral history, 29
Oral interpretation, 15, 38–40

Orality and Literacy (Ong), 26–27
Oral reading, 32, 33, 38
Oral vs. written texts, 56
Orpingalik (Netsilik Eskimo poet), *204–6*
Oxymoron, 111–12

Paralanguage, 68
Parry, Milman, 29
Participation, in aesthetic transactions, 147–50
Passion and nativity plays, 33
Patterning, 124–28
Pentad (dramatistic), 48–51, 55
Perceptual tendencies, of audience, 145
Performance, 3, 6, 10, 15, 20–21
    artistic, 8–12, 156–57
    challenge of, 23–24
    competitive, 164–65
    drama and dramatistic in, 7–8 (*See also*
        Dramatism)
    empathy and, 95–98
    as entertainment, 30, 33
    and evaluative issues, 163–65
    evaluative models of, 156–58
    in everyday life, 3–5, 12, 23–24
    forensic, 164–65
    history of, 29–41, 162
    human communication as, 3–6, 11, 15, 23
    as political act, 165–66
Performance norms, 11
Performance practice, 29, 39
    history of, 29–41
Performance studies, 40
    defined, 15–22
    history of, 15, 26–41
Performer(s), 24, 60–62
    as audience, 141–43
    and evaluative issues, 162–63
    mental processes of, 162–63
    in oral cultures, 29–30
    personal style of, 81
    in print cultures, 30
    sense of self, 17, 142, 143
    solo, 12–13, 59
    as speakers, 54, 55
    See also Speaker(s)
Persona(e)
    characterization of, 59, 64–68
    reliability of, 130

    as speakers, 52–53, 55, 61
Personification, 112
Philosophy of the Human Voice, The (Rush), 36
Piercy, Marge, *222–23*
Pitch, 69–70, 71, 72–73, 131
    optimum, 69
Plagiarism, 162
Plato, 31
Playing, in analytic process, 65, 78–80
Plot, 123
Poetry, 58, 59, 136, 161
    translation of, 21–22
Point of view, 90–92, 93, 120–21
Pope, Alexander, 35
Powers, Leland, 37
Presentational energy, 79–80
Presenting, in analytic process, 67–68, 84–85
Print cultures, 27, 28
    performance practice in, 30
    See also Literate (or script) cultures
Privilege, 91–92
Progressive relaxation, 78–79
Projection, 70
Projective identification, 94, 96
Pronunciation, 69, 72
Props, 75
Proxemics, 75, 77
Purpose (in pentad), 49

Questions, dramatistic, 7–8

Rag Doll (relaxation exercise), 79
Randall, Margaret, *176–77*
Ratzenberger, John, 95
Readers Theatre, 39
Reading aloud (oral reading), 32, 33, 38
Recognition, in empathic process, 90–92, 96
Rehearsal, 84, 143
Relaxation exercises, 78–79
Reliability, 130
Religion, 32–33, 127
Renaissance, performance practice in, 34–35
Repeating, in analytic process, 67, 83–84
Repetition, in language, 113
Rhapsode, 31
Rhyme, 133
Rhythm, 113, 125, 136
Riddles, 107–8

Roles, speaker/audience, 107–8. *See also* Audience; Speaker(s); Speaker/audience relationships
Role speech, 105
Roloff, Leland, 79–80
Romantic era, performance practice in, 36–38
Rome, ancient, performance practice in, 32
Rush, James, 36

St. Augustine, 32
Satire, 53
Scansion, 134
Scene(s), 49, 125–26
   closed, 58–59, 60, 129
   open, 60, 129
   presentational, 60
Schechner, Richard, 9
Scops (minstrels), 33
Scribes, 27
Script cultures. *See* Literate (or script) cultures
Second-person text, 91
Selectivity, as listening skill, 149
Sensitivity, critical, 154–55
Sequence, 124–28
Sequencing patterns, 124–28
   argumentative, 126
   perceptual, 124
   ritualistic, 127–28
   temporal/spatial, 124–25, 126
Shakespeare, William, 111, 113
Sheridan, Thomas, 36
Sign language, 75, 77
Simile, 111
Singers (performers), 29–30, 31
Social distance, 75
Social drama, 123
Solo performer, 12–13, 59
Sonnets, 115
Sound, 132–37
Sound effects, 132–33
Speaker(s), 48–50, 92, 119
   aesthetic, 19, 51–60
   central and characterized, 92
   as participant, 107–8
   relationship to audience, 58–60, 103, 107–8, 120, 129–30
   See also Performer(s)

Speaker/audience relationships, 58–60, 103, 107–8, 120, 129–30
Speech arts, 38–39
Speech Communication Association, 38
Speeches, 115
Speech play, 105
Speer, Jean Haskell, 40
Stage fright, 79–80
Stanislavski, Constantin, 94
Stereotypes
   adoptive, 94–95
   vocal, 71
Stories, 115
Structure(s), 115, 119–37
   and audience, 129–30
   and character, 130
   and character speech, 131–32
   and conflict, 121–24
   of the parts, 129–37
   and point of view, 120–21
   and sequence, 124–28
   and sound and rhythm, 132–37
   of the whole, 119–28
Summary, 126
Swift, Jonathan, 35, 112
Synedoche, 112

Tactile communication, 76, 77
Tallcott, Rollo Anson, 38
Tempo (rate), 70, 73
Tension, 78–79, 123–24
Terkel, Studs, *184–85*
Testing, in analytic process, 65–66, 80–81
Text, 48
   and evaluative issues, 159–61
   levels of meaning in, 159–60
   literary and nonliterary, 104
   See also Aesthetic text(s)
Textual study, performance as, 156
Theatrical conventions, 22–23, 144, 149
Third-person text, 91
Thompson, Jean, *191–200*
Tiwi society (Australia), 9
Tone, 105
Touching, 76
Traditional literary forms, 104

Translation process, 21–22, 83, 97
  page-to-stage, 160–61
Troubadours, 33
Turner, Victor, 123

Understatement, 112
Utterance. *See* Text

Verbal art, 11, 12
Verbal dueling, 8–9, 11
Video and tape recording, 81
Virgil, 32
Vocal clarity, 69, 72
Vocal quality, 71, 72, 73
Vocal variety, 69–70, 72
Voice
  as analytic tool, 64–68
  coordinating vocal and bodily behavior, 82–83

  dimensions of, 68–73
  working with, 78–85
Voices, 16, 17
Volume, 70, 72, 73
Vonnegut, Kurt, Jr., *223–28*

Walker, John, 36
Warm-ups, vocal and bodily, 80
Welty, Eudora, 92, 125
Werner's Magazine, 37, 38
Wilbur, Richard, 111
Williams, Miller, 21–22
Wordsworth, William, 37, 111, 112, *175–76*
Writing, 26–29
  technology of, 27

Zone of comfort, 75